QUIZ
OF THE
WORLD!

RICHARD ANDERSON

authorHOUSE·

AuthorHouse™ UK
1663 Liberty Drive
Bloomington, IN 47403 USA
www.authorhouse.co.uk
Phone: UK TFN: 0800 0148641 (Toll Free inside the UK)
        UK Local: 02036 956322 (+44 20 3695 6322 from outside the UK)

Published by AuthorHouse 01/08/2021

ISBN: 978-1-6655-8304-6 (sc)
ISBN: 978-1-6655-8303-9 (e)

Library of Congress Control Number: 2020924171

WELCOME TO THE QUIZ OF THE WORLD!

Here are 197 x 20 question quizzes on all the countries and sovereign states in the world!

With travel having proved difficult in recent months, I thought that you might like to travel round the world in a different way!

There are questions for all levels of 'quizzer' with extra hints included to help you with the harder questions.

I hope that this large compendium of questions will serve you well at pub and family quiz nights and that active participation will prove to be fun for you and your friends!

CONTENTS

AFGHANISTAN QUESTIONS

(1)   What is the capital city?

(2)   What are Dari and Pashto?

(3)   Name one of the three colours on the flag behind the national emblem.

(4)   Iran, Pakistan, Tajikistan, Turkmenistan and Uzbekistan are five of the countries with borders to Afghanistan. What is the large sixth country with the shortest border?

(5)   What is the name of the Islamic fundamentalist group which ruled Afghanistan in the late 1990s?

(6)   What religion do the vast majority of the population practise?

(7)   Which country invaded Afghanistan in December 1979?

(8)   What is the name of the mountain range in the north-east of the country?

(9)   The second biggest city in Afghanistan also begins with the letter K. What is it?

(10) What is the main ingredient of the national dish Kabuli palaw?

(11) What sort of animal is associated with the word Afghan?

(12) Of which illicit drug has Afghanistan been the world's leading producer since 2001?

(13) True or false: Afghanistan is not a member of the United Nations.

(14) Complete the name of the Afghan president from 2001 to 2014: Hamid K.....

(15) The name of the currency of Afghanistan is the same as part of the name of the country. What is it?

(16) What is the name of the famous pass in the north-east of Afghanistan which links the country with Pakistan?

(17) What name was given to the guerrilla-type militant groups led by Islamist Afghan fighters in the Soviet- Afghan War?

(18) What is the international vehicle registration code for Afghanistan?

(19) From which Western European country did Afghanistan gain independence in 1919?

(20) True or false: Afghanistan is the largest landlocked country in the world.

AFGHANISTAN ANSWERS

(1)   Kabul

(2)   The official languages of Afghanistan

(3)   One from black, red and green

(4)   China (91 km.)

(5)   Taliban

(6)   Islam

(7)   The Soviet Union

(8)   Hindu Kush

(9)   Kandahar

(10) Rice

(11) A dog

(12) Opium

(13) False. It joined in 1946.

(14) Karzai

(15) The afghani

(16) The Khyber Pass

(17) Mujahideen

(18) AFG

(19) The UK

(20) False. Kazakhstan is the largest. Afghanistan is the 9th largest.

ALBANIA QUESTIONS

(1) What is the official language of Albania?

(2) What was the name of the only king who ruled Albania from 1928 until 1939?

(3) The flag of Albania is red with a double-headed black what in the centre?

(4) What is Shqiperi?

(5) Albania has a coastline on the Ionian Sea and which other sea?

(6) Which country to the north-east of Albania with the capital Pristina contains a large majority of Albanians and a small minority of Serbians?

(7) What name is given to a range of mountains in Albania and to a famous military commander hero who led a rebellion against the Ottoman Empire?

(8) What was the name of the communist politician who served as head of state from 1944 until his death in 1985?

(9) What is the Lek?

(10) The city of Durres is the second most populous city of Albania. What is the most populous?

(11) What are Shköder and Ohrid?

(12) What are Gheg and Tosk?

(13) True or false: The majority of Albanians are Christian.

(14) Which international singing star, famous for Me, Myself and I with G-Eazy and In the Name of Love with Martin Garrix, was born in New York to Albanian parents?

(15) Against which Black Sea country did Albania score their first-ever win in the finals of an international football competition in the 2016 European Championships?

(16) Which country conquered Albania in 1939?

(17) With which country does Albania have its longest border?

(18) How many times has Albania won the Eurovision Song Contest?

(19) In which city can you find Mother Teresa Square?

(20) Which post did Ramiz Alia and Sali Berisha hold in the 1990s?

(1) Albanian

(2) Zog I

(3) Eagle

(4) The Albanian for Albania

(5) The Adriatic Sea

(6) Kosovo

(7) Skanderbeg

(8) Enver Hoxha

(9) The currency of Albania

(10) Tirana

(11) Lakes

(12) The two main dialects of Albanian

(13) False. The majority (59%) are Muslim.

(14) Bebe Rexha

(15) Romania

(16) Italy

(17) Greece (212 km.)

(18) Albania has never won. (Best position: 5th in 2012)

(19) Tirana

(20) The President of Albania

ALGERIA QUESTIONS

(1)   On which sea does Algeria have a coast?

(2)   What is the capital?

(3)   True or false: Algeria is the largest country in Africa in area.

(4)   What is the name of the desert which makes up a significant proportion of Algeria?

(5)   What is the name of the mountain range in Algeria separating the Mediterranean coastline from the Sahara Desert which also stretches through Morocco and Tunisia?

(6)   Apart from Berber, what is the other official language of Algeria?

(7)   Which other language, although not an official language, is widely used in Algeria?

(8)   What is the official currency, the dinar or the dirham?

(9)   To which ethnic group of Arabs do most Algerians belong?

(10) What city situated on the coast of Algeria is regarded as the second most important city in the country?

(11) Is Algeria considered to be part of the Maghreb region?

(12) Which Nobel Prize-winning writer, famous for the novel The Plague, was born in Algeria in 1913?

(13) In which of Camus's novels does the character Meursault appear?

(14) Which European nation colonized Algeria from 1830 until 1962?

(15) Who resigned as President of Algeria in 2019 following months of protest?

(16) Sonatrach based in Algeria is the largest company in Africa. What commodity does it deal in?

(17) Which city in Algeria used to be closely associated with the French Foreign Legion?

(18) Which Algerian-French film, directed by Costa-Gavras, won two Oscars at the 1970 Oscars?

(19) With which sport is Noureddine Morceli associated?

(20) With which country does Algeria have its longest border?

ALGERIA ANSWERS

(1) The Mediterranean Sea

(2) Algiers

(3) True

(4) The Sahara Desert

(5) The Atlas Mountains

(6) Arabic

(7) French

(8) The dinar

(9) Berbers

(10) Oran

(11) Yes; the Maghreb consists of the North African coastal countries (except for Egypt), which are predominantly Muslim.

(12) Albert Camus

(13) The Stranger (L'Étranger)

(14) France

(15) Abdelaziz Bouteflika

(16) Oil

(17) Sidi Bel Abbas

(18) Z (Best Foreign Language Film and Best Editing)

(19) Running (especially 1500 metres)

(20) Morocco (1,900 km.)

ANDORRA QUESTIONS

(1) Which two countries surround Andorra?

(2) In which mountain range is Andorra situated?

(3) The Principality of Andorra is headed by two "princes". Name one of them.

(4) True or false: The capital, Andorra la Vella, is the highest capital city in Europe.

(5) What is the official language of Andorra?

(6) True or false: Andorra is a member of the European Union.

(7) What is the official currency of Andorra?

(8) Which famous historical figure buried in the German city of Aachen is believed to have created Andorra?

(9) In which town is the New Parliament of Andorra situated?

(10) Is Andorra la Vella called Andorra la Ville or Andorra la Vieille in French?

(11) What is the mainstay of Andorra's economy?

(12) Apart from Catalan (38.8%), which three other languages are most used in Andorra?

(13) True or false: There are no universities in Andorra.

(14) The nearest airport for international flights is situated at which French city?

(15) What are Diari d'Andorra, El Periodic d'Andorra and Bondia?

(16) On 11ᵗʰ October 2018 Andorra had its first win in a European football championship qualifier against the country which has Chisinau as its capital. Which country?

(17) What are the Castellers d'Andorra?

(18) How many gold medals have Andorra won at the Summer Olympics?

(19) What is the international vehicle registration code for Andorra?

(20) What abbreviation is used as the Internet country code top-level domain for Andorra?

ANDORRA ANSWERS

(1)   France and Spain

(2)   Pyrenees

(3)   The Bishop of Urgell in Catalonia, Spain or the President of the French Republic

(4)   True (1,023 metres above sea level)

(5)   Catalan

(6)   False

(7)   The euro

(8)   Charlemagne

(9)   Andorra la Vella

(10) Andorra la Vieille

(11) Tourism

(12) Spanish (35.4%), Portuguese (15%) and French (5.4%)

(13) False. The Universitat d'Andorra was established in 1997.

(14) Perpignan

(15) Newspapers in Andorra

(16) Moldova

(17) A team of Catalan human tower builders

(18) None

(19) AND

(20) .ad

ANGOLA QUESTIONS

(1) Is Angola on the east or the west coast of Africa?

(2) Of which Western European country was Angola a colony for many years until 1975?

(3) What is Cabinda?

(4) Has Angola ever played in the football World Cup competition?

(5) What is the capital city of Angola?

(6) What is UNITA?

(7) Is the population of Angola about 30 million or about 60 million?

(8) Kwanza is the name of a river in Angola and also the name of what?

(9) Which famous member of the British Royal Family visited Angola in 1997 to speak out against landmines?

(10) What is the main official language of Angola?

(11) What cutting weapon is pictured in yellow on the Angolan flag?

(12) Is Angola a republic or a monarchy?

(13) The national anthem is called Angola Avante. What does this mean in English?

(14) What commodity is of utmost importance to Angola's economy?

(15) What is the Internet country code top level domain for Angola?

(16) True or false: Luanda is the most populous Portuguese-speaking capital city in the world.

(17) How often has Angola won the football African Cup of Nations?

(18) What is the major religion of Angola?

(19) Between 1580 and 1680 more than a million what were shipped from Angola to Brazil?

(20) In which sport has Angola won the African championship 11 times?

ANGOLA ANSWERS

(1) On the west coast

(2) Portugal

(3) An Angolan enclave surrounded by the Democratic Republic of the Congo and the Republic of the Congo

(4) Yes, in 2006. They were eliminated in the group stage.

(5) Luanda

(6) The National Union for the Total Independence of Angola, a political party, which fought together with the MPLA in the Angolan War for Independence (1961 – 75) and then against the MPLA in the civil war between 1975 and 2002

(7) About 30 million

(8) The Angolan currency

(9) Princess Diana

(10) Portuguese

(11) A machete

(12) A republic

(13) Forward Angola

(14) Oil

(15) .ao

(16) True

(17) Angola has never won

(18) Christianity

(19) Slaves

(20) Basketball

(1)   True or false: The island state of Antigua and Barbuda only consists of those two islands.

(2)   What is the capital, St. David's, St John's or St. Peter's?

(3)   97% of the population is resident on which of the two islands?

(4)   From which country did Antigua and Barbuda gain its independence in 1981?

(5)   Who is the head of state?

(6)   What is the meaning of the word barbuda in Spanish?

(7)   What is the national sport?

(8)   After which great Antiguan cricket batsman is the stadium on Antigua named?

(9)   The male of the national bird of Antigua and Barbuda is all-black with a scarlet throat pouch that is inflated like a balloon in the breeding season. What is its name?

(10)   Who explored the island of Antigua in 1493?

(11)   Are Antigua and Barbuda in the Leeward Islands or the Windward Islands?

(12)   Why did the inhabitants of Barbuda have to leave the island for a time in September 2017?

(13)   What is the official language of the islands?

(14)   What running distance does the athlete Daniel Bailey specialise in?

(15)   As a cricketer, was Antigua-born Curtly Ambrose famous as a batsman or a bowler?

(16)   Which of the two islands is bigger in area, Antigua or Barbuda?

(17)   Between which sea and which ocean are the islands situated?

(18)   One of the main sights on Antigua, the restored 18th-century British naval base in the south of the island is named after which famous British seafarer who spent the early years of his career there?

(19)   Who represents the Queen on Antigua and Barbuda?

(20)   What makes the main contribution to the economy of the islands?

ANTIGUA AND BARBUDA ANSWERS

(1)   False. It also includes a number of smaller islands.

(2)   St. John's

(3)   Antigua

(4)   The UK

(5)   Elizabeth II

(6)   Bearded

(7)   Cricket

(8)   Viv Richards

(9)   The frigate bird

(10) Christopher Columbus

(11) The Leeward Islands

(12) Because of the destruction caused by Hurricane Irma

(13) English

(14) 100m and 200m

(15) A (fast) bowler

(16) Antigua (280 sq. km.) Barbuda is 161 sq. km.

(17) Between the Caribbean Sea and the North Atlantic Ocean

(18) Lord Nelson; the site is called Nelson's Dockyard

(19) The governor-general

(20) Tourism

ARGENTINA QUESTIONS

(1) How can the name of the capital of Argentina be translated into English?

(2) How many times has Argentina won the football World Cup?

(3) What is the highest mountain in Argentina?

(4) What is the name of the waterfalls on the border between Brazil and Argentina, the largest waterfalls in the world?

(5) By what name is Argentina-born Jorge Mario Bergoglio better known?

(6) In terms of population, what is the second biggest city in Argentina?

(7) Which famous Argentinian wrote Ficciones in 1944, El Aleph in 1949 and The Book of Sand in 1975?

(8) Which popular dance is particularly associated with Argentina?

(9) With which sport do you associate Guillermo Vilas and Gabriela Sabatini?

(10) What can be seen in the middle of the Argentinian flag?

(11) By what name are the Islas Malvinas known in English?

(12) Which famous president died in 1974?

(13) Who was head of state when Argentina invaded the Falkland Islands in 1982?

(14) What is the name of the river which forms part of the border between Argentina and Uruguay, the scene of a famous battle in 1939?

(15) What is the name of the sparsely populated region at the southern end of South America, shared by Argentina and Chile?

(16) Who is the famous film composer and pianist, born in Buenos Aires in 1932, who is particularly well known for writing music for the Dirty Harry films?

(17) Which internationally successful 2017 film, based on a novel by Stephen King, was directed by the Argentinian filmmaker Andy Muschietti?

(18) What is pato?

(19) Which driver dominated the world of Formula One in the 1950s?

(20) What is the name of the southernmost city in the world, situated in Tierra del Fuego?

ARGENTINA ANSWERS

(1) Good airs or fair winds

(2) Twice

(3) Aconcagua (6,959m; 22,831 ft)

(4) The Iguazu Falls

(5) Pope Francis I

(6) Cordoba

(7) Jorge Luis Borges

(8) Tango

(9) Tennis

(10) The Sun of May

(11) The Falkland Islands

(12) Juan Peron

(13) General Leopoldo Galtieri

(14) The Rio de la Plata (River Plate)

(15) Patagonia

(16) Lalo Schifrin

(17) It

(18) The national sport of Argentina played on horseback with elements of polo and basketball

(19) Juan Manuel Fangio

(20) Ushuaia

ARMENIA QUESTIONS

(1) True or false: Armenia was the first state in the world to adopt Christianity as its official religion.

(2) In what year did Armenia become independent from the Soviet Union?

(3) During which war did the mass extermination and expulsion of 1.5 million ethnic Armenians within the Ottoman Empire start?

(4) What is the name of the enclave within Azerbaijan, mainly populated by Armenians?

(5) In what range of mountains is Armenia, along with Georgia and Azerbaijan, situated?

(6) Which mountain, situated in Turkey, but visible from Armenia is considered to be a symbol of the country and is featured on the Armenian coat of arms?

(7) What is the capital of Armenia?

(8) What is the official language of Armenia?

(9) What is the duduk, (a) the title of the president (b) a woodwind instrument or (c) a type of pancake eaten for breakfast?

(10) Although born in Tiflis, Georgia in 1903, the parents of this composer, noted for ballet and orchestral music, were Armenian. Who is he?

(11) Which French singer, of Armenian stock, had an international hit with the song She?

(12) Which yellow-orange fruit, similar to a small peach, is the national fruit of Armenia?

(13) Armenia has its longest border with the country whose capital is Baku. Which country?

(14) Does Armenia have a coastline or is it landlocked?

(15) What would you do with Oghi, eat it or drink it?

(16) True or false: The Armenian alphabet is the same as the English alphabet.

(17) Does Armenia participate in the Eurovision Song Contest?

(18) The father of which American singing star and actress, real name Cherilyn Sarkisian, had Armenian roots?

(19) Which famous American media personality, married to Kanye West, has Armenian ancestry?

(20) Which famous cartoon band was created by the Armenian-American Ross Bagdasarian, better known as David Seville?

ARMENIA ANSWERS

(1) True; the official date is 301 AD

(2) 1991

(3) The First World War

(4) Nagorno-Karabakh or Artsakh

(5) Transcaucasus

(6) Ararat

(7) Yerevan

(8) Armenian

(9) (b) A woodwind instrument indigenous to Armenia

(10) Aram Khachaturian

(11) Charles Aznavour

(12) The apricot

(13) Azerbaijan (996 km.)

(14) It is landlocked.

(15) Drink it. It's a sort of fruit spirit, similar to vodka.

(16) False; the Armenian alphabet was developed in 405 AD by Mesrop Mashtots.

(17) Yes, since 2006.

(18) Cher

(19) Kim Kardashian

(20) Alvin and the Chipmunks

AUSTRALIA QUESTIONS

(1)   What is the second biggest city in Australia as far as population is concerned?

(2)   Off the coast of which state is the Great Barrier Reef situated?

(3)   Which part of Australia used to be known as Van Diemen's Land?

(4)   What is the name of the Australian bird related to the kingfisher, known for its loud, distinctive call?

(5)   What is the name of the Australian-born actress who won a Best Actress Oscar for her role in Blue Jasmine?

(6)   What is the nearest large town to Uluru?

(7)   Which London-born Australian writer won the Nobel Prize for Literature in 1973?

(8)   What is the name of the large gulf in the north of Australia bounded by the Arafura Sea?

(9)   What are the names of the two men who led an expedition in 1860-61 to cross Australia from North to South?

(10) Of which state is Sydney the capital?

(11) What is bush tucker?

(12) What commodity is particularly associated with Hunter Valley and Barossa Valley?

(13) How many times has Australia hosted the Summer Olympic Games?

(14) What is the name of the carnivorous marsupial found only in Tasmania and nowadays threatened by a facial tumour disease?

(15) What is the highest mountain?

(16) Which office did Robert Menzies, Gough Whitlam, Malcolm Fraser and Julia Gillard hold?

(17) Australia has six states and two territories. Name the two territories.

(18) In which Australian city did Prince Charles go to school?

(19) With which of the arts was Dame Nellie Melba associated?

(20) With which sport do you associate Don Bradman, Ricky Ponting and Shane Warne?

AUSTRALIA ANSWERS

(1) Melbourne

(2) Queensland

(3) Tasmania

(4) Kookaburra

(5) Cate Blanchett

(6) Alice Springs

(7) Patrick White

(8) Gulf of Carpentaria

(9) Robert Burke and William Wills

(10) New South Wales

(11) Any food native to Australia which the Aborigines used

(12) Wine

(13) Twice: Melbourne (1956) and Sydney (2000)

(14) The Tasmanian devil

(15) Mount Kosciusko (2,228m; 7,310ft.)

(16) Prime Minister

(17) The Australian Capital Territory and the Northern Territory

(18) Geelong

(19) Opera

(20) Cricket

AUSTRIA QUESTIONS

(1) What name was given to the congress held in Vienna in 1814/1815 and chaired by Metternich?

(2) Who was the heir to the throne of Austria-Hungary who was shot in Sarajevo in 1914?

(3) What is the name of the large lake situated on the border between Austria and Hungary?

(4) In which city was Wolfgang Amadeus Mozart born?

(5) The Austrians call this state Kärnten. What do we call it?

(6) On which river is it possible to sail through the Wachau?

(7) Which Austrian singer had an international hit with Rock Me Amadeus?

(8) Which Austrian painter is particularly famous for his golden painting of Adele Bloch-Bauer?

(9) Which bodybuilder, actor and politician was born in the city of Graz in 1947?

(10) What is the name of the famous chocolate cake invented in Vienna in 1832?

(11) With which sport are Andreas Goldberger, Thomas Morgenstern and Gregor Schlierenzauer associated?

(12) What name is given to the former imperial palace of the Habsburgs in Vienna?

(13) What is the name of the Austrian family featured in the film The Sound of Music?

(14) Who wrote the novel The Third Man, set in post-war Vienna?

(15) What is the name of the controversial right-wing politician, member of the FPÖ party, who was killed in a car crash in 2008?

(16) Which country is linked with Austria by the Brenner Pass?

(17) What German word is used to describe the annexation of Austria into Nazi Germany in 1938?

(18) How often have the Winter Olympics been held in Innsbruck?

(19) The director of the film Metropolis was born in Vienna in 1890. Who was he?

(20) What was the name of the Austrian currency before the euro was introduced in 2002?

AUSTRIA ANSWERS

(1) The Congress of Vienna

(2) Archduke Franz Ferdinand

(3) Lake Neusiedl (Neusiedlersee)

(4) Salzburg

(5) Carinthia

(6) The Danube; the Wachau is a picturesque landscape on the river between Melk and Krems

(7) Falco

(8) Gustav Klimt

(9) Arnold Schwarzenegger

(10) Sachertorte

(11) Ski jumping

(12) The Hofburg

(13) Von Trapp

(14) Graham Greene

(15) Jörg Haider

(16) Italy

(17) Anschluss

(18) Twice; 1964 and 1976

(19) Fritz Lang

(20) The schilling

AZERBAIJAN QUESTIONS

(1) What is the capital of Azerbaijan?

(2) On which sea is Baku situated?

(3) The Walled City of Baku, the Gobustan Rock Art Cultural Landscape and the Historic Centre of Sheki are all UNESCO .... (complete the sentence)

(4) True or false: Azerbaijan does not share a border with Russia.

(5) What is the name of the disputed enclave in Azerbaijan where the majority of inhabitants are Armenian?

(6) Are the majority of Azerbaijanis Shia Muslims or Sunni Muslims?

(7) Which family have held the presidency of Azerbaijan since 1993?

(8) Called after an Alpine flower, what name was given to the German operation to conquer the oil fields of Baku in 1942?

(9) What are the Kura and the Aras?

(10) What is Yanar Dag?

(11) True or false: Azerbaijan is a member of OPEC.

(12) Which British driver won the Azerbaijan Grand Prix in 2018?

(13) Is the population of Azerbaijan about 10 million or about 15 million?

(14) What shorter word is sometimes used for the inhabitants instead of Azerbaijanis?

(15) What was the title of the song by Ell and Nikki which won the Eurovision Song Contest for Azerbaijan in 2011?

(16) The inaugural edition of which games was held in Baku in 2015?

(17) As a part of which nation did Azerbaijan compete at the Olympic Games between 1952 and 1988?

(18) In which sport has Azerbaijan won the most Olympic medals?

(19) Azerbaijan is sometimes known as the land of eternal (a) water (b) oil or (c) fire?

(20) Which fish from the Caspian Sea supplies Azerbaijan with caviar?

AZERBAIJAN ANSWERS

(1) Baku

(2) The Caspian Sea

(3) World Heritage Sites

(4) False

(5) Nagorno-Karabakh or the Republic of Artsakh

(6) Shia Muslims (89%)

(7) Aliyev: Heydar Aliyev 1993 – 2003, his son Ilham since 2003

(8) Operation Edelweiss

(9) The two major rivers of Azerbaijan

(10) A natural gas fire which blazes continuously on a hill on the Absheron Peninsula near Baku

(11) False

(12) Lewis Hamilton

(13) About 10 million

(14) Azeris

(15) Running Scared

(16) The European Games

(17) The Soviet Union

(18) Wrestling

(19) (c) Fire

(20) The sturgeon

BAHAMAS QUESTIONS

(1) Are the Bahamas in the Atlantic Ocean or the Caribbean Sea?

(2) What is the capital?

(3) On which island is Nassau?

(4) What is the currency, the Bahamian dollar or the Bahamian pound?

(5) Which member of the British Royal Family was governor of the Bahamas from 1940 to 1945?

(6) What disastrous event happened in the Bahamas on 1st September 2019?

(7) Name either the fish or the wading bird which are on the Bahamian coat of arms.

(8) Which American state is only 80 kilometres (50 miles) from the Bahamas?

(9) Which of the islands in the Bahamas has a feline-sounding name?

(10) Name one James Bond film with scenes shot in the Bahamas.

(11) Named after an imaginary island, what is the name of the famous resort situated on Paradise Island?

(12) Who was the first European to see the islands?

(13) Which Bahamian band recorded the song Who Let the Dogs Out?

(14) In honour of which King of England was Nassau named?

(15) What name is given to the colourful street parades which take place on Boxing Day and January 1st?

(16) The star of the films Lilies of the Field and In the Heat of the Night comes from a Bahamian family. Who is he?

(17) Goombay is a form of Bahamian music and a percussion instrument. Which percussion instrument?

(18) The writer of The Old Man and the Sea and Islands in the Stream lived on Bimini in the Bahamas from 1935 to 1937. Who is he?

(19) With which unexpected animals can one swim on Big Major Cay, pigs or sheep?

(20) The Bahamas were granted independence from the UK in the same year that the UK joined the European Economic Community. Which year?

BAHAMAS ANSWERS

(1) The Atlantic Ocean

(2) Nassau

(3) New Providence

(4) The Bahamian dollar

(5) The Duke of Windsor (Edward VIII)

(6) Hurricane Dorian struck the Abaco Islands and Grand Bahama.

(7) Marlin or flamingo

(8) Florida

(9) Cat Island

(10) Thunderball, You Only Live Twice, The Spy Who Loved Me, For Your Eyes Only, Never Say Never Again, Casino Royale

(11) Atlantis

(12) Christopher Columbus

(13) The Baha Men

(14) William III, Prince of Orange-Nassau (Reign: 1689 – 1702)

(15) Junkanoo

(16) Sidney Poitier

(17) A drum

(18) Ernest Hemingway

(19) Pigs

(20) 1973

BAHRAIN QUESTIONS

(1) With which country in Central America does the name of Bahrain's capital city rhyme?

(2) Which two colours feature on the flag (a) blue and green (b) red and white or (c) brown and orange?

(3) True or false: Bahrain is an island state.

(4) What construction joins Bahrain to Saudi Arabia?

(5) The causeway is named after a former king of Saudi Arabia. What was his name?

(6) Of which country did Bahrain become a protectorate in the nineteenth century?

(7) On which side of the road did Bahrain drive until 1967?

(8) In which gulf is Bahrain situated?

(9) Is Bahrain a kingdom or an emirate?

(10) What is the official language of Bahrain?

(11) What does Bahrain mean in Arabic?

(12) Which dynasty has ruled Bahrain since 1783?

(13) What championship race first took place in Bahrain in 2004?

(14) Which German driver won the Bahrain Grand Prix in 2012, 2013, 2017 and 2018?

(15) What is the name of the national airline of Bahrain?

(16) What adjective can be formed from the word Bahrain?

(17) True or false: There are more non-nationals living in Bahrain than Bahrainis.

(18) From which country do the largest number of non-nationals come?

(19) Apart from Bahrain, there are only two other Arab countries, beginning with I, which have a majority of Shiite Muslims living there. What are the other two countries?

(20) Ruth Jebet won a steeplechase gold medal for Bahrain in the 2016 Rio Olympics. In which country was she born?

BAHRAIN ANSWERS

(1)   Panama (Manama is the capital of Bahrain)

(2)   Red and white

(3)   True

(4)   A causeway (It is a series of bridges and causeways.)

(5)   King Fahd

(6)   The United Kingdom

(7)   On the left

(8)   The Persian Gulf

(9)   A kingdom (since 2002)

(10) Arabic

(11) Two seas

(12) Al Khalifa

(13) The Bahrain Grand Prix, a Formula One Championship race

(14) Sebastian Vettel

(15) Gulf Air

(16) Bahraini

(17) True; c. 570,000 Bahraini and 667,000 non-nationals

(18) India (c. 290,000)

(19) Iraq and Iran

(20) Kenya

BANGLADESH QUESTIONS

(1)   How do you spell the capital city of Bangladesh?

(2)   What name did Bangladesh have prior to independence in 1971?

(3)   Into which bay does the Ganges delta empty its waters?

(4)   What is the predominant language in Bangladesh?

(5)   The second city of Bangladesh is an important seaport. What is its name?

(6)   What is the name of the ethnic minority persecuted in Myanmar, the majority of whom found refuge in Bangladesh?

(7)   What is the name of the Bangladeshi entrepreneur who was awarded the Nobel Peace Prize in 2006 for founding the Grameen Bank?

(8)   With which two countries does Bangladesh share a border?

(9)   How did the first President of Bangladesh, Sheikh Mujibur Rahman, die?

(10) What is the name of the historical region to which Bangladesh and parts of north- eastern India belong?

(11) In what year did the Bangladesh Liberation War take place?

(12) What type of storm killed about 140,000 people in Bangladesh in 1991?

(13) The delta of two important rivers is situated in Bangladesh and the Indian state of West Bengal and is the largest in the world. What are the two rivers?

(14) Is the population of the metropolitan area of Dhaka 10 million or 20 million?

(15) What colour is the circle in the middle of the Bangladeshi flag?

(16) Which tropic runs through Bangladesh?

(17) The national animal of Bangladesh is the Bengal what?

(18) What is Bangladesh's largest manufacturing sector?

(19) What is the Bangladesh Awami League?

(20) How many countries in the world have a bigger population than Bangladesh?

BANGLADESH ANSWERS

(1) Dhaka (not to be confused with Dakar, the capital of Senegal)

(2) East Pakistan

(3) The Bay of Bengal

(4) Bengali

(5) Chittagong

(6) Rohingya

(7) Muhammad Yunus

(8) India and Myanmar

(9) He was assassinated by army officers.

(10) Bengal

(11) 1971

(12) A cyclone

(13) The Ganges and the Brahmaputra

(14) 20 million

(15) Red (on a green field)

(16) The Tropic of Cancer

(17) Tiger

(18) The textile industry

(19) A major political party in Bangladesh which has provided a number of Bangladeshi presidents and prime ministers

(20) 7: China, India, USA, Indonesia, Pakistan, Brazil and Nigeria

BARBADOS QUESTIONS

(1)   What is the capital of Barbados?

(2)   Is Barbados one of the Greater Antilles or the Lesser Antilles?

(3)   The three countries which chronologically claimed Barbados as a colony have as their capitals Madrid, Lisbon and London. What are the three countries?

(4)   Who was King of England when the ship, the Olive Blossom, arrived in Barbados in 1625 and claimed the island for England?

(5)   The majority of the people living on Barbados claim descent from the people of which continent?

(6)   True or false: The name Barbados comes from the Spanish or Portuguese and means the bearded ones?

(7)   What word is used to describe the inhabitants of Barbados and also the creole which many of them speak?

(8)   Which Grammy Award winning female singer with the real name Robyn Fenty was born on Barbados?

(9)   One of the most famous Bajans was Errol Barrow. Was he a musician or a politician?

(10)   Which Bridgetown-born cricketer was knighted for his services to cricket in 1975?

(11)   Against which Welsh county was Sobers playing for Nottinghamshire when he hit six sixes in an over for the first time in history?

(12)   Is the Grantley Adams International Airport named after a politician or a sportsman?

(13)   What was the title of the 2012 UK number one single by the Bajan group Cover Drive?

(14)   The father of which English international footballer who played for Arsenal, Chelsea and Roma was from Barbados?

(15)   Barbados is sometimes known as the land of the flying what?

(16)   What is the name of the group which had a number one UK hit in 1975 with the song Barbados?

(17)   Which hip hop artist, famous for the song The Message was born in Bridgetown in 1958?

(18)   True or false: Barbados is a member of the Commonwealth.

(19)   Is the currency of Barbados the Barbados dollar or the Barbados pound?

(20)   Which island group is closest to Barbados?

BARBADOS ANSWERS

(1) Bridgetown

(2) The Lesser Antilles

(3) Spain, Portugal and the UK

(4) James I

(5) Africa

(6) True

(7) Bajan

(8) Rihanna

(9) A politician; he was the first Prime Minister of independent Barbados (1966 – 76), having previously been premier.

(10) Garfield Sobers

(11) Glamorganshire

(12) A politician; Grantley Adams was the first premier of Barbados (1953 – 58)

(13) Twilight

(14) Ashley Cole

(15) Fish

(16) Typically Tropical

(17) Grandmaster Flash (Joseph Saddler)

(18) True

(19) The Barbados dollar

(20) St. Vincent and the Grenadines

BELARUS QUESTIONS

(1) True or false: Belarus is a landlocked country.

(2) What is the capital?

(3) What sport does the Belarusian athlete Victoria Azarenka play?

(4) What are the two official languages of Belarus?

(5) What is the name of the city opposite the Polish city of Terespol where an important treaty was signed in 1918?

(6) The 1918 Treaty of Brest-Litowsk ended the participation of which country in World War I?

(7) True or false: Capital punishment still exists in Belarus.

(8) What important prize was the Belarusian journalist, essayist and historian Svetlana Alexievich awarded in 2015?

(9) Who became President of Belarus in 1994?

(10) The winter sportswoman Darya Domracheva has won 4 Olympic gold medals. In which winter sport?

(11) The River Neman rises in Belarus. By what German name is it often better known?

(12) Which is the only one of the three Baltic states, Latvia, Lithuania and Estonia, without a border to Belarus?

(13) By what archaic name involving a colour is Belarus still sometimes known?

(14) Which gymnast known as the Sparrow from Minsk won four Olympic gold medals?

(15) The Council of the Republic and the House of Representatives are the two chambers of what?

(16) In which decade did Belarus gain independence from the Soviet Union?

(17) Which is the only Belarusian football club to have qualified for the group stage of the UEFA Champions League?

(18) In which Belarusian city were the 2019 European Games held?

(19) The Belarusian currency has the same name as the currency in Russia. What is it?

(20) Which famous painter, famous for his work with stained glass, was born in Liozna, nowadays in Belarus, in 1887 and died in France in 1985 aged 97?

BELARUS ANSWERS

(1)   True

(2)   Minsk

(3)   Tennis

(4)   Russian and Belarusian

(5)   Brest (formerly Brest-Litowsk)

(6)   Russia

(7)   True; Belarus is the only European country where capital punishment still exists.

(8)   The Nobel Prize for Literature

(9)   Alexander Lukashenko

(10) Biathlon

(11) The Memel

(12) Estonia

(13) White Russia (e.g. the German for Belarus is Weißrussland – White Russia)

(14) Olga Korbut

(15) The National Assembly of Belarus

(16) The 1990s

(17) FC Bate Borisov

(18) Minsk

(19) The (Belarusian) ruble or rouble

(20) Marc Chagall

BELGIUM QUESTIONS

(1)   What is the French spelling of the Belgium capital?

(2)   What is La Brabançonne?

(3)   There are three official Belgian languages. What are they?

(4)   Who is King of the Belgians?

(5)   What is the name of the city on the River Scheldt or Schelde, famous for its diamond industry?

(6)   What is the name of the Belgian cartoonist who created The Adventures of Tintin?

(7)   What are Walloons?

(8)   The European Commission is based in Brussels. Who is the President of it?

(9)   Which province in south Belgium has the same name as a neighbouring country?

(10) Which city in the province of West Flanders is noted for its canals and its lace?

(11) True or false: Belgium has never hosted the Olympic Games.

(12) What is the name of the geographer and cartographer from Flanders who created a world map in 1569 based on a new projection?

(13) What is the full name of the detective created by Belgian writer Georges Simenon?

(14) By what name is the former Belgian Congo known today?

(15) In which Belgian city can you see St. Bavo Cathedral, the Gravensteen and the River Leie?

(16) What are Tripel Karmeliet, Duvel Tripel Hop and Duchesse de Bourgogne?

(17) With which sport is the name Jacky Ickx associated?

(18) The Germans know this city as Lüttich. What do the French call it?

(19) Which Belgian football club has won more international trophies than any other?

(20) The 1974 international hit Seasons in the Sun by Terry Jacks was based on a song by which Belgian chansonnier?

BELGIUM ANSWERS

(1) Bruxelles

(2) The national anthem of Belgium

(3) Dutch (Flemish), French and German

(4) Philippe

(5) Antwerp

(6) Hergé

(7) The French-speaking inhabitants of Belgium

(8) The German Ursula von der Leyen

(9) Luxembourg

(10) Bruges or Brugge

(11) False; Antwerp hosted the games in 1920.

(12) Gerardus Mercator

(13) Jules Maigret

(14) The Democratic Republic of the Congo (DRC)

(15) Ghent

(16) Types of Belgian beer

(17) Motor racing (Formula One and the 24 Hours of Le Mans)

(18) Liège

(19) R.S.C. Anderlecht

(20) Jacques Brel

BELIZE QUESTIONS

(1) What was the former name of Belize?

(2) Belize has a border with Guatemala and which other Central American country?

(3) What is the capital of Belize?

(4) True or false: Belmopan is the largest city in Belize.

(5) True or false: Belmopan was specifically built as a new capital.

(6) What is the official language of Belize?

(7) About 53% of Belizeans are Mestizos. This means they are of mixed Mayan and which European country descent?

(8) The Belize Barrier Reef is the second largest coral reef system in the world. What is the largest?

(9) With which neighbouring country does Belize have an ongoing territorial dispute?

(10) Who is the head of state?

(11) The most decorated female American gymnast has Belize citizenship through her mother. Who is she?

(12) Belize was badly affected by Hurricane Hattie. In which decade, the 1960s or 1970s?

(13) True or false: The British Union Jack still features on the Belizean flag.

(14) On which sea does Belize have a coastline?

(15) How many countries in Central America have a smaller population than Belize?

(16) In which century did British Honduras become a British Crown colony?

(17) What is the Great Blue Hole?

(18) A favourite dish of the Garifuna, some of whom live in Belize, is hudut, made from plantains. What is a plantain?

(19) Of which civilisation is the Caracol archaeological site in Belize a good example?

(20) How many other countries in Central America do not have a coastline on the Pacific Ocean, like Belize?

(1)   British Honduras

(2)   Mexico

(3)   Belmopan

(4)   False; Belize City is by far the largest (c. 58,000). Belmopan has a population of about 20,000.

(5)   True; it was founded in 1970. The previous capital, Belize City, had had problems with hurricanes.

(6)   English

(7)   Spanish

(8)   The Great Barrier Reef off Australia

(9)   Guatemala, which claims about 53% of the mainland of Belize.

(10) Queen Elizabeth II

(11) Simone Biles

(12) The 1960s (1961)

(13) False

(14) The Caribbean Sea

(15) None

(16) In the nineteenth century (1862)

(17) A giant marine sinkhole off the coast of Belize

(18) A cooking banana

(19) The Mayan civilization

(20) None

BENIN QUESTIONS

(1)   What is the capital of Benin?

(2)   What does Porto-Novo mean in English?

(3)   From which language does the name Porto-Novo come?

(4)   What is the official language of Benin?

(5)   What was the previous name of Benin until 1975?

(6)   What is the largest city of Benin?

(7)   Which country, with Abuja as its capital, lies to the east of Benin?

(8)   What is the Bight of Benin?

(9)   What fibre accounts for 40% of Benin's GDP?

(10) Which Benin-born actor received Oscar nominations for his performance in In America and Blood Diamond?

(11) From which country did Dahomey achieve independence in 1960?

(12) Does Benin have a coastline on the Atlantic or Indian Ocean?

(13) What is considered to be the most popular sport in Benin?

(14) Which trade was particularly active on the coast of Benin from the early 16th century to the late 19th century?

(15) What are the Fon, the Aja, the Yoruba and the Bariba?

(16) National Day in Benin coincides with St. Andrews Day in the UK. What is the date?

(17) What "religion", which is practised in Haiti, originated in Benin?

(18) What is the adjective created from the word Benin?

(19) Which Beninese singer-songwriter was called "Africa's premier diva" by Time magazine in 2007?

(20) What royal buildings can be seen at Abomey, the former capital of Dahomey?

BENIN ANSWERS

(1) Porto-Novo

(2) New port

(3) Portuguese

(4) French

(5) Dahomey

(6) Cotonou

(7) Nigeria

(8) A bay in the Gulf of Guinea

(9) Cotton

(10) Djimon Hounsou

(11) France

(12) The Atlantic Ocean

(13) Football

(14) The slave trade

(15) Tribes in Benin

(16) 30th November

(17) Vodou or voodoo

(18) Beninese

(19) Angélique Kidjo

(20) Royal palaces

BHUTAN QUESTIONS

(1) Is Bhutan a kingdom or a republic?

(2) Bhutan is surrounded by the two most populous countries on earth. Which two?

(3) In which range of mountains is Bhutan situated?

(4) What is the capital?

(5) What is the national sport of Bhutan which toxophilites enjoy?

(6) What is the role of Jigme Khesar Namgyel Wangchuck?

(7) What is the dominant religion in Bhutan, Buddhism or Hinduism?

(8) A 2010 Control Act of Bhutan made it illegal to sell this addictive substance or to use it in public. What substance?

(9) Is the gho the national dress for Bhutanese men or women?

(10) What is Phuntsholing?

(11) True or false: Thimphu is the highest capital in the world.

(12) Which colonial powers have ruled Bhutan?

(13) What mythical animal appears on Bhutan's flag?

(14) Is Dzongkha the official language of Bhutan or the currency?

(15) In Bhutan, what is more important than gross national product?

(16) In the north, Bhutan has a border with which autonomous region of China?

(17) Which university in Texas has adopted Bhutanese architecture for its campus buildings?

(18) What is the ngultrum?

(19) To which neighbouring country's currency is the ngultrum fixed?

(20) What is the Internet country code top level domain for Bhutan?

BHUTAN ANSWERS

(1) A kingdom

(2) China and India

(3) The Himalayas

(4) Thimphu

(5) Archery

(6) He's the King of Bhutan

(7) Buddhism

(8) Tobacco

(9) For men (the kira is for women)

(10) The second biggest town in Bhutan

(11) False; it's the fourth highest, after Quito, Bogota and Addis Ababa. Sucre, the constitutional capital of Bolivia is also higher.

(12) None; Bhutan has never been colonised.

(13) A dragon

(14) The official language

(15) Happiness

(16) Tibet

(17) The University of Texas at El Paso

(18) The currency

(19) India's currency, the rupee

(20) .bt

BOLIVIA QUESTIONS

(1) Which city is the seat of government and the de facto national capital of Bolivia?

(2) Which city is the constitutional capital of Bolivia?

(3) Apart from Bolivia, which other South American country is landlocked?

(4) What is the name of the president who resigned after widespread protests that the 2019 general election had been rigged?

(5) What is the name of the lake, often called the highest navigable lake in the world, situated on the border between Bolivia and Peru?

(6) The constitution of Bolivia recognizes 36 official languages, but which one is spoken most?

(7) Does Bolivia have a border with Paraguay or Uruguay?

(8) Is the majority of the population Protestant or Roman Catholic?

(9) Is the currency of Bolivia (a) the boliviano or (b) the Bolivian peso?

(10) What three colours are the three horizontal stripes of the Bolivian flag? Clue: almost a traffic light!

(11) What are Uros, Suriki and Isla del Sol?

(12) True or false: La Paz is the city in Bolivia with the biggest population.

(13) Although traditionally famous for tin and silver, Bolivia has nine million tons of which element used in the production of batteries?

(14) Which famous Argentine-born Marxist revolutionary who played a major role in the Cuban Revolution, was killed in Bolivia in 1967?

(15) What sort of mineral would you expect to see at the Salar de Uyuni?

(16) True or false: Bolivia is the only South American country never to have won an Olympic medal.

(17) To which country did Bolivia lose its Pacific coast in 1879?

(18) One of the main festivals in Bolivia is the Carnival of Oruro which ends on Ash Wednesday, just before which period of abstinence and penance?

(19) True or false: Simon Bolivar who led the independence of several South American countries against the Spanish Empire was Bolivian by birth.

(20) The father of the star of the film Myra Breckinridge was born in Bolivia. Who is the star?

BOLIVIA ANSWERS

(1) La Paz

(2) Sucre

(3) Paraguay

(4) Evo Morales

(5) Lake Titicaca

(6) Spanish

(7) Only with Paraguay

(8) Roman Catholic (c. 78%); Protestant (19%)

(9) The boliviano

(10) Red, yellow and green

(11) Islands in Lake Titicaca

(12) False; Santa Cruz de la Sierra is the biggest city.

(13) Lithium

(14) Che Guevara

(15) Salt. It's the largest salt flat in the world.

(16) True

(17) To Chile; Bolivia still asserts its claim today to the Department of the Litoral, as the coast is known.

(18) Lent

(19) False; he was born in Venezuela. Bolivia is named after him, however.

(20) Raquel Welch

BOSNIA AND HERZEGOVINA QUESTIONS

(1) On which peninsula is Bosnia and Herzegovina situated?

(2) True or false: It is a landlocked country.

(3) On which sea is the coastal strip?

(4) Archduke Franz Ferdinand was assassinated in the capital city in 1914. What is its name?

(5) Is Herzegovina in the north or the south of the country?

(6) To which country did Bosnia and Herzegovina belong from the end of World War I until 1992?

(7) What is the name of the town where a massacre of more than 8,000 took place in 1995 during the Bosnian War?

(8) What is the name of the town on the River Neretva famous for its old bridge which was destroyed in 1993 and subsequently rebuilt?

(9) Into which river does the River Sava, which forms part of the border between Bosnia and Croatia, flow?

(10) Which three nationalities make up the majority of the inhabitants of Bosnia and Herzegovina?

(11) What is the majority religion?

(12) In which year did the Winter Olympics take place in Sarajevo?

(13) With which of the arts are the names Emir Kusturica and Danis Tanovic associated?

(14) Are there stars or stripes on the country's flag?

(15) With what sport is Sarajevo-born Edin Dzeko associated: football, basketball or tennis?

(16) What is the name of the film festival, founded in 1995, the largest one in Southeast Europe?

(17) What is the second biggest city whose name in English means Ban's meadow?

(18) Which empire occupied Bosnia and Herzegovina from 1878 until the end of World War I?

(19) For which Bavarian team did Hasan Salihamidzic play from 1998 – 2007?

(20) What was Bosnian writer Ivo Andric awarded in 1961?

BOSNIA AND HERZEGOVINA ANSWERS

(1)   The Balkan Peninsula

(2)   False; it has a narrow strip of coast of about 20 kms.

(3)   On the Adriatic

(4)   Sarajevo

(5)   In the south

(6)   Yugoslavia

(7)   Srebrenica

(8)   Mostar

(9)   The Danube

(10) Bosniaks, Serbs and Croats

(11) Islam (c. 51%)

(12) 1984

(13) Cinema

(14) Stars

(15) Football; he has captained the national team.

(16) The Sarajevo Film Festival

(17) Banja Luka

(18) The Austro-Hungarian Empire

(19) FC Bayern München

(20) The Nobel Prize for Literature

BOTSWANA QUESTIONS

(1) By what name was Botswana known until 1966?

(2) Of which country was Bechuanaland a protectorate?

(3) Which desert makes up about 70% of Botswana's territory?

(4) Which precious stone is of particular importance to Botswana's economy?

(5) What is the capital of Botswana?

(6) The pula is the currency of Botswana. Pula is also used as the word for a type of weather which does not happen very often in Botswana. What sort of weather?

(7) What is the name of the famous delta named as one of the Seven Natural Wonders of Africa in 2013?

(8) Are the majority of the inhabitants Protestant or Catholic?

(9) Which river made famous by Rudyard Kipling's Just So stories forms the border between Botswana and South Africa?

(10) What are the Tswana, the BaKalanga and the San?

(11) By what other name are the San people known?

(12) What is the name of the series of novels by Alexander McCall Smith set in Botswana?

(13) True or false: Botswana is totally surrounded by South Africa.

(14) The border with one of the countries – South Africa, Namibia, Zimbabwe and Zambia – is very short, only 156 metres. Which country is it?

(15) What is the name of the first President of Botswana from 1966 – 1980 who married the British woman, Ruth Williams?

(16) What is the name of the 2016 film starring David Oyelowo and Rosamund Pike which told the story of Khama's controversial marriage?

(17) The Botswanan dish of seswaa is a meat dish made from beef and which other meat?

(18) After whom is the international airport in Gaborone named?

(19) Botswana has the largest population in Africa of which huge land mammal?

(20) A mokoro is often used in the Okavango Delta as transport. What is it?

BOTSWANA ANSWERS

(1)   Bechuanaland

(2)   The United Kingdom

(3)   The Kalahari Desert

(4)   The diamond

(5)   Gaborone

(6)   Rain

(7)   The Okavango Delta

(8)   Protestant (c. 66%)

(9)   The Limpopo

(10) The main ethnic groups in Botswana

(11) Bushmen

(12) The No. 1 Ladies' Detective Agency

(13) False; it also has borders with Namibia, Zimbabwe and Zambia

(14) Zambia

(15) Sir Seretse Khama

(16) A United Kingdom

(17) Goat

(18) Sir Seretse Khama

(19) The elephant

(20) A dugout canoe

BRAZIL QUESTIONS

(1)   Which city in Brazil has the largest population?

(2)   Who commanded the Portuguese fleet that arrived in Brazil in 1500 and claimed the country for Portugal?

(3)   True or false: Brazil is the only country in the world with the Equator and Tropic of Capricorn running through it.

(4)   What is the name of the president who came to power in January 2019?

(5)   What is the currency of Brazil?

(6)   On which mountain is the statue of Christ the Redeemer in Rio situated?

(7)   With which two South American countries does Brazil not share a border?

(8)   In how many Football World Cups did Pele play and how many times was he on the winning side?

(9)   Rio was the second city in Latin America to host the Summer Olympics. Which city was the first?

(10) What is the largest Brazilian city on the River Amazon?

(11) Of all the Brazilian Formula One drivers, which one won the most races?

(12) When does the Rio Carnival begin?

(13) What is the name of Brazil's national cocktail made with the sugarcane spirit cachaca?

(14) Which colour features most on the Brazilian flag?

(15) What was the profession of the famous Brazilian Oscar Niemeyer?

(16) Which important Brazilian city did Niemeyer help to design?

(17) What is the name of the region containing the world's largest wetlands on the border of Bolivia and Paraguay?

(18) What is the name of the martial art which combines elements of dance, acrobatics and music which was developed by enslaved Africans in Brazil?

(19) What is the title of the bossa nova song with music by Antonio Carlos Jobim which became an international hit in the 1960s for Stan Getz and Astrud Gilberto?

(20) Which former member of the Monty Python troupe directed the 1985 dystopian science fiction film Brazil starring Jonathan Pryce?

BRAZIL ANSWERS

(1) Sao Paulo

(2) Pedro Cabral

(3) True

(4) Jair Bolsonaro

(5) The real

(6) Corcovado (not to be confused with the Sugar Loaf Mountain)

(7) Chile and Ecuador

(8) He played in four World Cups (1958, 1962, 1966 and 1970) and won three. Brazil failed to win in 1966.

(9) Mexico City

(10) Manaus

(11) Ayrton Senna (41) followed by Nelson Piquet (23)

(12) The Friday before Ash Wednesday

(13) Caipirinha

(14) Green

(15) Architect

(16) The capital Brasilia

(17) Pantanal

(18) Capoeira

(19) The Girl from Ipanema

(20) Terry Gilliam

BRUNEI QUESTIONS

(1)   In which continent is Brunei located?

(2)   On which island is Brunei located?

(3)   Which other two nations share the island of Borneo with Brunei?

(4)   True or false: Borneo is the largest island in Asia.

(5)   Which of the three countries, Brunei, Indonesia and Malaysia, has the most territory on Borneo?

(6)   Does Brunei have a border with both Indonesia and Malaysia?

(7)   Of which country did Brunei become a protectorate in 1888?

(8)   What two commodities have contributed greatly to Brunei's wealth?

(9)   What is the capital of Brunei?

(10) Which country occupied Brunei during the Second World War?

(11) Is Brunei an emirate or a sultanate?

(12) What is the official language?

(13) On which sea does Brunei have a coastline?

(14) How does Malaysia come between Brunei geographically?

(15) What has Brunei been building in order to connect the two parts?

(16) What is the official religion of Brunei?

(17) What is unusual about the housing of Kampong Ayer on the Brunei River?

(18) Which of the words in the name of the capital, Bandar Seri Begawan, means city or port?

(19) The long form of the country's name is Brunei Darussalam. What does Darussalam mean?

(20) What strict Islamic law did Brunei adopt in 2014?

BRUNEI ANSWERS

(1) Asia

(2) On Borneo

(3) Indonesia and Malaysia

(4) True; 743,330 km²

(5) Indonesia (c. 73%). Malaysia has about 26% and Brunei only 1%.

(6) No, only with Malaysia

(7) The United Kingdom

(8) Petroleum and natural gas

(9) Bandar Seri Begawan

(10) Japan

(11) A sultanate

(12) Malay (English, however, is widely used.)

(13) The South China Sea

(14) Brunei has two unconnected parts which are separated by Malaysia (Sarawak).

(15) A 30-kilometre bridge (The Temburong Bridge)

(16) Islam

(17) It consists of traditional stilt villages built on the river. Kampong Ayer means "water village".

(18) Bandar

(19) The Abode of Peace

(20) Sharia law

BULGARIA QUESTIONS

(1) The director and former actress Coppola shares her first name with the Bulgarian capital. What is it?

(2) Which Empire ruled Bulgaria for almost 500 years until 1878?

(3) With which country does Bulgaria have a border to the north?

(4) What river constitutes the border between Bulgaria and Romania?

(5) Of what did Bulgaria become a member on 1st January 2007?

(6) Does Bulgaria have a Black Sea or a Caspian Sea coast?

(7) What is the biggest city on the Black Sea?

(8) Which minority, often discriminated against in Europe, makes up about 5% of the population in Bulgaria and is the largest of such a minority in Europe?

(9) What is the name of the script used in written Bulgarian?

(10) Which two sports, both beginning with W, have produced the most medals for Bulgaria at the Summer Olympics?

(11) What is the name of the last king or tsar of Bulgaria from 1943 to 1946 who later served as prime minister from 2001 to 2005?

(12) Vasil Levski, a revolutionary and national hero of Bulgaria today, who was executed in 1873, tried to free the country from whose rule?

(13) Which Bulgarian football player played for CSKA Sofia and Barcelona and 83 times for the national team?

(14) Who or what is Uncle Bulgaria?

(15) With which sport is Grigor Dimitrov associated?

(16) What name is given to a major seaside resort on the Black Sea Coast near a national park of the same name?

(17) What is the name of the largest and most famous Eastern Orthodox monastery situated in the Rila Mountains?

(18) The second city of Bulgaria was selected as co-host of the 2019 European Capital of Culture. What is its name?

(19) What stage of the 1994 football World Cup did Bulgaria reach: the final, semi-final or quarter-final?

(20) Which Bulgarian-born writer, who lived most of his life in Austria and the UK, was awarded the Nobel Prize for Literature in 1981?

BULGARIA ANSWERS

(1)   Sofia

(2)   The Ottoman Empire

(3)   Romania

(4)   The Danube

(5)   The European Union

(6)   A Black Sea coast

(7)   Varna

(8)   The Roma or Romani people

(9)   Cyrillic script

(10) Weightlifting and wrestling

(11) Simeon

(12) The Ottoman Empire

(13) Hristo Stoichkov

(14) The oldest and wisest of the Wombles of Wimbledon

(15) Tennis

(16) Golden Sands

(17) The Rila Monastery (The Monastery of Saint Ivan of Rila)

(18) Plovdiv

(19) The semi-final. Bulgaria was beaten by Italy 2 – 1.

(20) Elias Canetti

BURKINA FASO QUESTIONS

(1) By what name was Burkina Faso known from 1958 – 1984?

(2) What is the capital city?

(3) True or false: Ouagadougou is the only capital city in the world which begins with O.

(4) What is pictured in the middle of the country's flag, (a) a star (b) a sun?

(5) Which European language is the official language of Burkina Faso?

(6) What is the name of the major river which flows through Burkina Faso into Ghana?

(7) The River Volta has three main parts named after colours: La Volta Blanche, La Volta Noire et La Volta Rouge. What are the three colours in English?

(8) True or false: Burkina Faso has a coast on the Gulf of Guinea and the Atlantic Ocean.

(9) The currency of Burkina Faso is the West African CFA franc. What is the subunit of it?

(10) Who or what are Burkinabé?

(11) Is Bobo-Dioulasso the name of a city in Burkina Faso or the name of a famous DJ?

(12) What is the harmattan?

(13) True or false: Part of Burkina Faso is in the Sahel, the region between the Sahara in the north and the savanna to the south.

(14) In what area of the arts are Gaston Kaboré, Idrissa Ouedraogo and Dani Kouyate internationally known?

(15) What are Mossi, Dyula, Fulfulde and Gourmanché?

(16) Which sport is celebrated in the Tour du Faso?

(17) Burkina Faso has a border with which other country beginning with B?

(18) What was the name of the federation of eight French colonial territories including Burkina Faso which existed from 1895 to 1960?

(19) True or false: Burkina Faso received its first UNESCO World Heritage site in 2009.

(20) "Faso" comes from the Dyula language and has a similar meaning to the German word Vaterland. What is the equivalent in English?

BURKINA FASO ANSWERS

(1)   Upper Volta

(2)   Ouagadougou

(3)   False: There is also Oslo, the capital of Norway, and Ottawa, the capital of Canada

(4)   (a) A star

(5)   French

(6)   The River Volta

(7)   White, black and red

(8)   False; it is landlocked.

(9)   The centime

(10) It's the name of the citizens of Burkina Faso.

(11) It's the name of the second biggest city in the country.

(12) A hot, dry wind which blows from the Sahara in Burkina Faso and other West African nations

(13) True (Northern Burkina Faso)

(14) Film; they are all filmmakers.

(15) Languages spoken in Burkina Faso

(16) Cycling

(17) Benin

(18) French West Africa

(19) True: the ruins of Loropéni

(20) Fatherland

BURUNDI QUESTIONS

(1)   What is the capital of Burundi?

(2)   What is the largest city?

(3)   In which year was the capital of Burundi officially changed to Gitega?

(4)   Which major lake lies along Burundi's southwestern border?

(5)   Which country colonised Burundi before the First World War?

(6)   Which country took over from Germany after World War I?

(7)   On which side of the road do they drive in Burundi?

(8)   With which country to the north was Burundi linked during colonial times?

(9)   In which European country did Burundian footballer Mohamed Tchité play most of his professional football?

(10) True or false: Most of the population are Muslim.

(11) Lake Tanganyika is the second deepest lake in the world. What is the deepest?

(12) Are Burundi's two main exports (a) coffee and tea or (b) wine and beer?

(13) Which large country borders Burundi to the west?

(14) The two main ethnic groups are well known because of the genocide both in Burundi and Rwanda. What are the two groups?

(15) Which ethnic group is larger in Burundi, the Hutu or the Tutsi?

(16) Kirundi and which two European languages are official languages of Burundi?

(17) What was the title of the minor hit single recorded by Burundi Steiphenson Black in 1971?

(18) Do most of the inhabitants live in towns or on the land?

(19) The source of the southernmost tributary of which great African river is in Burundi?

(20) What is the name of the well-known percussion ensemble from Burundi?

BURUNDI ANSWERS

(1)   Gitega

(2)   Bujumbura

(3)   In 2019

(4)   Lake Tanganyika

(5)   Germany

(6)   Belgium

(7)   On the right

(8)   Rwanda (as Ruanda-Urundi until 1962)

(9)   Belgium

(10) False; most are Christian.

(11) Lake Baikal in Russia

(12) (a) Coffee and tea

(13) The Democratic Republic of the Congo

(14) Hutu and Tutsi

(15) The Hutu (85%), the Tutsi (14%)

(16) French and English

(17) Burundi Black

(18) On the land

(19) The Nile

(20) The (Royal) Drummers of Burundi

CAMBODIA QUESTIONS

(1)   What is the alternative name for Cambodia?

(2)   On which peninsula is it located?

(3)   Which group was responsible for the genocide which took place in Cambodia in the 1970s?

(4)   What is the capital of Cambodia?

(5)   The world's twelfth longest river flows through the city. What is its name?

(6)   What is the name of the famous Hindu temple complex, the largest religious monument in the world?

(7)   What 1984 film directed by Roland Joffé takes place during the civil war with the Khmer Rouge and tells the story of American journalist Sydney Schanberg and his Cambodian assistant Dith Pran?

(8)   Who won a best supporting actor Oscar for his performance as Dith Pran?

(9)   Is Cambodia a kingdom or a republic?

(10)   What article of clothing is the traditional Cambodian krama?

(11)   What is the predominant religion in Cambodia?

(12)   Born in 1922, this man became head of state of Cambodia several times, including king. Who is he?

(13)   What is the name of the coastal city named in honour of Sihanouk?

(14)   Is the Khmer language written in the same script as English?

(15)   Who plays the renegade colonel Kurtz who goes AWOL in Cambodia in the 1979 film Apocalypse Now?

(16)   Cambodia has a border with Laos, Thailand and which other country?

(17)   Which British singer had a hit with the song Cambodia in 1981?

(18)   Is the Internet country code top level domain .cm or .kh?

(19)   Who was the infamous leader of the Khmer Rouge who was prime minister of Democratic Kampuchea from 1976 – 1979 and who was responsible for millions of deaths?

(20)   Do Cambodians normally run amok or do they eat it?

CAMBODIA ANSWERS

(1) Kampuchea

(2) Indochina

(3) Khmer Rouge

(4) Phnom Penh

(5) The Mekong

(6) Angkor Wat

(7) The Killing Fields

(8) Haing S. Ngor

(9) A kingdom

(10) A type of scarf or bandanna

(11) Buddhism (95%)

(12) Norodom Sihanouk

(13) Sihanoukville

(14) No

(15) Marlon Brando

(16) Vietnam

(17) Kim Wilde

(18) .kh

(19) Pol Pot

(20) They eat it. It's a coconut milk curried dish made with chicken, fish or shrimp and vegetables.

CAMEROON QUESTIONS

(1) Between which two countries was Cameroon divided after World War I?

(2) Is the capital city Douala or Yaoundé?

(3) Because it possesses all major climates and vegetation of Africa, Cameroon is sometimes called "Africa in what"?

(4) Does Cameroon have a border with the Democratic Republic of the Congo or the Republic of the Congo or both?

(5) Which lake, which is named after another African country, is situated on the Northernmost border of Cameroon?

(6) Is Douala situated on the coast or inland?

(7) Did Cameroon gain independence from Britain and France in the 1960s or the 1970s?

(8) Which country colonised the country in 1884 and called it Kamerun?

(9) The country got its name from sailors who named a river there Rio dos Camaroes because it contained a lot of shrimps. What nationality were they?

(10) True or false: Cameroon is a member of the Commonwealth.

(11) The Cameroon national football team won the gold medal at the 2000 Summer Olympics. In which city did the games take place?

(12) What position did Paul Biya take over in Cameroon in 1982?

(13) Is the highest mountain in Cameroon named after the country or the capital?

(14) Which Cameroonian footballer, who played for Barcelona, Inter Milan and Chelsea, was African Player of the Year a record four times?

(15) Cameroon is situated on the Bight of Biafra. What is the Bight of Biafra?

(16) Cameroon shares its longest border with this country and also problems with the terrorist group Boko Haram. Which country?

(17) Which Cameroon footballer was one of the stars of the 1990 World Cup and was famous for dancing around the corner flag after having scored a goal?

(18) True or false: Cameroon has the same time as the United Kingdom.

(19) Makossa is a Cameroonian urban music style. Who recorded the song Soul Makossa in 1972?

(20) The chant "mamako, mamasa, maka makossa" was used by which artist in the song Wanna Be Startin' Something?

CAMEROON ANSWERS

(1) Between France and the United Kingdom

(2) Yaoundé

(3) Miniature

(4) Only the Republic of the Congo

(5) Lake Chad

(6) On the coast

(7) In the 1960s

(8) Germany

(9) Portuguese

(10) True; it joined in 1995.

(11) Sydney

(12) President

(13) The country: Mount Cameroon (4,100m)

(14) Samuel Eto'o

(15) A bay in the Gulf of Guinea, named after a part of Nigeria

(16) Nigeria

(17) Roger Milla

(18) False; it has GMT + one hour

(19) Manu Dibango

(20) Michael Jackson

CANADA QUESTIONS

(1) What colour is the maple leaf on the Canadian flag?

(2) True or false: Canada is the world's largest country.

(3) What is the biggest Canadian city as far as population is concerned?

(4) What is Canada's smallest province?

(5) Which city in Nova Scotia has the same name as a town in Yorkshire?

(6) Which capital city was founded in 1826 as Bytown?

(7) Which 16th century explorer claimed Canada for France?

(8) Apart from Saskatchewan, which other Canadian province is landlocked?

(9) Which country did Canadian-born singer Celine Dion represent in the 1988 Eurovision Song Contest?

(10) In and around which city were the 1988 Winter Olympics held?

(11) Which Canadian writer wrote the novel The Handmaid's Tale?

(12) What is Nunavut?

(13) True or false: Justin Bieber and Shawn Mendes were born in Canada.

(14) What is Canada's largest island?

(15) What is the name of the father and son, both of whom have been prime minister of Canada?

(16) In which year were the Summer Olympics held in Montreal?

(17) Which city in British Columbia is often named as one of the top five cities worldwide for quality of life?

(18) True or false: Canada has the longest coastline in the world.

(19) What is the national animal of Canada?

(20) What is the largest lake entirely in Canada?

CANADA ANSWERS

(1)   red

(2)   False; Russia is bigger.

(3)   Toronto

(4)   Prince Edward Island

(5)   Halifax

(6)   Ottawa

(7)   Jacques Cartier

(8)   Alberta

(9)   Switzerland (She won the competition.)

(10)   Calgary

(11)   Margaret Atwood

(12)   The largest and most northerly territory of Canada

(13)   True

(14)   Baffin Island

(15)   Pierre and Justin Trudeau

(16)   1976

(17)   Vancouver

(18)   True

(19)   The beaver

(20)   Great Bear Lake

CAPE VERDE QUESTIONS

(1)   In which ocean is Cape Verde located?

(2)   True or false: Cape Verde consists of only one island.

(3)   To which continent does Cape Verde belong?

(4)   What is the capital?

(5)   The capital of Chile and the island on which Praia is located have the same name. What is it?

(6)   What is the official language of Cape Verde?

(7)   What does Cape Verde mean in English?

(8)   True or false: Before the arrival of Europeans, the Cape Verde islands were uninhabited.

(9)   What is the nearest African country to Cape Verde?

(10) True or false: Praia, the capital, has a population of more than 100,000.

(11) Which group which had hits in the 1970s with Heaven Must Be Missing an Angel and Don't Take Away the Music has Cape Verdean roots?

(12) The currency of Cape Verde is the same as the previous currency of Portugal. What is it?

(13) True or false: More than a million people live in Cape Verde.

(14) In which country in Africa with the capital city Dakar is the Cape Verde Peninsula?

(15) What international award did the singer Cesária Évora, known as the Barefoot Diva, win in 2004?

(16) Instead of Cape Verde, the country prefers to be called by the Portuguese name. What is it?

(17) After which singer is the airport on the island of Sao Vicente named?

(18) True or false: More Cape Verdeans live abroad than in Cape Verde.

(19) Is morna a music and dance genre or a tradition of oral story telling from Cape Verde?

(20) Cape Verde consists of the Barlavento and the Sotavento Islands. Which ones are the northern islands?

CAPE VERDE ANSWERS

(1) The Atlantic Ocean

(2) False; there are 10 main islands and several islets.

(3) Africa

(4) Praia

(5) Santiago

(6) Portuguese

(7) Green cape

(8) True

(9) Senegal

(10) True

(11) Tavares

(12) The (Cape Verdean) escudo

(13) False; the population is about 550,000.

(14) Senegal

(15) A grammy for her album Voz d'Amor

(16) Cabo Verde

(17) Cesária Évora

(18) True

(19) A music and dance genre

(20) The Barlavento Islands

CENTRAL AFRICAN REPUBLIC QUESTIONS

(1)   The capital of the Central African Republic (CAR) is situated on the Ubangi River. What is its name?

(2)   Which country colonized CAR in the late 19th century?

(3)   The motto of the country is Unité, Dignité, Travail. What does this mean?

(4)   There are five different colours on the CAR flag. Name two of them.

(5)   Is CAR landlocked or does it have a coast?

(6)   What precious stone is the most important export of CAR?

(7)   In which sport has CAR won the African Championship twice?

(8)   What is Sangho?

(9)   Apart from Sangho, which other European language is an official language of CAR?

(10) Paris has 20 of these urban districts and Bangui eight. What name is usually used for them?

(11) Is the Dzanga-Sangha National Park located in a desert area or a rain forest area?

(12) CAR has a border with a country which came into being in 2011. Which country?

(13) Into which major river does the Ubangi River flow?

(14) True or false: CAR has been in a state of civil war for many years.

(15) Is the Seleka rebel group mostly Muslim or Christian?

(16) Is CAR situated north or south of the Equator?

(17) What natural catastrophe struck the country in October/ November 2019, drought or flooding?

(18) The national anthem of CAR has the same name as a European cultural movement spanning the 14th to the 17th century. What is its name?

(19) True or false: There are no railways in CAR.

(20) What is the name of the political and military leader who proclaimed himself Emperor of Central Africa in 1976?

CENTRAL AFRICAN REPUBLIC ANSWERS

(1) Bangui

(2) France

(3) Unity, dignity, work

(4) Blue, white, green, yellow, red

(5) It's landlocked.

(6) The diamond

(7) Basketball

(8) A creole language widely spoken in CAR.

(9) French

(10) Arrondissements

(11) In a rain forest area

(12) South Sudan

(13) The Congo

(14) True

(15) Mostly Muslim

(16) North of the Equator

(17) Flooding

(18) La Renaissance

(19) True

(20) Jean-Bédel Bokassa

CHAD QUESTIONS

(1) The capital city N'Djamena faces the city of Kousséri on the other side of the Chari River. In which country is Kousséri?

(2) Into which lake does the Chari River flow?

(3) The flag of Chad is identical to a country on the Black Sea, the capital of which is Bucharest. Which country?

(4) The three zones of Chad are the Savanna in the south, the Sahelian belt in the middle and what in the north?

(5) Was Chad part of French West Africa or French Equatorial Africa?

(6) Lake Chad is surrounded by four countries: 2 Cs, Chad and Cameroon, and 2 Ns. What are the 2 Ns?

(7) What is the French spelling of the Country Chad?

(8) In recent years many refugees have fled from Darfur to Chad. In which country is Darfur?

(9) Apart from French, what is the other official language of Chad?

(10) All Chad's borders with other countries are over one thousand kilometres in length, except for which country, the capital of which is Abuja?

(11) Which cereal crop is most widely used in Chadian cuisine?

(12) Are the majority of people in Chad Christian or Muslim?

(13) Do most of the Muslim population live in the north or the south of the country?

(14) What catastrophic development has happened to Lake Chad in recent decades, similar to what has happened to the Sea of Aral in Central Asia?

(15) Since 2003 oil has replaced what soft, fluffy fibre as the main export?

(16) What are Moundou and Sarh?

(17) By what name was N'Djamena known from 1900 to 1973?

(18) Which city in Cameroon is the nearest seaport to N'Djamena?

(19) Chad has never won any Olympic medals, but what special honour for their country did Bibiro Ali Taher in 2016 and Carine Ngarlemdana in 2012 carry out?

(20) The name Chad comes from the Kanuri language and means (a) a desert or (b) a lake. Which one is correct?

CHAD ANSWERS

(1) Cameroon

(2) Lake Chad

(3) Romania (Both flags have vertical stripes of blue, yellow and red.)

(4) The Sahara Desert

(5) French Equatorial Africa

(6) Niger and Nigeria

(7) Tchad

(8) Sudan

(9) Arabic

(10) Nigeria

(11) Millet

(12) Muslim (55%), Christian (41%)

(13) In the north

(14) The drying up of the lake

(15) Cotton

(16) The second and third biggest cities in Chad

(17) Fort-Lamy

(18) Douala (1,060 km. away)

(19) They carried the flag of Chad at the opening ceremonies.

(20) (b) A lake

CHILE QUESTIONS

(1) What is the full name of the capital city?

(2) What is the unit of currency in Chile?

(3) Is Chile (a) 3,200 (b) 4,200 or (c) 5,200 km. long?

(4) True or false: Chile has a border with Brazil.

(5) What is the name of Chile's second city?

(6) For which Bavarian football team did the Chilean Arturo Vidal play from 2015 to 2018?

(7) Who was the first European to set foot in Chile?

(8) True or false: Aconcagua, the highest mountain in South America, is situated in Chile.

(9) Who was the head of the military dictatorship which ruled Chile between 1973 and 1990?

(10) What is the name of Chile's most famous poet who was one of the main characters in the award-winning 1994 film Il Postino?

(11) What is the name of the desert in the north of Chile, one of the driest places on earth, which contains great mineral wealth?

(12) With which sport do you associate the Chilean Marcelo Rios?

(13) In which year did Chile host the football World Cup?

(14) True or false: Easter Island belongs to Chile.

(15) What record does the 6,893m. high volcano Ojos del Salado hold?

(16) What is the name of the novelist who wrote The House of Spirits and who is related to the man who was President of Chile from 1970 to 1973?

(17) In which decade did the Great Chilean earthquake, the most powerful earthquake ever recorded, take place?

(18) Which Irish-sounding independence leader freed Chile from Spanish rule in the Chilean War of Independence in the early 19ᵗʰ century?

(19) What name is given to the indigenous inhabitants of south-central Chile who traditionally lived in the region of Araucania?

(20) The increase in the price of what transport system was one of the catalysts for the country-wide protests in 2019?

(1)   Santiago de Chile

(2)   The peso

(3)   4,200 km.

(4)   False

(5)   Valparaiso

(6)   FC Bayern München

(7)   Ferdinand Magellan

(8)   False; it's in Argentina.

(9)   Augusto Pinochet

(10) Pablo Neruda

(11) The Atacama Desert

(12) Tennis

(13) 1962

(14) True

(15) It's the highest active volcano in the world.

(16) Isabel Allende

(17) In the 1960s (22 May 1960)

(18) Bernardo O'Higgins

(19) The Mapuche

(20) The Santiago Metro's subway fare

CHINA QUESTIONS

(1)   How many stars are there on the Chinese flag?

(2)   The renminbi is the name of the Chinese currency, but what name refers to the currency's primary unit?

(3)   What is the longest river in China?

(4)   During which dynasty was gunpowder invented: (a) Tang (b) Ming?

(5)   What is the name of the controversial telecommunications and electronics giant with its headquarters in Shenzhen, Guangdong?

(6)   What was the name of the economic and social campaign carried out by the Communist Party of China from 1958 to 1962 which resulted in millions of deaths?

(7)   True or false: the giant panda can only be found in the wild in China.

(8)   What is the name of the square in Beijing where student-led demonstrations were brutally suppressed in 1989?

(9)   In which year did Beijing host the Summer Olympics?

(10)   What name is given to the imperial palaces of the Ming and Qing Dynasties in Beijing?

(11)   To which country did the city of Macau belong before it was transferred to China in 1999?

(12)   Who was China's most famous philosopher born in 551 BC?

(13)   Puxi, the Bund, Lujiazui and Pudong: Which Chinese city are we in?

(14)   Which politician became the fourth Chief Executive of Hong Kong in 2017?

(15)   Who wrote the play The Good Person of Szechwan?

(16)   The Chinese call it Zhongguo. What do we call it?

(17)   What is the name of the martial art involving a form of moving meditation?

(18)   Who directed the film The Last Emperor which told of the life of Puyi, the last emperor of China?

(19)   Which US president did Mao Zedong welcome to China in 1972?

(20)   What is the meaning of the word Beijing – very appropriate considering its geographical position and its status in China?

CHINA ANSWERS

(1)   Five: one big one and four smaller ones

(2)   The yuan

(3)   The Yangtze

(4)   (a) Tang – in the 9th century

(5)   Huawei

(6)   The Great Leap Forward

(7)   True

(8)   Tiananmen Square

(9)   2008

(10) The Forbidden City

(11) Portugal

(12) Confucius

(13) Shanghai

(14) Carrie Lam

(15) Bertolt Brecht

(16) China; it's the official Chinese name of the country.

(17) Tai chi

(18) Bernardo Bertolucci

(19) Richard Nixon

(20) Northern capital

COLOMBIA QUESTIONS

(1) Colombia has a coast on an ocean and a sea. What are their names?

(2) Why was President Juan Manuel Santos awarded the 2016 Nobel Peace Prize in 2016?

(3) What is the abbreviation used to describe the main guerrilla movement in the civil war?

(4) What is the capital city?

(5) The second-biggest city is named after a small village in Spain where the explorer Hernán Cortés was born. What is its name?

(6) How many countries in South America have a bigger population than Colombia?

(7) True or false: The three horizontal stripes on the Colombian flag are all the same size.

(8) Laundry Service, Oral Fixation, Vol. 2 and She Wolf were albums by this singer. Who is she?

(9) With which Central American country does Colombia have a border?

(10) What is Pico Cristóbal Colón?

(11) What is the name of the Nobel Literature prizewinner who wrote One Hundred Years of Solitude and Love in the Time of Cholera?

(12) Is Tejo (a) a Columbian sport or (b) a Columbian river?

(13) Because it has such a large number of different species, Colombia is one of the 17 megadiverse countries in the world. There are four other South American countries in the list. Can you name two of them?

(14) With which sport do you associate Juan Pablo Montoya?

(15) Is the historic city of Cartagena (UNESCO World Heritage Site) on the Pacific or the Caribbean coast?

(16) What is the name of the Colombian national footballer who was loaned to Bayern München by Real Madrid in 2017?

(17) The airport in Bogota is named after the mythical golden realm of South America. What realm?

(18) What is the name of the Colombian cyclist who became the first Latin American to win the Tour de France in 2019?

(19) What would you do with a chiva, (a) eat it (b) drink it or (c) travel in it?

(20) Colombian singer Juanes had a number one single in Germany and France in 2005 with the song La Camisa Negra. What does the title of the song mean?

COLOMBIA ANSWERS

(1)   The Pacific Ocean and the Caribbean Sea

(2)   "For his resolute efforts to bring the country's more than 50-year-long civil war to an end."

(3)   FARC: Fuerzas Armadas Revolucionarias de Colombia

(4)   Bogota

(5)   Medellin

(6)   Only Brazil (212 million); Colombia's population is 51 million

(7)   False; the top yellow stripe is bigger than the other two.

(8)   Shakira

(9)   Panama

(10) The highest mountain in Colombia (5,700m)

(11) Gabriel Garcia Márquez

(12) (a) A sport. It's a throwing sport.

(13) Two from Brazil, Ecuador, Peru, Venezuela

(14) Motor racing

(15) On the Caribbean coast

(16) James (Rodriguez)

(17) El Dorado

(18) Egan Bernal

(19) (c) Travel in it; it's a colourful, rustic bus used in rural Colombia.

(20) The Black Shirt

COMOROS QUESTIONS

(1)   True or false: Comoros is an island country.

(2)   In which ocean are the islands situated?

(3)   What is the capital?

(4)   Are the majority of the inhabitants Christian or Muslim?

(5)   True or false: Comoros is a member of the Arab league.

(6)   What are Grande Comore, Mohéli and Anjouan?

(7)   What is the name of the fourth island which rejected independence in 1974 and decided to remain with France, even though Comoros still lays claim to it?

(8)   Apart from Comorian, which are the two other official languages of the islands?

(9)   True or false: Comoros has had a stable government since independence from France.

(10) Which large African island is situated near to Comoros?

(11) The channel in which the islands are located is named after the closest country on the African continent. Which country?

(12) Of the three islands, Grande Comore, Anjouan and Mohéli, which is the biggest?

(13) Which fish, thought for many years to be extinct, is sometimes found in the vicinity of the Comoros?

(14) On which of the three islands is the capital Moroni located?

(15) True or false: The Comorian language is a dialect of Swahili.

(16) Name two of the five colours featured on the flag.

(17) Is the majority of the population Sunni Islam or Shi'ite?

(18) Which bat, named after a famous British Africa explorer, can now only be found on the island of Anjouan and nowhere else?

(19) What nationality were the European explorers who first visited Comoros in 1503?

(20) What are Ngazidja, Nduzwani and Mwali?

COMOROS ANSWERS

(1) True

(2) The Indian Ocean

(3) Moroni

(4) Muslim

(5) True

(6) The three main islands of Comoros

(7) Mayotte

(8) Arabic and French

(9) False; there have been over 20 coups since 1974.

(10) Madagascar

(11) Mozambique

(12) Grande Comore

(13) The coelacanth

(14) Grande Comore

(15) True

(16) Two from yellow, white, red, blue, green

(17) Sunni Islam

(18) The Livingstone bat

(19) Portuguese

(20) The three islands, Grande Comore, Anjouan and Mohéli, in the local language

COSTA RICA QUESTIONS

(1) What is the literal translation of the name Costa Rica?

(2) Is the capital San Juan or San José?

(3) What is the official language?

(4) Which country borders Costa Rica to the north?

(5) True or false: The Costa Rican flag consists of the same colours as the Union Jack.

(6) From which country do the most tourists come from who visit Costa Rica?

(7) On a clear day from the top of the highest mountain, Mount Chirripó, it is possible to see which two bodies of water?

(8) What is the furthest that the Costa Rican national football team has progressed in the World Cup?

(9) To whom or to what do the words Ticos and Ticas refer?

(10) Which famous novel written by Michael Crichton in 1990 and made into a film by Steven Spielberg, takes place on the fictional Costa Rican island of Isla Nublar?

(11) With which sport do you associate Costa Rican Paulo Wanchope?

(12) The currency of Costa Rica sounds like an English punctuation mark. What is it?

(13) Is the important resort of Puntarenas on the Caribbean or on the Pacific?

(14) True or false: Dionne Warwick's song Do You Know the Way to San José written by Burt Bacharach and Hal David is about the Costa Rican capital.

(15) Gallo Pinto, the national dish of Costa Rica, consists of beans and which cereal grain?

(16) In which aquatic sport did Claudia Poll win Costa Rica's first Olympic gold medal in the 1996 Olympics?

(17) Which important prize was the then President of Costa Rica, Oscar Arias Sanchez, awarded in 1987 for his efforts to end the Central American crisis of civil wars and communist revolutions?

(18) What percentage of the land in Costa Rica consists of national parks and protected areas?

(19) True or false: Costa Rica does not have an army.

(20) What important transport hub in San José is named after the national hero of Costa Rica, Juan Santamariá, a drummer boy who died in 1856 defending his country against forces led by US filibuster William Walker?

(1) Rich coast

(2) San José

(3) Spanish

(4) Nicaragua

(5) True: red, white and blue

(6) The United States (c. 1 million)

(7) The Pacific Ocean and the Caribbean Sea

(8) The quarter finals in 2014

(9) They are the colloquial words for the male and female inhabitants of Costa Rica.

(10) Jurassic Park

(11) Football; he played for Derby County, West Ham United and Manchester City, amongst other teams.

(12) The (Costa Rican) colon

(13) On the Pacific

(14) False; it's about San José in California.

(15) Rice

(16) Swimming (200 metres freestyle)

(17) The Nobel Peace Prize

(18) About 25%

(19) True

(20) The airport

COTE D'IVOIRE QUESTIONS

(1) What does Cote d'Ivoire mean in English?

(2) In which part of Africa is it situated – north, south, east or west?

(3) What is the country's biggest city?

(4) Is Abidjan or Yamoussoukro the political capital?

(5) True or false: The Cote d'Ivoire flag is identical to the Irish flag.

(6) On which gulf does Abidjan lie?

(7) What is the official language?

(8) Cote d'Ivoire is bordered by Guinea to the west and by which G to the east?

(9) What is the shape of the famous building in Abidjan designed by the Italian architect Rinaldo Olivieri. Is it (a) a rectangle (b) a pyramid or (c) an obelisk?

(10) Which Ivorian footballer played for Chelsea between 2004 and 2012?

(11) Of which bean is Cote d'Ivoire the world's largest exporter?

(12) The cathedral in Abidjan has the same name as a famous cathedral in London. Which one?

(13) True or false: Cote d'Ivoire qualified for the 1995 Rugby World Cup.

(14) Which part of the country is predominantly Muslim, the north or the south?

(15) True or false: Over 50% of Ivorians are Muslim.

(16) For which English football club, sometimes known as the Sky Blues, did Yaya Touré of Cote d'Ivoire play between 2010 and 2018?

(17) What is the nickname of the Cote d'Ivoire national football team?

(18) In which language is the country known as Elfenbeinküste?

(19) The head of which animal can be seen on the country's coat-of-arms?

(20) What world record does the Basilica of Our Lady of Peace in Yamoussoukro hold?

(1) Ivory Coast

(2) West Africa

(3) Abidjan

(4) Yamoussoukro

(5) The colours are the same, but are in a different order: Ivory Coast – orange, white, green; Ireland – green, white, orange

(6) The Gulf of Guinea

(7) French

(8) Ghana

(9) A pyramid

(10) Didier Drogba

(11) The cocoa bean

(12) St. Paul's Cathedral

(13) True

(14) The north

(15) False: The figure is about 43%

(16) Manchester City

(17) Les Éléphants

(18) In German

(19) The head of an elephant

(20) It's the largest Christian church in the world.

CROATIA QUESTIONS

(1)   Which country was Croatia a part of from 1918 to independence in 1991?

(2)   Apart from Kosovo, which other former Yugoslav state does Croatia not have a border with?

(3)   True or false: Zagreb, the capital of Croatia, is on the River Danube.

(4)   Which British rock star portrayed Croatian-born scientist Nikola Tesla in the film The Prestige in 2006?

(5)   What is the name of the city on the Adriatic Sea right in the south of Croatia which is one of the most visited tourist destinations in the Mediterranean?

(6)   Which city was historically known as Agram?

(7)   Name either the Croatian group or the title of the song which won the Eurovision Song Contest for Yugoslavia in 1989.

(8)   Which peninsula in the northern Adriatic does Croatia share with Slovenia and Italy?

(9)   Why is the international car registration for Croatia HR?

(10) What is the second biggest city in Croatia?

(11) What are Hvar, Cres, Krk, Rab and Pag?

(12) What is the name of the Croatian tennis player who won the 2001 Wimbledon men's singles title as a wildcard?

(13) Which city on the Adriatic coast was frequently used as a location for the TV series Game of Thrones?

(14) True or false: Croatia is a member of the European Union.

(15) Which Croatian football player won the Golden Ball award for Best Player at the 2018 World Cup Finals?

(16) Who became the first President of Croatia in 1990 until his death in 1999?

(17) The roots of which breed of dog can be traced back to a historical region of Croatia?

(18) What national park in central Croatia near the border with Bosnia and Herzegovina, famous for its lakes, became a UNESCO World Heritage Site in 1979?

(19) Which city on the Danube was heavily damaged during the Croatian War of Independence in the early 1990s?

(20) What is the name of the traditional a cappella singing in Dalmatia which in 2012 was inscribed in UNESCO Intangible Cultural Heritage of Humanity?

CROATIA ANSWERS

(1)   Yugoslavia

(2)   North Macedonia

(3)   False; it's on the River Sava.

(4)   David Bowie

(5)   Dubrovnik

(6)   Zagreb

(7)   The song: Rock Me, the group: Riva

(8)   Istria

(9)   It stands for Hrvatska, the Croatian for Croatia.

(10) Split

(11) Islands off the coast of Croatia

(12) Goran Ivanisevic

(13) Dubrovnik

(14) True: It joined in 2013.

(15) Luka Modric

(16) Franjo Tud(j)man

(17) The dalmatian

(18) Plitvice Lakes National Park

(19) Vukovar

(20) Klapa

CUBA QUESTIONS

(1) Who recorded the international hit song Havana in 2017?

(2) True or false: Cuba is the largest island in the Caribbean.

(3) In which year did the Cuban Missile Crisis break out?

(4) Who was US President at the time of the crisis?

(5) Who took over as First Secretary of the Central Committee of the Communist Party of Cuba after Fidel Castro's retirement from the post?

(6) What name is given to the failed invasion in 1961 of northern Cuba by US-sponsored Cuban exiles who hoped to reverse Fidel Castro's Cuban Revolution?

(7) Who was the Cuban-born singer of the Miami Sound Machine?

(8) Who was the US-backed military dictator who was President of Cuba between 1952 and 1959, having already served as president between 1940 and 1944?

(9) Which American comedienne was married to Cuban-born bandleader, actor and producer Desi Arnaz for twenty years?

(10) What is the most popular sport in Cuba?

(11) With what world-famous Cuban product are Torcedores connected?

(12) Which city in central Cuba, a UNESCO World Heritage site since 1988, has the same name as an island in the Caribbean?

(13) What is the name of the US naval base which has a famous detention centre for terrorists?

(14) Why is the country sometimes called El Cocodrilo in Spanish?

(15) What genre of Cuban dance music was particularly associated with the bandleader Pérez Prado?

(16) Who is the star of the 1990 film Havana about an American professional gambler who decides to visit the city on the eve of the Cuban Revolution in 1958?

(17) Which ensemble of Cuban musicians, established in 1996 to revive the music of pre-revolutionary Cuba, was featured in an award-winning documentary by Wim Wenders?

(18) Who wrote the novel Our Man in Havana?

(19) With which sport do you associate the Olympic gold medal winner Teófilo Stevenson?

(20) The city of Hialeah has the highest percentage of Cuban and Cuban-American residents in the USA. In which state is it?

CUBA ANSWERS

(1)   Camila Cabello

(2)   True (105,006 km²)

(3)   1962

(4)   John F. Kennedy

(5)   His brother, Raúl Castro

(6)   The Bay of Pigs

(7)   Gloria Estefan

(8)   Fulgencio Batista

(9)   Lucille Ball

(10) Baseball

(11) Cigars; they are the people who hand-roll them.

(12) Trinidad

(13) Guantanamo Bay Naval Base

(14) Because the outline of the island looks a bit like a crocodile.

(15) Mambo

(16) Robert Redford

(17) The Buena Vista Social Club

(18) Graham Greene

(19) Boxing

(20) Florida

CYPRUS QUESTIONS

(1) What are the two official languages of Cyprus?

(2) True or false: Cyprus is a member of the European Union.

(3) True or false: Lefkosia is the capital of Cyprus.

(4) What adjective and noun can be formed from the name Cyprus?

(5) True or false: Cyprus is the largest island in the Mediterranean.

(6) True or false: The euro is the unit of currency.

(7) Does Cyprus drive on the right or left side of the road?

(8) The highest mountain in Cyprus has the same name as the highest mountain in Greece. What is it?

(9) What is the name of the second biggest city situated on the southern coast of Cyprus?

(10) Is the United Nations Buffer Zone in Cyprus, a demilitarized zone between the Greek part of the country and the Turkish part, known as (a) the green line (b) the red line or (c) the blue line?

(11) Who was the archbishop who became first President of Cyprus in 1960?

(12) Which other nation apart from Cyprus includes a map of itself on its flag?

(13) Which nation did EOKA, the Greek Cypriot nationalist guerrilla organisation, fight against in their campaign for self-determination and eventual union with Greece?

(14) True or false: Nicosia is the only divided capital in the world.

(15) What is the name of the tourist resort at the far eastern end of the southern coast of Cyprus, famous for its international festival?

(16) Do more Greek Cypriots live on Cyprus or more Turkish Cypriots?

(17) In which decade did Turkey invade Cyprus?

(18) With which sport do you associate Limassol-born Marcos Baghdatis?

(19) Name one of the two bases in Cyprus retained by Britain as British Overseas Territories after Cyprus was granted independence.

(20) Which Cypriot football club reached the quarter finals of the UEFA Champions League in 2011- 2012?

(1)   Greek and Turkish

(2)   True (since 2004)

(3)   True; Nicosia is also known as Lefkosia.

(4)   Cypriot

(5)   False; both Sicily and Sardinia are larger.

(6)   True

(7)   On the right

(8)   Mount Olympus (1,952m)

(9)   Limassol

(10) (a) The green line

(11) Archbishop Makarios

(12) Kosovo

(13) The United Kingdom

(14) True

(15) Ayia (or Agia) Napa

(16) More Greek Cypriots (c. 77%), Turkish Cypriots (c. 18%)

(17) In the 1970s (1974)

(18) Tennis

(19) Akrotiri and Dhekelia

(20) APOEL FC of Nicosia

CZECH REPUBLIC QUESTIONS

(1) What is the short-form name for the Czech Republic?

(2) What is the Czech for the capital city Prague?

(3) What name is given to the westernmost and largest historical region of the Czech Republic?

(4) The Czechs call this river the Labe. What do we call it?

(5) Famous for writing The Trial and The Castle, which German-speaking writer was born in Prague?

(6) In which year was the union between the Czech Republic and Slovakia dissolved?

(7) For what alcoholic beverage is the city of Pilsen famous?

(8) What and where is Hradcany?

(9) Which writer became the first President of the Czech Republic in 1993?

(10) What is the most popular winter sport in the Czech Republic?

(11) Which Czech filmmaker directed the films One Flew Over the Cuckoo's Nest and Amadeus?

(12) Which war did the Defenestration of Prague in 1618 help to set off?

(13) How many of these Czech-born tennis players have won a Wimbledon singles title: Ivan Lendl, Martina Navratilova, Petra Kvitova, Tomas Berdych and Jana Novotna?

(14) Who was the First Secretary of the Communist Party of Czechoslovakia during the Prague Spring in 1968?

(15) Who composed the opera The Bartered Bride and the symphonic cycle Má vlast which contains the famous symphonic poem The Moldau?

(16) What name is given to the revolution in 1989 which peacefully ended communist rule?

(17) Which city in Moravia, the second biggest in the Czech Republic, is well known as a city of culture?

(18) What is the historical German name of the region from which many ethnic Germans were expelled at the end of the Second World War?

(19) What is the name of the Czech theologian and philosopher, born in 1372, who was a seminal figure in the Bohemian Reformation?

(20) What are Karlovy Vary (Karlsbad) and Mariánské Lázne (Marienbad) particularly famous for?

CZECH REPUBLIC ANSWERS

(1)   Czechia

(2)   Praha

(3)   Bohemia

(4)   The Elbe

(5)   Franz Kafka

(6)   1993

(7)   Pilsner beer

(8)   The castle district in Prague

(9)   Václav Havel

(10) Ice hockey

(11) Milos Forman

(12) The Thirty Years' War

(13) Three of them: Navratilova, Kvitova and Novotna

(14) Alexander Dubcek

(15) Bedrich Smetana

(16) The Velvet Revolution

(17) Brno

(18) Sudetenland

(19) Jan Hus

(20) For being spa towns

DEMOCRATIC REPUBLIC OF THE CONGO QUESTIONS

(1) By what name was the DR Congo known between 1971 and 1997?

(2) Which European nation colonised the DR Congo region?

(3) What is the capital city?

(4) True or false: The DR Congo has a population of over 100 million.

(5) Which is the only other country in Africa which is bigger in area than the DR Congo?

(6) True or false: The Congo is the third-longest river in Africa.

(7) True or false: The DR Congo is a landlocked country.

(8) Which Belgian monarch first sponsored the exploration of the Congo in the 1870s?

(9) Which city in the DR Congo used to be known as Léopoldville?

(10) With which country does the DR Congo share Lake Albert, Africa's seventh largest lake?

(11) What was the name of the Congolese politician who became the first Prime Minister of the then Republic of the Congo in 1960 and who was executed by a firing squad in 1961?

(12) What was the name of the Congolese politician who was the military dictator President of Zaire from 1965 to 1997?

(13) What was the name of the breakaway state that proclaimed its independence in 1960 under Moise Tshombe?

(14) Which famous diplomat and Irish nationalist wrote a report about abuses in the Congo in 1904?

(15) Which capital city is located opposite Kinshasa on the other side of the Congo?

(16) True or false: Kinshasa and Brazzaville are the closest pair of capital cities in the world.

(17) Which two boxers fought in Zaire in the famous Rumble in the Jungle fight?

(18) Who recorded two songs about the fight, Black Superman (Muhammad Ali) and 'In Zaire'?

(19) What animal do visitors particularly hope to meet in the Parc National des Virungas?

(20) Famous for writing Jurassic Park, who also wrote the 1980 science fiction novel Congo which was made into a film in 1995?

DEMOCRATIC REPUBLIC OF THE CONGO ANSWERS

(1) Zaire

(2) Belgium

(3) Kinshasa

(4) False; it's about 86 million.

(5) Algeria

(6) False; it's the second-longest.

(7) False; it has a short coastline on the South Atlantic Ocean.

(8) Leopold II

(9) Kinshasa

(10) Uganda

(11) Patrice Lumumba

(12) Joseph-Désiré Mobutu (Mobutu Sese Seko)

(13) Katanga

(14) Roger Casement

(15) Brazzaville, the capital of the Republic of the Congo.

(16) False; Rome and the Vatican City are the closest!

(17) Muhammad Ali and George Foreman (Ali won by knockout.)

(18) Johnny Wakelin

(19) Mountain gorillas

(20) Michael Crichton

DENMARK QUESTIONS

(1) What colour is the cross on the Danish flag, the oldest state flag in the world?

(2) What name is given to the Danish peninsula which is joined to Germany?

(3) In which year did the Battle of Jutland take place?

(4) What is the second largest city in Denmark, Odense or Aarhus?

(5) True or false: The currency of Denmark is the euro.

(6) How many islands make up Denmark, (a) 206, (b) 306 (c) 406?

(7) What is the name of the bridge which together with a tunnel joins Denmark to Sweden?

(8) Which famous Danish brewery was founded by J.C. Jacobsen in 1847?

(9) Which famous 11th century Danish king was also King of England and of Norway?

(10) What is the name of the islands about halfway between Norway and Iceland which are an autonomous territory within the Kingdom of Denmark?

(11) Which team did Denmark surprisingly defeat in the final of the 1992 UEFA European Championships?

(12) What is the name of the Danish island situated closer to the coast of Sweden than Denmark, the capital of which is Rønne?

(13) Lars Ulrich, a member of a famous heavy metal band, was born in Denmark. Which band?

(14) Since 1513, Kings of Denmark have only been called one of two names. What are the two names?

(15) Who in 1952 sang the song The Ugly Duckling based on the fairy tale by Odense-born Hans Christian Andersen?

(16) What product is particularly associated with the small town of Billund in Jutland?

(17) Denmark has won the Eurovision Song Contest three times. Name one of the artists who has/have won.

(18) Which famous building in Australia was designed by the Dane Jorn Utzon?

(19) Which physicist famous for his work on atomic structure and quantum theory was awarded the Nobel Prize for Physics in 1922?

(20) Which Icelandic singer starred in Danish-born director Lars von Trier's 2000 film Dancer in the Dark?

DENMARK ANSWERS

(1)   white

(2)   Jutland

(3)   1916

(4)   Aarhus (273,077). Odense is the third biggest city (179,601).

(5)   False; it's the krone.

(6)   (c) 406

(7)   The Øresund Bridge

(8)   Carlsberg

(9)   Canute

(10) The Faroe Islands

(11) Germany (The score was 2-0).

(12) Bornholm

(13) Metallica

(14) Christian or Frederick

(15) Danny Kaye

(16) Lego

(17) Grethe & Jørgen Ingmann (1963), the Olsen Brothers (2000) and Emmelie de Forest (2013)

(18) Sydney Opera House

(19) Niels Bohr

(20) Björk

DJIBOUTI QUESTIONS

(1) In which continent is Djibouti located?

(2) What is the predominant religion in the country?

(3) Djibouti has a border with two countries beginning with E. What are they?

(4) On which sea is Djibouti situated?

(5) What is the name of the gulf to the west of Djibouti?

(6) Was Djibouti called French Ethiopia or French Somaliland until 1967?

(7) True or false: The capital of Djibouti is Djibouti.

(8) Djibouti is predominantly inhabited by two ethnic groups: the Afars and which people from a neighbouring country?

(9) True or false: As well as Arabic, English is the other official language.

(10) What name is given to the part of Africa in which Djibouti is situated?

(11) Which Arab country is situated opposite Djibouti across the Gulf of Aden?

(12) Djibouti as a port handles about 95% of which other African country's trade?

(13) Which economically powerful Asian nation established a military base in Djibouti in 2017?

(14) In 1958 a referendum was held to decide whether to join the Somali Republic or to remain with France. What was the decision?

(15) By what name was Djibouti known between 1967 and 1977?

(16) True or false: Djibouti gained independence in 1977.

(17) What sort of creature is the Djibouti francolin, which is only found in Djibouti?

(18) What is pictured on the flag, a half moon or a star?

(19) Is the saline Lake Assal the lowest point in Africa or the highest situated lake in Africa?

(20) True or false: Djibouti is the smallest country in area on the African mainland.

DJIBOUTI ANSWERS

(1) Africa

(2) Islam

(3) Ethiopia and Eritrea

(4) The Red Sea

(5) The Gulf of Aden

(6) French Somaliland

(7) True

(8) Somalis

(9) False. It's French.

(10) The Horn of Africa

(11) Yemen

(12) Ethiopia

(13) China

(14) To remain with France.

(15) The French Territory of the Afars and the Issas

(16) True

(17) A bird

(18) A star

(19) The lowest point in Africa (155m below sea level). It's the third lowest point on earth after the Dead Sea and the Sea of Galilee.

(20) False: both Gambia and Eswatini are smaller.

DOMINICA QUESTIONS

(1) Is Dominica in the East Indies or the West Indies?

(2) In which sea is Dominica situated?

(3) Are the vast majority of Dominicans of African or European descent?

(4) Is Dominica part of the Lesser Antilles or the Greater Antilles?

(5) What is the capital?

(6) Great Britain took possession of the island in 1763 at the end of which war?

(7) The French name for the island is the same as the Singing Nun's worldwide hit in 1963. What is it?

(8) Is the currency the East Caribbean dollar or the East Caribbean pound?

(9) On which day of the week did the Spanish first see the island, giving it the name Dominica as a result?

(10) True or false: The Boiling Lake on Dominica is the largest hot lake in the world.

(11) The second-largest town on Dominica has the same name as an important naval port on the south coast of England. What is its name?

(12) The sisserou, which can only be found on Dominica, is featured on the flag and the coat of arms. What sort of bird is it?

(13) Which yellow fruit is important for Dominica's economy?

(14) What do Dominicans think of when they hear the names David, Dean, Erika and Maria?

(15) The parents of the singer who had a UK number one with Dreams in 1993 come from Dominica. What is the singer's name?

(16) A famous pool on the island is named after a green precious stone. Which stone?

(17) True or false: The British monarch is the head of state.

(18) The writer of the novel Wide Sargasso Sea was born and brought up on Dominica. What is her name?

(19) What is the name of the woman who became prime minister in 1980, the Caribbean's first female prime minister?

(20) What are Morne aux Diables, Morne Diablotins and Morne Trois Pitons?

DOMINICA ANSWERS

(1) The West Indies

(2) The Caribbean

(3) African descent

(4) The Lesser Antilles

(5) Roseau

(6) The Seven Years' War

(7) Dominique

(8) The East Caribbean dollar

(9) Sunday (after the Latin dies Dominica)

(10) False, it's the second-largest; the largest is the Frying Pan Lake in New Zealand

(11) Portsmouth

(12) A parrot

(13) The banana

(14) Hurricanes which all struck Dominica.

(15) Gabrielle

(16) The emerald

(17) False; the president is the head of state.

(18) Jean Rhys

(19) Eugenia Charles

(20) Volcanic mountains on Dominica (Morne is an old French word for a small mountain.)

DOMINICAN REPUBLIC QUESTIONS

(1) On which island is the Dominican Republic located?

(2) With which country does it share the island?

(3) Which country occupies more of the island, Haiti or the Dominican Republic?

(4) Apart from Hispaniola, which other Caribbean island is shared by two sovereign states?

(5) What is the capital?

(6) Is the most popular sport baseball, basketball or football?

(7) The motto of the country is Dios, Patria, Libertad. What does it mean in English?

(8) True or false: The founder of Santo Domingo, Bartholomew Columbus, was the elder brother of Christopher Columbus.

(9) Is the currency the Dominican dollar or the Dominican peso?

(10) In what field was Santo Domingo-born Oscar de la Renta famous?

(11) To play what sport do many tourists travel to the Dominican Republic?

(12) What precious metal is mined at the Pueblo Viejo mine, the largest in the Americas?

(13) True or false: The Cuidad Colonial or Colonial Zone, the historic centre of Santo Domingo, is a UNESCO World Heritage Site.

(14) Which dictator ruled the Dominican Republic from 1930 until his assassination in 1961?

(15) Santo Domingo stands on the Ozama River. Into which sea does it empty?

(16) The parents of American baseball player Alex Rodriguez come from the Dominican Republic. Which famous singer-actress did Alex start dating in 2017?

(17) In which century did the Dominican War of Independence against Haiti take place?

(18) Merengue and Bachata both originated in the Dominican Republic. What are they?

(19) True or false: The Dominican Republic is the most visited destination in the Caribbean.

(20) The second-largest city in the Dominican Republic has the same name as the capital of Chile. What is it?

DOMINICAN REPUBLIC ANSWERS

(1) Hispaniola

(2) Haiti

(3) The Dominican Republic (48,671 km²). Haiti (27,750 km²)

(4) Saint Martin (shared by France 53 km² and the Netherlands 20 km²)

(5) Santo Domingo

(6) Baseball

(7) God, Homeland, Freedom

(8) False: He was the younger brother.

(9) The Dominican peso

(10) Fashion design

(11) Golf

(12) Gold

(13) True

(14) Rafael Trujillo

(15) The Caribbean

(16) Jennifer Lopez

(17) The nineteenth century

(18) Types of dance and music

(19) True

(20) Santiago (de los Caballeros)

ECUADOR QUESTIONS

(1) Which ocean borders Ecuador to the west?

(2) True or false: Ecuador's capital is the only capital city in the world which begins with Q.

(3) What does the word ecuador mean in Spanish?

(4) True or false: The Ecuadorean and the Colombian flags are the same colour.

(5) Which country borders Ecuador to the south?

(6) What is the name of the mountain range which runs through central Ecuador?

(7) True or false: Quito is the capital city which is closest to the Equator.

(8) The national tree of Ecuador is the cinchona, the bark of which can yield something beginning with q which was used to treat malaria. What is the q?

(9) What is the name of the group of islands belonging to Ecuador famous for their large number of endemic species studied by Charles Darwin?

(10) True or false: Oil is very important as far as Ecuador's exports are concerned.

(11) A monument to what can be seen at Ciudad Mitad del Mundo?

(12) True or false: Cotopaxi is the highest mountain in Ecuador.

(13) Which civilization started to expand from Peru into Ecuador in the 15th century?

(14) After what sort of creature are the Galapagos Islands named?

(15) What is Ecuador's second-largest city and its main port?

(16) Cuy is an animal which is often eaten in Ecuador. What is it?

(17) Ecuador now has the US dollar as its currency. What was the name of the previous currency, which had the same name as a big city in Bolivia?

(18) Which German DJ group had a big hit with the song Ecuador in 1997?

(19) What is the name of the city located at about 2,500 metres above sea level which was declared a UNESCO World Heritage Site because of its many historical buildings?

(20) The first name of the Ecuadorean athlete Perez who won a gold medal in the Men's 20 km walk at the 1996 Olympics is the same as the surname of the third President of the United States. What is the name?

ECUADOR ANSWERS

(1) The Pacific

(2) True (Quito)

(3) Equator

(4) True: horizontal stripes of yellow, blue and red

(5) Peru

(6) The Andes

(7) True

(8) Quinine

(9) The Galapagos Islands

(10) True (about 40%)

(11) A monument to the Equator

(12) False, it's Chimborazo (6,263m) (Cotopaxi, 5,897m)

(13) The Inca civilization

(14) A giant tortoise (known as galápago in Spanish)

(15) Guayaquil

(16) Guinea pig

(17) Sucre

(18) Sash

(19) Cuenca

(20) Jefferson

EGYPT QUESTIONS

(1) Which sea borders Egypt to the east?

(2) What is the name of the peninsula between Egypt and Israel?

(3) Which city is known as Al-Qahirah in Arabic?

(4) Who wrote the whodunnit Death on the Nile?

(5) How many of the Seven Wonders of the Ancient World were situated in Egypt?

(6) What is the name of the port situated on the Mediterranean Sea at the entrance to the Suez Canal?

(7) Which President of Egypt was assassinated by an Islamic extremist in 1981?

(8) The third-largest city in Egypt is also the site of the Great Pyramid and the Great Sphinx. What is its name?

(9) What is the name of the dam built on the River Nile in the 1960s?

(10) Which Ancient Egyptian deity is usually depicted with a canine head?

(11) Which Cairo-born diplomat and politician was Secretary General of the United Nations from 1992 – 1997?

(12) Which Alexandria-born actor starred in Lawrence of Arabia and Dr Zhivago?

(13) Whose gold burial mask can be seen in The Museum of Egyptian Antiquities in Cairo?

(14) What is the name of the tourist resort on the Red Sea beginning with the letter H, which is famous for water sports?

(15) For which English club did professional footballer Mohamed Salah start playing in 2017?

(16) What name is given to Egyptian Christians?

(17) Who was President of Egypt during the Suez Crisis in 1956?

(18) Which 1898-born Egyptian singer, known for her vocal dexterity and unique style, was sometimes called The Voice of Egypt or Egypt's Fourth Pyramid?

(19) The ruins of the ancient Egyptian city of Thebes lie within which modern Egyptian city?

(20) What is the name of the Egyptian writer who won the Nobel Prize for Literature in 1988, the first Arabic-language writer to do so?

EGYPT ANSWERS

(1) The Red Sea

(2) The Sinai Peninsula

(3) Cairo

(4) Agatha Christie

(5) Two: The Great Pyramid of Giza and The Lighthouse of Alexandria

(6) Port Said

(7) Anwar Sadat

(8) Giza

(9) The Aswan (High) Dam

(10) Anubis

(11) Boutros Boutros-Ghali

(12) Omar Sharif

(13) Tutankhamun's

(14) Hurghada

(15) Liverpool

(16) Copts

(17) Gamal Abdel Nasser

(18) Umm Kulthum

(19) Luxor

(20) Naguib Mahfouz

EL SALVADOR QUESTIONS

(1) True or false: El Salvador is a landlocked country.

(2) What is the capital city?

(3) What does the name El Salvador mean in English?

(4) True or false: The capital San Salvador is situated on the Pacific coast.

(5) How many countries in Central America are smaller in area than El Salvador?

(6) What colour blue is the flag: light blue, dark blue or cobalt blue?

(7) What nationality was the conquistador Pedro de Alvarado who first entered El Salvador in 1524?

(8) True or false: El Salvador is the only Central American country which does not have a Caribbean coastline.

(9) Which country is most important to El Salvador as far as imports and exports are concerned?

(10) Are most Salvadorans Protestant or Catholic?

(11) What type of natural disaster is El Salvador particularly prone to, for example in 1854, 1986 and 2001?

(12) The parents of Rosemary Casals emigrated to the USA from El Salvador. With which sport is she associated?

(13) Pupusa is the national dish of El Salvador. Is it a thick flatbread or a fruit similar to a papaya?

(14) What devastating event took place in El Salvador between 1979 and 1992?

(15) The father of which famous White House intern of the 1990s was born in San Salvador?

(16) Is the unit of currency the colon or the US dollar?

(17) With which country did El Salvador briefly go to war in 1969 in the Football War?

(18) The Monumento al Divino Salvador del Mundo in San Salvador consists of a statue of whom standing on top of a global sphere of planet earth?

(19) What is the name of the Archbishop of San Salvador who was assassinated in 1980 while celebrating Mass?

(20) Alicia Nash, the wife of the Nobel Prize-winning economist and mathematician John Forbes Nash, was born in El Salvador. In the film A Beautiful Mind she was played by Jennifer Connelly. Who played her husband?

EL SALVADOR ANSWERS

(1) False: It has a Pacific coast.

(2) San Salvador

(3) The Saviour

(4) False: It is situated inland.

(5) None; it is the smallest.

(6) Cobalt blue

(7) Spanish

(8) True

(9) The USA

(10) Catholic

(11) Earthquakes

(12) Tennis

(13) It's a thick flatbread usually filled with cheese, squash or beans.

(14) A civil war

(15) Monica Lewinsky

(16) The US dollar; the colon was used until 2001.

(17) Honduras

(18) Jesus Christ

(19) Oscar Romero

(20) Russell Crowe

EQUATORIAL GUINEA QUESTIONS

(1) True or false: Equatorial Guinea is the only sovereign state in Africa which has Spanish as an official language.

(2) What is the capital, Lavabo or Malabo?

(3) True or false: Malabo is situated on an island.

(4) Is the island of Bioko off the coast of Cameroon or Equatorial Guinea?

(5) True or false: the island of Annobon which belongs to Equatorial Guinea is north of the Equator.

(6) Which Portuguese-speaking island nation lies between the islands of Bioko and Annobon?

(7) Which part of Equatorial Guinea is known as Rio Muni?

(8) Equatorial Guinea shares a border with the country the capital of which is Libreville. Which country?

(9) Apart from Spanish, Equatorial Guinea has two other European languages as its official languages. What are they?

(10) The discovery of large reserves of what in the 1990s has increased government revenue dramatically?

(11) By what name was the island Bioko formerly known?

(12) What nationality was the explorer Fernando Pó?

(13) True or false: Fang which is spoken by over 80% of the population is a Bantu language.

(14) What role will the city of Ciudad de la Paz, formerly known as Oyala, play in the future in Equatorial Guinea?

(15) Who is Teodoro Obiang?

(16) The son of which British prime minister was named as a financial backer of the 2004 coup d'état attempt organized by Simon Mann?

(17) What does the name of the island Annobon mean?

(18) Is the unit of currency the CFA franc or the Spanish peseta?

(19) What is pictured on the country's flag: a tree, a flower or a bird?

(20) What is the name of the biggest city on mainland Equatorial Guinea?

(1)   True

(2)   Malabo

(3)   True; it is situated on Bioko Island.

(4)   Off the coast of Cameroon

(5)   False; it is south of the Equator.

(6)   Sao Tomé and Principe

(7)   The mainland part

(8)   Gabon

(9)   Portuguese and French

(10) Oil

(11) Fernando Pó

(12) Portuguese

(13) True

(14) It will be the new capital city, replacing Malabo.

(15) The country's infamous president since 1979

(16) The son of Margaret Thatcher, Mark Thatcher

(17) Good Year; it was discovered by the Portuguese on New Year's Day (Portuguese Dia do Ano Bom) in 1473.

(18) The CFA franc

(19) A tree

(20) Bata

ERITREA QUESTIONS

(1) On which sea is Eritrea situated?

(2) Is the capital Asmara or Astana?

(3) From which neighbouring country did Eritrea finally achieve independence in 1993?

(4) Of which European country was Eritrea a colony between 1890 and 1947?

(5) What is Eritrea's smallest neighbouring country?

(6) Is Asmara known for its modernist architecture or for its old traditional historic buildings?

(7) Which European city was Asmara modelled on in the early part of the 20th century?

(8) Is Nakfa the currency or the language of Eritrea?

(9) With which sport is the Eritrean Ghirmay Ghebreslassie associated?

(10) Which country in Europe has the most exiled Eritreans?

(11) True or false: Both the Prime Minister of Ethiopia and the President of Eritrea were awarded the Nobel Peace Prize for their work in the 2018 Eritrea-Ethiopia peace summit.

(12) Which two religions are predominant in Eritrea?

(13) Which desert animal is featured on the national emblem of Eritrea?

(14) True or false: Eritrea is situated in the Horn of Africa.

(15) Which Italian monarch was "King of Eritrea" from 1900 to 1941?

(16) Which famous English suffragette wrote a book entitled Eritrea on the Eve?

(17) Zersenay Tadese won a bronze medal in the 10,000 metres in the 2004 Olympic Games. In which city did the games take place?

(18) What is Tigrinya?

(19) The branch of what tree, which is particularly associated with Mediterranean countries, is pictured on the Eritrean flag?

(20) What sort of fishing for gems has taken place in the Dahlak Archipelago in the Red Sea near the city of Massawa since Roman times?

ERITREA ANSWERS

(1) The Red Sea

(2) Asmara

(3) Ethiopia

(4) Italy

(5) Djibouti

(6) Its modernist architecture (It was declared a UNESCO World Heritage Site in 2017).

(7) Rome

(8) The currency; Eritrea has no official language, but has nine national languages plus English

(9) Long-distance running, especially the marathon

(10) Germany (more than 55,000)

(11) False; only the Prime Minister of Ethiopia, Abiy Ahmed, was awarded the Nobel Peace Prize.

(12) Christianity and Islam

(13) The camel

(14) True

(15) Victor Emmanuel III

(16) Sylvia Pankhurst

(17) Athens

(18) One of the main languages of Eritrea

(19) The olive tree

(20) Pearl fishing

ESTONIA QUESTIONS

(1) Which Estonian city was known by the German name Reval until the first half of the 20th century?

(2) On which sea is Estonia situated?

(3) What is the official language of Estonia?

(4) To which Scandinavian language is it closely related?

(5) Which one of these colours does not feature on the Estonian flag: black, blue, green, white?

(6) What is the name of the gulf in the Baltic Sea between Estonia and Finland?

(7) True or false: Estonia has never won the Eurovision Song Contest.

(8) What are Saaremaa and Hiiumaa?

(9) In which year did Estonia gain independence from the Soviet Union?

(10) What is the name of the second-largest city in Estonia, home to the country's oldest and most renowned university?

(11) True or false: Estonia was the first country in the world to adopt online voting in an election.

(12) What created the famous crater in the village of Kaali on Saaremaa?

(13) What percentage of the population belong to the Russian ethnic group?

(14) What is the name of the lake on the border between Estonia and Russia, the fifth largest in Europe?

(15) How often is the Estonian Song Festival, one of the largest amateur choral events in the world, held?

(16) Which telecommunications app specializing in video chat was co-created by Estonians?

(17) Estonian Ado Kosk invented the sport of Kiiking in 1993. Is it (a) a type of indoor football or (b) 360 degree swinging?

(18) The national flower of Estonia is often used to describe the blue of the flag. What is the flower?

(19) Gerd Kanter won the gold medal at the 2008 Summer Olympics. In which athletics field event?

(20) In which month is Jaanipäev, the Estonian midsummer celebration, held?

ESTONIA ANSWERS

(1)   Tallinn, the capital

(2)   On the Baltic Sea

(3)   Estonian

(4)   Finnish

(5)   Green

(6)   The Gulf of Finland

(7)   False; Estonia won in 2001 with the song Everybody by Tanel Padar, Dave Benton and 2XL.

(8)   The two biggest Estonian islands in the Baltic

(9)   1991

(10) Tartu

(11) True; in 2005

(12) A meteorite

(13) About 25%

(14) Lake Peipus

(15) Every five years

(16) Skype

(17) 360 degree swinging (in other words, doing a complete circle on a swing)

(18) The cornflower

(19) The discus

(20) June

ESWATINI QUESTIONS

(1) By what name is Eswatini also known?

(2) Is Eswatini landlocked or does it have a coast?

(3) Name one of the two countries with which it has a border.

(4) Of which country was Swaziland a protectorate from 1903 to 1968?

(5) Is Eswatini a kingdom or a republic?

(6) What is the executive capital and largest city of Eswatini?

(7) Is Lobamba the judicial or the legislative capital of Eswatini?

(8) To which African currency is the Eswatini currency, the lilangeni, fixed?

(9) Is the Incwala, the Kingship Ceremony, the most important cultural event in Eswatini, usually held in December or August?

(10) Which country is most important for Eswatini as far as imports and exports are concerned?

(11) What name is given to a native of Eswatini?

(12) How is the name Eswatini sometimes written?

(13) The title of the ruler is Ngwenyama. To which majestic animal does the title refer?

(14) What are the Lomati, the Komati, the Umbuluzi and the Usutu, tribes or rivers in Eswatini?

(15) Which actor, who was nominated for a Best Supporting Actor Oscar in the 2018 film Can You Ever Forgive Me?, was born in Mbabane in 1957?

(16) Which infection of the immune system is prevalent in Eswatini?

(17) Sibebe Rock in Eswatini is the world's second largest monolith. What is the largest?

(18) What colour are the feathers which can only be worn by members of the royal family in Eswatini, red, white or black?

(19) What sort of festival is the MTN Bushfire, held annually in May?

(20) Every year thousands of young women perform for the Queen Mother at the Umhlanga. Is it also known as (a) the Kingship Ceremony (b) the Bushfire Fest or (c) the Reed Dance Festival?

ESWATINI ANSWERS

(1)   Swaziland

(2)   It's landlocked.

(3)   Mozambique or South Africa

(4)   The United Kingdom

(5)   It's a kingdom. (King Mswati III)

(6)   Mbabane

(7)   The legislative capital (The Parliament is situated in the town.)

(8)   The South African rand

(9)   In December

(10) South Africa

(11) A Swazi

(12) eSwatini

(13) The lion

(14) Rivers

(15) Richard E. Grant

(16) AIDS (about 25% of the population have it.)

(17) Uluru in Australia

(18) Red

(19) A festival of African music

(20) (c) The Reed Dance Festival

ETHIOPIA QUESTIONS

(1) What is the capital and largest city of Ethiopia?

(2) Does Ethiopia have a sea coast?

(3) True or false: Ethiopia is the most populous landlocked country in the world.

(4) Which Ethiopian city is also known as Finfinne?

(5) Who was Emperor of Ethiopia from 1930 to 1974?

(6) True or false: Haile Selassie died a natural death.

(7) By what name beginning with the letter A is Ethiopia sometimes known?

(8) About 60% of foreign income in Ethiopia comes from one crop. Which crop?

(9) Is Lake Tana in Ethiopia the source of the Blue Nile or the White Nile?

(10) Ethiopia was never colonized by a European nation, but which European country occupied it between 1936 – 1941?

(11) What is the name of the Ethiopian athlete who won the marathon Olympic gold medal in 1960 and 1964?

(12) In which year did the Live Aid Concert for famine relief in Ethiopia organised by Bob Geldof take place?

(13) What is the official language of Ethiopia?

(14) What sort of animal is the endangered walia ibex which can only be found in the mountains of Ethiopia?

(15) The parents of the successful singer with the real name Abel Testaye emigrated to Canada from Ethiopia in the 1980s. By what name is the singer better known?

(16) Which organisation consisting of 55 member states has its headquarters in Addis Ababa?

(17) Ethiopia shares its border with Somalia, Sudan, South Sudan, Eritrea, Kenya and which other country?

(18) From which song did Lucy, an early australopithecine skeleton found in Ethiopia in 1974, get her name?

(19) Which French poet, famous for his relationship with Paul Verlaine, worked as a merchant in the Ethiopian city of Harar between 1880 and 1881?

(20) Which religion, particularly practised in Jamaica, gives great importance to Haile Selassie, often seeing him as Jah incarnate?

(1) Addis Ababa

(2) No, it doesn't.

(3) True. (c 110 million)

(4) Addis Ababa

(5) Haile Selassie

(6) False; he was strangled to death aged 83 following a coup on 27 August 1975.

(7) Abyssinia

(8) Coffee

(9) The Blue Nile

(10) Italy

(11) Abebe Bikila

(12) 1985

(13) Amharic

(14) A mountain goat

(15) The Weeknd

(16) The African Union

(17) Djibouti

(18) Lucy in the Sky with Diamonds by the Beatles

(19) Arthur Rimbaud

(20) Rastafarianism

FEDERATED STATES OF MICRONESIA QUESTIONS

(1) In which ocean are the Federated States of Micronesia (FSM) situated?

(2) What are Yap, Chuuk, Pohnpei and Kosrae?

(3) What is the capital?

(4) In which of the four states is Palikir situated?

(5) True or false: Palikir is the biggest city in the FSM?

(6) In which decade did the FSM become independent under a Compact of Free Association with the USA: the 1960s, the 1970s or the 1980s?

(7) What is the official language?

(8) What international currency is used by the FSM?

(9) Roughly how many islands make up the FSM, just over (a) 500 (b) 600 (c) 700?

(10) Which of the four island states, Yap, Chuuk, Pohnpei and Kosrae, is noted for its stone money (Rai stones)?

(11) To which archipelago does the FSM belong, the Caroline Islands or the Mariana Islands?

(12) Which of the four states has the biggest population?

(13) True or false: The language Yapese really exists.

(14) Name one other sovereign nation apart from the FSM which is part of the region known as Micronesia.

(15) Nan Madol is an archaeological site off the island of Pohnpei, consisting of 92 artificial islets linked by a network of canals. It is often likened to which Italian city?

(16) How many time zones are there in the FSM, one, two or three?

(17) Not a true nut, but rather the seed of a fruit categorized as a berry, what "nut" is often chewed in the FSM?

(18) Which of the four states is the most easterly, Kosrae or Yap?

(19) What is the Internet country code top level domain?

(20) Which town on Pohnpei Island was capital of the FSM until replaced by Palikir in1989?

(1) In the Pacific

(2) They are the four states of the Federated States of Micronesia or four islands of FSM.

(3) Palikir

(4) Pohnpei

(5) False; Weno on Chuuk Atoll is the largest city.

(6) The 1980s

(7) English

(8) The US dollar

(9) (b) Just over 600

(10) Yap

(11) The Caroline Islands

(12) Chuuk

(13) True

(14) One from Kiribati, Marshall Islands, Nauru or Palau

(15) Venice; it's often called the Venice of the Pacific.

(16) Two; Yap and Chuuk are 10 hours ahead of GMT and the other two states 11 hours.

(17) Betel nut

(18) Kosrae

(19) .fm

(20) Kolonia

FIJI QUESTIONS

(1) Is Fiji situated in the North Pacific or the South Pacific Ocean?

(2) Is Fiji in Melanesia, Micronesia or Polynesia?

(3) What are Viti Levu and Vanua Levu?

(4) True or false: Viti Levu and Vanua Levu and one other island make up Fiji.

(5) On which continent is Fiji?

(6) Do they drive on the left or right side of the road in Fiji?

(7) Of which country was Fiji a colony until 1970?

(8) True or false: The British Union Jack features on the Fijian flag.

(9) What is the most popular team sport played in Fiji?

(10) From which country do the most tourists come to Fiji?

(11) The strait between the islands of Viti Levu and Vanua Levu is named after the captain of the infamous HMS Bounty. What is his name?

(12) From which organisation was Fiji suspended from 2009 to 2014 because of failure to hold democratic elections after the 2006 coup?

(13) Is Fiji's second city Lautoka known as Sugar City or Banana City?

(14) Which 2000 film starring Tom Hanks and a volleyball was largely filmed in Fiji?

(15) Two military coups took place in 1987 caused by concern over a government dominated by descendants of which nation?

(16) Fiji won its first gold medal at the 2016 Rio Olympics for which rugby competition?

(17) Is the unit of currency the Fijian dollar or the Fijian pound?

(18) True or false: Fiji has a history of cannibalism.

(19) Would Fijians drink or eat kava?

(20) Which island nation is closest to Fiji?

FIJI ANSWERS

(1) The South Pacific

(2) In Melanesia

(3) The two major islands of Fiji with 87% of the population

(4) False; Fiji consists of over 300 islands and 500 small islets.

(5) Oceania

(6) On the left

(7) The United Kingdom

(8) True

(9) Rugby Union

(10) Australia (c 365,000 per year)

(11) William Bligh

(12) The Commonwealth of Nations

(13) Sugar City; it's situated in the heart of Fiji's sugarcane-growing region.

(14) Cast Away

(15) India

(16) The men's rugby sevens

(17) The Fijian dollar

(18) True

(19) They would drink it. It's a mildly intoxicating drink made from the pounded roots of a pepper plant mixed with water.

(20) Tonga (c 745 kms.)

FINLAND QUESTIONS

(1) True or false: Helsinki is the northernmost capital of an EU state.

(2) What is the Finnish for Finland?

(3) What are the two official languages of Finland?

(4) Does Finland share a border with Denmark, Norway and Sweden?

(5) What colour is the cross on the Finnish flag?

(6) With which sport do you associate the names Paavo Nurmi and Lasse Viren?

(7) Does Finland have the world's highest consumption of coffee or tea?

(8) With which steam and high heat bath is Finland particularly associated?

(9) Which Finnish Formula 1 driver won the World Championship in 2007?

(10) In which year were the Summer Olympics held in Helsinki?

(11) What is the name of the gulf in the Baltic Sea which is situated between the west coast of Finland and the east coast of Sweden?

(12) Which city in Finland is called Abo in Swedish?

(13) What is the name of the multinational telecommunications and IT company founded in 1865, with its headquarters in Espoo?

(14) Who composed the tone poem Finlandia?

(15) What is the name of the Swedish-speaking group of islands at the entrance to the Gulf of Bothnia which belong to Finland?

(16) Why do would-be rock and heavy metal guitar players descend on the city of Oulu in Northern Finland in August?

(17) What was the title of the song with which the group Lordi won the 2006 Eurovision Song Contest?

(18) Is Pesäpallo something you eat, something you drink or something you play?

(19) Which town in Northern Finland is considered by Finns to be the home of Santa Claus and has a Santa Claus Village and Santa Park?

(20) The Finnish director Renny Harlin was married to one of the stars of the film Thelma and Louise in the 1990s. Who is she?

FINLAND ANSWERS

(1)   True

(2)   Suomi

(3)   Finnish and Swedish

(4)   No, it doesn't share a border with Denmark.

(5)   Blue (on a white background)

(6)   Athletics: long-distance running

(7)   Coffee

(8)   The sauna

(9)   Kimi Räikkönen

(10) 1952

(11) The Gulf of Bothnia

(12) Turku

(13) Nokia

(14) Jean Sibelius

(15) The Aland Islands

(16) For the Air Guitar World Championships

(17) Hard Rock Hallelujah

(18) Something you play; it's a fast-moving bat and ball sport often considered to be the national sport of Finland

(19) Rovaniemi

(20) Geena Davis

FRANCE QUESTIONS

(1) Liberté, égalité and what are the three words of the French motto?

(2) What is the name of France's third-biggest city, situated on the Rhone and noted for its cuisine and gastronomy?

(3) France won the FIFA World Cup in 1998 and which other year?

(4) Is the cheese Roquefort made from cow's, goat's or sheep's milk?

(5) With what industry are Thierry Mugler, Christian Lacroix and Jean-Paul Gaultier connected?

(6) Why was the Eiffel Tower built?

(7) Name the last three French Presidents.

(8) From whose painting, Impression, soleil levant, did the Impressionist movement derive its name?

(9) What is the name of the French overseas department and region in South America?

(10) Which river flows through the Camargue and the city of Arles before it flows into the Mediterranean Sea?

(11) What relation was Napoleon III to Napoleon?

(12) What is the name of the island off Marseille, in whose prison the Count of Monte Cristo was incarcerated in the novel by Alexandre Dumas?

(13) What is the name of the highland region in the middle of Southern France, consisting of mountains and plateaus, with the Puy de Sancy as its highest peak?

(14) Which of these well-known DJs is/are not French: David Guetta, Bob Sinclar, Martin Solveig?

(15) What is the name of the fortified city in the department of Aude which became a UNESCO World Heritage Site in 1997?

(16) From what fruit is the brandy Calvados principally made?

(17) Which cardinal served as chief minister to Louis XIII and Louis XIV from 1642 until his death in 1661?

(18) Which two French brothers are credited with creating the cinema in 1895?

(19) The Frenchman Maurice Garin won the inaugural race of this famous competition in 1903. What competition?

(20) During which war did Joan of Arc lead the French army to several important victories?

FRANCE ANSWERS

(1) Fraternité

(2) Lyon

(3) 2018

(4) Sheep's milk

(5) The fashion industry

(6) It was constructed from 1887 to 1889 as the entrance to the 1889 World's Fair.

(7) Emmanuel Macron, Francois Hollande and Nicolas Sarkozy

(8) Claude Monet

(9) French Guiana

(10) The Rhone

(11) His nephew

(12) If (The count was imprisoned in the Chateau d'If).

(13) Massif Central

(14) All of them are French

(15) Carcassonne

(16) Apples

(17) Cardinal Mazarin

(18) Auguste and Louis Lumière

(19) The Tour de France

(20) The Hundred Years' War

GABON QUESTIONS

(1) Is Gabon located on the west coast or the east coast of Africa?

(2) Is the capital city Freetown or Libreville?

(3) What is Gabon's only official language?

(4) Is the population just over 1 million, 2 million or 3 million?

(5) How many different colours make up the flag: one, two or three?

(6) What adjective can be made from the word Gabon?

(7) Gabon's name originates from the word gabao meaning cloak in which language?

(8) Which commodity is vital to Gabon's economy?

(9) True or false: There is a city called Franceville in Gabon.

(10) Was the Omar Bongo University in Libreville named after a former president or a famous drummer from Gabon?

(11) With which of the Guinea countries does Gabon share a border?

(12) With which sport do you associate the name Pierre-Emerick Aubameyang?

(13) Which British club did Aubameyang join from Borussia Dortmund in 2018?

(14) Which Alsatian humanitarian set up a hospital in Gabon in 1912?

(15) In which Gabonese town did Schweitzer set the hospital up?

(16) With which neighbouring country with Malabo as its capital is Gabon in dispute over Mbane Island?

(17) What animals have become famous for surfing in Loango National Park, elephants or hippos?

(18) True or false: The Equator runs through Gabon.

(19) In which Korean martial art did Anthony Obame win a silver medal at the 2012 Olympics, the first Gabonese athlete to win an Olympic medal?

(20) Born in Gabon, 2.03 metre-tall Chris Silva plays his sport in the USA. Which sport?

GABON ANSWERS

(1)　On the west coast

(2)　Libreville

(3)　French

(4)　Just over 2 million

(5)　Three: green, yellow and blue

(6)　Gabonese

(7)　Portuguese

(8)　Oil

(9)　True

(10)　A former president (from 1967 until 2009)

(11)　Equatorial Guinea

(12)　Football

(13)　Arsenal

(14)　Albert Schweitzer

(15)　In Lambaréné

(16)　Equatorial Guinea

(17)　Hippos

(18)　True

(19)　Taekwondo

(20)　Basketball

THE GAMBIA QUESTIONS

(1)   Which country almost entirely surrounds the Gambia?

(2)   On which ocean does the Gambia have a coastline?

(3)   True or false: The Gambia is the smallest country on mainland Africa.

(4)   Is the capital Bangui or Banjul?

(5)   What is the official language?

(6)   True or false: The British monarch is the head of state.

(7)   How wide is the Gambia at its widest point (a) less than 50 kms. (b) less than 75 kms, (c) less than 100 kms.?

(8)   Which European nation dominated trade in the area in the 15th and 16th centuries before the British took over?

(9)   Which river flows through the centre of the Gambia into the Atlantic?

(10)   True or false: Most of the inhabitants are Christians.

(11)   Who wrote the 1976 novel Roots, the story of Kunta Kinte, a young man from the Gambia sold as a slave?

(12)   The nickname of the Gambian national football team is the same as the name of a variety of arachnid with a venomous sting in its tail. What is the arachnid?

(13)   True or false: Banjul is the largest city in the Gambia.

(14)   What was the former name of the city of Banjul?

(15)   Is the national sport boxing, football or wrestling?

(16)   What was the aim of the Senegambia confederation in the 1980s?

(17)   What is the dalasi?

(18)   True or false: Banjul is situated on an island at the estuary of the Gambia River.

(19)   What is the most important crop of the Gambia, coffee or peanuts?

(20)   Which institution did the then president, Yahya Jammeh, withdraw from in 2013 describing it as "a neo-colonial institution"?

THE GAMBIA ANSWERS

(1)   Senegal

(2)   The Atlantic Ocean

(3)   True

(4)   Banjul

(5)   English

(6)   False: The Gambia is a republic with a president.

(7)   (a) less than 50 kms.

(8)   Portugal

(9)   The Gambia River

(10)   False: 96% are Muslims.

(11)   Alex Haley

(12)   A scorpion

(13)   False; the largest city is Serekunda

(14)   Bathurst

(15)   Wrestling

(16)   A confederation of the Gambia and Senegal; The Gambia's growing concern about its autonomy led to the confederation's dissolution in 1989.

(17)   The unit of currency

(18)   True

(19)   Peanuts

(20)   The Commonwealth of Nations

GEORGIA QUESTIONS

(1) The Germans call the capital city Tiflis. What do the British call it?

(2) What is the name of the mountainous region beginning with the letter C in which Georgia is situated?

(3) To the west, Georgia has a coastline on which sea?

(4) From which country did Georgia gain independence in 1991?

(5) Which famous Russian leader was born in Georgia in 1878?

(6) What colour is the cross on the Georgian flag?

(7) Georgia has the same patron saint as England. Who is it?

(8) True or false: Georgia is the only country to have the lari as its currency.

(9) Awarded the title Grandmaster in 1984, in what board game was Kutaisi-born Maia Chiburdanidze seven times women's world champion?

(10) With which neighbouring country did Georgia go to war in 2008?

(11) Mikhail Gorbachev's Minister of Foreign Affairs became President of Georgia in 1995. Who was he?

(12) Kvevri are large earthenware vessels traditionally used for the fermentation, storage and ageing of which alcoholic beverage for which Georgia is famous?

(13) In which martial art did Georgia win its only gold medal at the 2012 Olympics?

(14) Which singer, whose first album Call Off the Search was a multi-million selling smash in Europe, was born in Georgia in 1984?

(15) A lot of surnames in Georgia end in -dze or -shvili. Which ending means son and which ending means child?

(16) Which peaceful revolution forced Eduard Shevardnadze to resign as president in 2003, (a) carnation (b) rose (c) tulip?

(17) Nicknamed the Lelos, in what sport's World Cup has the Georgian national team participated since 2003?

(18) In which Bavarian town, famous for Audi, is the Georgian Chamber Orchestra based?

(19) Name one of the two autonomous regions of Georgia backed by Russia which claim independence.

(20) Which port on the Black Sea, Georgia's third-largest city, is sometimes called "The Las Vegas of the Black Sea" because of its casinos?

(1)   Tbilisi

(2)   The Caucasus

(3)   The Black Sea

(4)   The USSR

(5)   Joseph Stalin

(6)   Red

(7)   St. George

(8)   True

(9)   Chess

(10)   Russia

(11)   Eduard Shevardnadze

(12)   Wine

(13)   Judo (won by Lasha Shavdatuashvili)

(14)   Katie Melua

(15)   -dze means son and -shvili means child.

(16)   The Rose Revolution (The Tulip Revolution was in Kyrgyzstan in 2005 and the Carnation Revolution in Portugal in 1974).

(17)   Rugby

(18)   Ingolstadt

(19)   Abkhazia and South Ossetia

(20)   Batumi

(1) Which city became capital of West Germany in 1949?

(2) Which city is Germany's financial centre and location of the busiest airport?

(3) How many times has Germany won the FIFA World Cup?

(4) Which film festival awards the Golden Bear as its main prize?

(5) What did Wilhelm Conrad Röntgen discover in 1895?

(6) True or false: Bavaria is the biggest state in area and population.

(7) In which year was Adolf Hitler appointed Chancellor of Germany by Hindenburg?

(8) With which country does Germany have its longest border?

(9) In which city on the River Elbe was Angela Merkel born in 1954?

(10) Which famous festival is associated with the Theresienwiese and the cry of O'zapft is?

(11) By what name is the Emperor Karl I better known in English?

(12) How many theses is Luther supposed to have posted on the door of All Saints' Church, Wittenberg?

(13) What did the Two Plus Four Agreement make possible?

(14) The Rivers Isar, Inn, Lech and Altmühl all flow into which great river?

(15) In which city are the headquarters of Volkswagen?

(16) How many horses are there in the Quadriga on the top of the Brandenburg Gate?

(17) What is the largest lake entirely in Germany?

(18) To whom did Beethoven originally dedicate his Eroica Symphony?

(19) What is ARD?

(20) Which famous writer, born in 1749, married Christiane Vulpius in 1806?

GERMANY ANSWERS

(1) Bonn

(2) Frankfurt am Main

(3) Four times: 1954, 1974, 1990, 2014

(4) The Berlin International Film Festival or Berlinale

(5) X-rays

(6) False; it's the biggest in area, but Nordrhein-Westfalen has a bigger population.

(7) 1933

(8) Austria

(9) Hamburg

(10) The Oktoberfest

(11) Charlemagne

(12) 95

(13) The reunification of Germany

(14) The Danube

(15) Wolfsburg

(16) Four

(17) Müritz

(18) Napoleon Bonaparte

(19) The joint organisation of Germany's public service broadcasters (similar to the BBC in the UK).

(20) Johann Wolfgang von Goethe

GHANA QUESTIONS

(1) By what name was Ghana known from 1867 to its independence in 1957?

(2) From which country did it gain independence in 1957?

(3) Who was the first President of Ghana who led Ghana to independence?

(4) What is the capital city?

(5) Which diplomat who served as the seventh Secretary-General of the United Nations was born in Ghana in 1938?

(6) What is the official language of Ghana?

(7) True or false: The name Accra comes from the Akan word Nkran and means ants.

(8) What is the name of the gulf on which Ghana has a coastline?

(9) What is the name of the country on the northern border of Ghana, with the capital city Ouagadougou?

(10) The basin of which great river which rises in Burkina Faso covers about 45% of Ghana's total land surface?

(11) The Ghanaian national football team reached the quarter finals of the FIFA World Cup in 2010. In which country did the competition take place?

(12) True or false: Lake Volta is the largest lake in Africa by area.

(13) What is in the middle of the Ghanaian flag: a black star, a red star or a white star?

(14) Is kente the currency of Ghana or a type of silk and cotton fabric used to make Ghanaian clothes?

(15) Which country, whose capital is Lome, is situated to the east of Ghana?

(16) True or false: Ghana was the first sub-Saharan country to gain independence.

(17) Do Ghanaians eat or drink banku?

(18) An American singer who had hits with the songs Foolish and Rock Wit U has the same name as an ancient kingdom and people of Ghana. What is the name?

(19) Which Scottish novelist, famous for Any Human Heart and A Good Man in Africa and for writing the James Bond continuation novel Solo was born in Accra in 1952?

(20) Ozwald Boateng's parents emigrated to the UK from Ghana in the 1950s. In which field is he particularly famous?

GHANA ANSWERS

(1) The Gold Coast

(2) United Kingdom

(3) Kwame Nkrumah

(4) Accra

(5) Kofi Annan

(6) English

(7) True

(8) The Gulf of Guinea

(9) Burkina Faso

(10) The Volta

(11) South Africa

(12) False; it is the largest artificial lake in the world by surface area. The largest lake in Africa by area is Lake Victoria.

(13) A black star

(14) It's a type of silk and cotton fabric. The cedi is the currency.

(15) Togo

(16) True (in 1957)

(17) They eat it; it's a paste made of fermented corn and cassava dough.

(18) Ashanti

(19) William Boyd

(20) Fashion design

GREECE QUESTIONS

(1) In which two years did Athens host the modern Summer Olympic Games?

(2) What is the native Greek name for the country of Greece?

(3) Which two texts of world literature are believed to have been composed by Homer in the 7th or 8th centuries BC?

(4) From which animal is feta cheese made?

(5) What is the name of the sea off the west coast of Greece, the Aegean or the Ionian Sea?

(6) What name was given in Ancient Greece to a settlement, especially a citadel, built upon an elevated piece of ground for purposes of defence, as in Athens?

(7) Which team did Greece beat in the final of the 2004 UEFA European Football Championship?

(8) The second-largest city of Greece is situated in the region of Macedonia. What is its name?

(9) What is the highest mountain in Greece?

(10) Which city won the Peloponnesian War, the Delian League led by Athens or the Peloponnesian League led by Sparta?

(11) What are the three defined orders of Ancient Greek architecture?

(12) What name is given to the group of islands that includes Rhodes, Kos and Patmos?

(13) Did Aristophanes write comedies or tragedies?

(14) On which Greek island is the city of Heraklion?

(15) Who was the last King of Greece who fled the country in 1973?

(16) For which film did Giorgos Provias invent the choreography of the sirtaki?

(17) What name is given to the dish of small pieces of meat and sometimes vegetables grilled on a skewer?

(18) Who is the wife of the chief Greek god Zeus, who is also his sister?

(19) In which town in western Greece did Lord Byron die in 1824?

(20) Which Greek actress won a Best Supporting Actress Oscar for her role in the 1943 film For Whom the Bell Tolls?

GREECE ANSWERS

(1)   1896 and 2004

(2)   Hellas

(3)   The Iliad and the Odyssey

(4)   Goat

(5)   The Ionian Sea

(6)   Acropolis

(7)   Portugal

(8)   Thessaloniki

(9)   Mount Olympus (2,918 metres)

(10) The Peloponnesian League led by Sparta

(11) Doric, Ionic and Corinthian

(12) The Dodecanese

(13) Comedies (e.g. The Birds, The Frogs, The Clouds)

(14) Crete

(15) King Constantine II

(16) Zorba the Greek (1964)

(17) Souvlaki

(18) Hera

(19) Missolonghi

(20) Katina Paxinou

GRENADA QUESTIONS

(1) In which sea is the island state of Grenada situated?

(2) Is the capital St. George's or St. John's?

(3) Is the unit of currency the East Caribbean dollar or the West Caribbean dollar?

(4) What are Carriacou and Petite Martinique?

(5) The capital of Carriacou has the same name as the stadium of the English football team Sheffield Wednesday. What is it?

(6) Which South American country is closest to Grenada?

(7) Who is the head of state?

(8) Grenada is particularly known for a spice which is used to flavour many kinds of baked goods, puddings, sauces and eggnog. What is the spice?

(9) Ivan hit Grenada in 2004. Who or what is Ivan?

(10) What is the most popular sport in Grenada?

(11) Grenada was ceded to Great Britain by France in the 1763 Treaty of Paris. Which war did this treaty end?

(12) Which country invaded Grenada in 1983 to help to restore democratic government to the island?

(13) Who was President of the United States at the time of the invasion?

(14) What is the popular tourist attraction on Grenada called Grand Etang?

(15) What is Grenada's Internet country code top level domain?

(16) True or false: Nutmeg features on the flag of Grenada.

(17) What is unusual about Grenada's sculpture park?

(18) The Zika virus was identified as being on Grenada in August 2016. What insect transmits the virus?

(19) Why are the Grenada dove and the bougainvillea flower important to Grenada?

(20) True or false: The majority of Grenadians are of African descent.

GRENADA ANSWERS

(1)   In the Caribbean Sea

(2)   St. George's

(3)   The East Caribbean dollar

(4)   Islands belonging to Grenada

(5)   Hillsborough

(6)   Venezuela

(7)   Queen Elizabeth II

(8)   Nutmeg

(9)   Hurricane Ivan, which destroyed or damaged 90% of the buildings on Grenada.

(10) Cricket

(11) The Seven Years' War

(12) The USA

(13) Ronald Reagan

(14) A (volcanic) lake

(15) .gd

(16) True

(17) It's underwater.

(18) The mosquito

(19) They are the national symbols.

(20) True: about 82%

GUATEMALA QUESTIONS

(1)   Is Guatemala in Central America or South America?

(2)   True or false: Guatemala is the most populous country in Central America.

(3)   What is the capital of Guatemala?

(4)   True or false: Guatemala is the only country where the capital and the country have the same name.

(5)   Which ancient civilization's territory covered all of Guatemala, including the city of Tikal?

(6)   True or false: Guatemala has a border with Mexico.

(7)   Does Guatemala have a Caribbean coast?

(8)   What is the official language of Guatemala?

(9)   The southernmost point of Guatemala is on the border with which small Central American country?

(10) Which country has more Guatemalan immigrants, the USA or Mexico?

(11) Erick Barrondo won the silver medal in the Men's 20km Racewalk at the 2012 Olympics. In which city?

(12) Which American fruit company had a great influence on Guatemala, particularly in the first half of the 20th century?

(13) Is Guatemala the world's largest producer of Cardamom or coriander?

(14) Which international prize was the Guatemalan human rights activist Rigoberta Menchú awarded in 1992?

(15) What bird, beginning with Q, is the national bird of Guatemala?

(16) Did the Guatemala Civil War in the second half of the 20th century between the government and various leftist groups last about (a) 16 years (b) 26 years or (c) 36 years?

(17) A city in the central highlands of Guatemala known for its Spanish Baroque-influenced architecture has the same name as a Caribbean island beginning with A. What island?

(18) The greatest Guatemalan footballer of all time, Carlos Ruiz, who played for the national team from 1998 to 2016, is nicknamed Pescado. What does the nickname mean?

(19) Which Guatemalan writer won the Nobel Prize for Literature in 1967?

(20) What is the name of the actor born in Guatemala City who played the title role in the 2013 film Inside Llewyn Davis and Poe Dameron in the last three Star Wars films?

GUATEMALA ANSWERS

(1) In Central America

(2) True; the population is over 17 million.

(3) Guatemala City

(4) False; there are several other countries, such as Mexico and Mexico City, Luxembourg and Luxembourg, Panama and Panama City etc.

(5) The Mayan civilization

(6) True

(7) Yes

(8) Spanish

(9) El Salvador

(10) The USA

(11) London

(12) The United Fruit Company

(13) Cardamom

(14) The Nobel Peace Prize

(15) Quetzal

(16) (c) 36 years

(17) Antigua

(18) Fish

(19) Miguel Ángel Asturias

(20) Oscar Isaac

GUINEA QUESTIONS

(1) What is the capital of Guinea?

(2) True or false: Conakry was originally built on an island.

(3) Does Guinea share a border with Equatorial Guinea or Guinea-Bissau?

(4) Is French or Spanish the official language of Guinea?

(5) Does the flag have horizontal or vertical stripes?

(6) Which of the three countries, Guinea, Guinea-Bissau and Equatorial Guinea, has the biggest population?

(7) Does Guinea have a king or a president as its head of state?

(8) True or false: 50% of the population are Muslim and about 50% Christian.

(9) Guinea has 25% of the world's bauxite reserves. Of which metal is bauxite the main source?

(10) How many of these rivers have their source in Guinea: the Niger, the Gambia and the Senegal?

(11) Which Guinean singer had an international hit in 1987 with Yé ké yé ké?

(12) Which virus disease broke out in Guinea in March 2014?

(13) The city of Kankan is home to the Julius Nyerere University. Of which country was Nyerere president?

(14) The parents of which famous footballer who has played for Juventus and Manchester United and the French national team originally come from Guinea?

(15) In which ocean are the Iles de Los, off the coast of Guinea?

(16) Who was Sekou Toure?

(17) How many times has the Guinean national football team qualified for the FIFA World Cup?

(18) By what name was Guinea known before it gained independence in 1958?

(19) Freetown is the closest capital of another country to Conakry. Which country?

(20) The man who became President of Guinea in 2010 has a first name which is the same as a Greek letter. Is it alpha, beta or gamma?

GUINEA ANSWERS

(1) Conakry

(2) True; on Tombo Island

(3) With Guinea-Bissau

(4) French

(5) Vertical stripes

(6) Guinea (about 13 million)

(7) A president

(8) False: the majority (85%) are Muslim.

(9) Aluminium

(10) All three

(11) Mory Kante

(12) Ebola

(13) Tanzania (1964 – 1985)

(14) Paul Pogba

(15) The Atlantic Ocean

(16) Guinea's first president

(17) They have never qualified for it.

(18) French Guinea

(19) Sierra Leone

(20) Alpha (Condé)

GUINEA-BISSAU QUESTIONS

(1) True or false: Guinea-Bissau is an alternative name for Equatorial Guinea.

(2) Was Guinea-Bissau colonized as Portuguese Guinea or Spanish Guinea in the 19th century?

(3) Why was Bissau added to the name of the country when it became independent in 1973/74?

(4) What is Bissau?

(5) What is the official language?

(6) Is Portuguese or Creole spoken by a majority of inhabitants?

(7) Does Guinea-Bissau have a border with both Guinea and Equatorial Guinea?

(8) True or false: Guinea-Bissau is a very mountainous country.

(9) The capital city Bissau is situated on the Geba River estuary. Into which ocean does the river flow?

(10) Is the currency the Portuguese escudo or the West African CFA franc?

(11) The Portuguese call these islands off the coast of Guinea-Bissau the Bijagós. How are the islands known in English?

(12) Amilcar Cabral was the leader of the nationalist movement of Guinea-Bissau during the war of independence in the 60s and 70s. Did he die a natural death or was he assassinated?

(13) Are the inhabitants of the country called Bissau-Guineans or Guinea-Bissauans?

(14) Apart from ground nuts, which other type of kidney-shaped nut is one of the main exports of Guinea-Bissau?

(15) Are the months December to May the dry season or the rainy season?

(16) What features on the country's flag, a black star or a white star?

(17) The PAIGC is a political party in Guinea-Bissau, originally formed to campaign for independence from Portugal. The abbreviation stands for The African Party for the Independence of Guinea – and which other former island colony of Portugal?

(18) True or false: It is possible to see saltwater hippos on the Bissagos Islands.

(19) After which revolutionary leader is the university in Bissau named?

(20) The motto of the country is Unidade, Luta, Progresso. What do the three words mean?

GUINEA-BISSAU ANSWERS

(1)   False; they are two separate countries.

(2)   As Portuguese Guinea

(3)   To avoid confusion with Guinea (formerly French Guinea).

(4)   It's the capital.

(5)   Portuguese

(6)   Creole (Crioulo)

(7)   No, only with Guinea.

(8)   False; the highest elevation is 300 metres above sea level.

(9)   The Atlantic Ocean

(10) The West African CFA franc

(11) The Bissagos Islands

(12) He was assassinated in 1973.

(13) Bissau-Guineans

(14) The cashew nut

(15) The dry season

(16) A black star

(17) Cape Verde

(18) True

(19) Amilcar Cabral

(20) Unity, struggle, progress

GUYANA QUESTIONS

(1) In which continent is the country of Guyana?

(2) Apart from Guyana, how many English-speaking countries are there in South America?

(3) True or false: Guyana is the smallest country in South America in area.

(4) What was the name of the country as a British colony?

(5) Is the capital Georgetown or Bridgetown?

(6) Who is the famous British actor, who starred in Alfie and Educating Rita, whose wife Shakira was Miss Guyana and runner-up at the Miss World Pageant in 1967?

(7) About 40% of the population of Guyana can trace their ancestry to which large southern Asian country?

(8) Which Guyanese-born singer had a number one hit in the UK in 1982 with I Don't Wanna Dance?

(9) Is the unit of currency the Guyanese dollar or the Guyanese pound?

(10) What is the name of the Guyanese-born businesswoman who initiated a court case against the British government over its authority to implement Brexit without the approval of the British parliament?

(11) Guyana is a member of CARICOM. What is it?

(12) Before Guyana became a British colony in 1814, was it part of Dutch or French Guiana?

(13) In what field has Guyanese-born CCH Pounder made a name for herself?

(14) What happened in "Jonestown" Guyana in November 1978?

(15) The third largest town in Guyana has the same name as New York in the 17th century. What is its name?

(16) Guyana's highest mountain, Mount Roraima and Guyana's table-top mountains are said to be the inspiration for the 1912 novel The Lost World. Who wrote it?

(17) Name one of the two neighbouring countries with which Guyana has a border dispute.

(18) The river on which Georgetown is situated has the same name as a famous brown sugar. What is the river's name?

(19) Which famous Guyanese cricketer captained the West Indies side between 1974 and 1985 and was knighted in the 2020 New Year's Honours for services to cricket?

(20) The Kaieteur Falls are the world's largest single drop waterfall. Are they about two times or four times as high as Niagara Falls?

GUYANA ANSWERS

(1) South America

(2) None

(3) False; both Suriname and Uruguay are smaller.

(4) British Guiana

(5) Georgetown

(6) Michael Caine

(7) India

(8) Eddy Grant

(9) The Guyanese dollar

(10) Gina Miller

(11) The Caribbean Community, an organisation of 15 Caribbean nations promoting economic co-operation among its members.

(12) Dutch Guiana (1667 – 1814)

(13) Acting

(14) The mass murder-suicide of 909 people from The People's Temple Agricultural Project led by Jim Jones.

(15) New Amsterdam

(16) Sir Arthur Conan Doyle

(17) Either Venezuela or Suriname

(18) The Demerara River

(19) Sir Clive Lloyd

(20) Four times as high (226 metres)

HAITI QUESTIONS

(1) On which Caribbean island is Haiti situated?

(2) With which country does Haiti share the island of Hispaniola?

(3) What is the capital?

(4) Which alcoholic drink made from sugar cane is produced by the Barbancourt company?

(5) Which island, with Kingston as its capital, is situated to the west of Haiti?

(6) The parents of which American singer who has had hits with Want to Want Me and Whatcha Say were born in Haiti?

(7) Apart from Haiti, which is the only other nation in the Americas to have French as an official language?

(8) What is the name of the syncretic religion widely practised in Haiti based on a West African religion?

(9) Which autocratic ruler was President of Haiti from 1957 until his death in 1971?

(10) What was the name of Papa Doc's son who took over from his father and ruled until 1986?

(11) A word which describes crop plants like pumpkins, cucumbers and melons is very similar to the name of the Haitian currency. What is the word?

(12) Which black general of the French army led the Haitian Revolution between 1791 and 1803?

(13) What was the name of Papa Doc Duvalier's infamous secret police?

(14) Which member of the pop group the Fugees was actually born in Haiti?

(15) In which year did a deadly earthquake hit Haiti, (a) 2005 (b) 2010 (c) 2015?

(16) Who wrote the novel The Comedians which is set in Haiti and which was made into a 1967 film starring Elizabeth Taylor and Richard Burton?

(17) Is a tap tap (a) a brightly painted share taxi in Haiti or (b) a voodoo drum?

(18) The second largest city in Haiti has the same name as an international supermarket chain with its headquarters in France. What is the name of the city?

(19) The father of tennis player Naomi Osaka is Haitian. What nationality is her mother?

(20) What is the name of the Roman Catholic priest who was Haiti's first democratically elected president in the 1990s?

HAITI ANSWERS

(1) Hispaniola

(2) Dominican Republic

(3) Port-au-Prince

(4) Rum

(5) Jamaica

(6) Jason Derulo

(7) Canada

(8) Haitian Vodou or Voodoo

(9) Francois "Papa Doc" Duvalier

(10) Jean-Claude "Baby Doc" Duvalier

(11) Gourd (The currency is the gourde.)

(12) Toussaint Louverture

(13) Tonton Macoute

(14) Wyclef Jean

(15) (b) 2010

(16) Graham Greene

(17) (a) A brightly painted share taxi

(18) Carrefour

(19) Japanese

(20) Jean-Bertrand Aristide

HONDURAS QUESTIONS

(1) True or false: Honduras was formerly known as British Honduras.

(2) What is the official language of Honduras?

(3) What is the capital city?

(4) Does Honduras have a longer Caribbean coast or a longer Pacific coast?

(5) True or false: The name Honduras means "depths".

(6) Is the currency the US dollar, the lempira or the peso?

(7) True or false: Honduras has never qualified for the finals of the FIFA World Cup.

(8) Who was the first European to reach Honduras?

(9) In Spanish they are called Islas de la Bahia. What are they called in English?

(10) The parents of American actress America Ferrera were born in Honduras. In which award-winning comedy drama did Ferrera appear on TV between 2006 and 2010?

(11) Honduras is the second largest country in Central America. What is the largest?

(12) Is Copán an archaeological site of the Inka civilization or the Maya civilization?

(13) Against which country did Honduras fight the football war in 1969?

(14) The flag of Honduras contains five stars representing the five nations of the former Federal Republic of Central America, which existed from 1823 to 1841. Apart from Honduras, name two other countries which were part of the federal republic.

(15) Would a Honduran eat or drink a baleada?

(16) What is the name of the second-biggest city in Honduras, once dubbed "the murder capital of the world"?

(17) True or false: Central Americans refer to a person from Honduras as a Catracho.

(18) What is the name of the gulf on the Pacific Ocean on which Honduras has a coastline, the Gulf of Fonseca or the Gulf of Honduras?

(19) What was the name of the hurricane in 1998 which caused much damage to Honduras?

(20) True or false: Honduras actually has a joint capital, Tegucigalpa and Comayaguela.

HONDURAS ANSWERS

(1) False; the former name of Belize was British Honduras.

(2) Spanish

(3) Tegucigalpa

(4) A longer Caribbean coast (823 km) (Pacific 163 km)

(5) True

(6) The lempira

(7) False; Honduras qualified for the finals in 1982, 2010 and 2014.

(8) Christopher Columbus

(9) The Bay Islands

(10) Ugly Betty

(11) Nicaragua

(12) The Maya civilization

(13) El Salvador

(14) Two from: El Salvador, Costa Rica, Nicaragua and Guatemala

(15) He would eat it. It's a flour tortilla usually filled with mashed fried red beans.

(16) San Pedro Sula

(17) True

(18) The Gulf of Fonseca (The Gulf of Honduras is on the Caribbean.)

(19) Hurricane Mitch

(20) True, the 1982 constitution names the two cities as a central district to serve as a permanent national capital.

(1)   On which river is the capital city Budapest situated?

(2)   The flag of Hungary consists of the same three colours as the flag of Italy. What are the three colours?

(3)   What is the unit of currency?

(4)   True or false: Budapest has the oldest metro in the world.

(5)   Which Hungarian patented the first commercially successful modern ballpoint pen?

(6)   Erik Weisz was born in Budapest in 1874. By what name is he better known?

(7)   What is the name of the 3-D combination puzzle invented in 1974 by a Hungarian professor of architecture?

(8)   In what year was the Austro-Hungarian Empire dissolved?

(9)   In which year did the Hungarian Revolution against the Hungarian People's Republic and its Soviet-imposed policies take place?

(10) With which sport is the name Ferenc Puskás associated?

(11) The Germans know the largest lake in Central Europe as Plattensee. By what name do the Hungarians and the British know it?.

(12) Which composer, particularly known for his piano music, was born in Hungary in 1811?

(13) What is the name of the Hungarian wine largely made from Furmint and Hárslevelü grapes, the sweet wine of which is particularly famous?

(14) With what recreational activity are the names Gellert, Király and Széchenyi associated?

(15) How many times was Hungarian-born actress Zsa Zsa Gabor married?

(16) A csárda is an old Hungarian term for a roadside tavern, but what is the csárdas?

(17) Only two languages in Europe are related to Hungarian. One of them is Finnish, what is the other one?

(18) What was the title of the 1981 film directed by István Szábo and starring Klaus Maria Brandauer as Hendrik Hoefgen?

(19) What are Vizsla, Puli, Komondor, Pumi and Mudi?

(20) What name is given to the vast treeless plains famous for their cowboys and shepherds?

HUNGARY ANSWERS

(1) The Danube

(2) Red, white and green

(3) The forint

(4) False; London is the oldest, Budapest the second-oldest.

(5) László Bíró

(6) Harry Houdini

(7) Rubik's Cube (invented by Ernö Rubik).

(8) 1918

(9) 1956

(10) Football

(11) Lake Balaton

(12) Franz Liszt

(13) Tokay or Tokaji

(14) Thermal bathing (spa treatment)

(15) Nine times

(16) A traditional Hungarian folk dance

(17) Estonian

(18) Mephisto

(19) Types of Hungarian dog

(20) Puszta

ICELAND QUESTIONS

(1) What is the capital of Iceland?

(2) True or false: Reykjavik is the world's northernmost capital of a sovereign state.

(3) Is a person with the name Jónsdóttir a man or a woman?

(4) Is the unit of currency the euro or the krona?

(5) True or false: The closest land to Iceland is Greenland.

(6) Which group of islands in Europe is closest to Iceland?

(7) Between 1918 and 1944 Iceland was an independent state in a personal union with which other country?

(8) What is the name of the Icelandic parliament, the oldest surviving parliament in the world?

(9) Which American president met Mikhail Gorbachev in Reykjavik in 1986?

(10) What is the name of the Icelandic dairy product, a fresh sour milk cheese, similar to yoghurt?

(11) Which famous Icelandic singer appeared in the film Dancer in the Dark in 2000?

(12) With which other country was Iceland involved in a number of disputes in the 1950s, 1960s and 1970s, known as the Cod Wars?

(13) What is the only native land mammal that lives in Iceland?

(14) What was the name of the volcano which erupted in 2010, causing chaos to air travel?

(15) Which country did Iceland beat in the Round of 16 in the UEFA Euro 2016?

(16) What is the name of the geothermal spa in southwestern Iceland which has the same name as a film starring Brooke Shields and Christopher Atkins?

(17) What is the name of the island which rose above the ocean in a series of volcanic eruptions between 1963 and 1968?

(18) Which two chess players played in the famous world chess championship matches in Reykjavik in 1972?

(19) Where is Iceland's international airport situated?

(20) Which Nobel Prize was Halldór Laxness awarded in 1955?

ICELAND ANSWERS

(1) Reykjavik

(2) True (Nuuk, the capital of Greenland is further north, but Greenland is not a sovereign state).

(3) A woman (Jón's daughter)

(4) The krona

(5) True

(6) The Faroe Islands

(7) Denmark

(8) The Althing

(9) Ronald Reagan

(10) Skyr

(11) Björk

(12) United Kingdom

(13) The arctic fox

(14) Eyjafjallajökull

(15) England (2-1)

(16) The Blue Lagoon

(17) Surtsey

(18) Bobby Fischer and Boris Spassky

(19) Keflavik

(20) The Nobel Prize for Literature

INDIA QUESTIONS

(1) What is the capital of India?

(2) What animal is considered to be a sacred symbol of life in Hinduism?

(3) True or false: India is the most populous democracy in the world.

(4) True or false: The River Ganges does not rise in India.

(5) What object can be seen in the middle of the Indian flag?

(6) The Hindu trinity of deities is made up of Brahma, Vishnu and who else?

(7) By what name is the city of Madras now usually known?

(8) In which language is India known as Bharat?

(9) What is the name of the state on the southwestern coast of India which used to be part of the Portuguese Empire?

(10) What would you do with a dhoti: eat it, sail it or wear it?

(11) What is the name of the religion based on the teachings of Guru Nanak?

(12) Which former Indian test cricketer and captain of the national team is the highest run scorer of all time in international cricket?

(13) What is the name of the Hindu festival of lights held somewhere between mid-October and mid-November?

(14) How was Mrs Gandhi killed?

(15) What is garam masala?

(16) What name is given to the bay, part of the Indian Ocean, off the east coast of India?

(17) Which actor played the role of Gandhi in the 1982 film of the same name?

(18) Who commissioned the Taj Mahal to house the tomb of his favourite wife, Mumtaz Mahal?

(19) Which strategy board game with 64 squares is believed to be derived from the Indian game chaturanga?

(20) What is the name of the territory right in the north of the Indian subcontinent which is a disputed territory between India and Pakistan?

INDIA ANSWERS

(1) New Delhi

(2) The cow

(3) True

(4) False; it does.

(5) A 24-spoke wheel

(6) Shiva

(7) Chennai

(8) Hindi

(9) Goa

(10) Wear it. It's a traditional men's garment in India.

(11) Sikhism

(12) Sachin Tendulkar

(13) Diwali

(14) She was assassinated in 1984 by her own bodyguards (Sikh nationalists).

(15) A blend of ground spices commonly used in Indian cooking.

(16) The Bay of Bengal

(17) Ben Kingsley

(18) Shah Jahan

(19) Chess

(20) Kashmir

INDONESIA QUESTIONS

(1) Which of Indonesia's islands has the biggest population?

(2) Which city was known as Batavia in the Dutch East Indies?

(3) True or false: Indonesia has no land borders with other countries.

(4) Roughly how many islands make up Indonesia, (a) 7,000 (b) 17,000 (c) 27,000?

(5) The Indonesian part of which island is known as Kalimantan?

(6) The four islands known as the Greater Sunda Islands are Java, Borneo, Sulawesi and…?

(7) Which volcano famously erupted in 1883 in the Sunda Strait?

(8) With which two other countries does Indonesia share the island of Borneo?

(9) Who was the first President of Indonesia who was the leader of the Indonesian struggle for independence from the Dutch Empire?

(10) The flag of Indonesia shares its colours with the flag of Poland. What are the colours?

(11) What is the name of the largest species of lizard named after one of the islands on which it is found?

(12) Known also as Celebes, the 11th largest island in the world has a landmass which includes four peninsulas. What is the island's more usual name?

(13) Which tourist island, east of Java, is the only Hindu-majority province in Muslim Indonesia?

(14) What name is given to the Indonesian technique of wax-resist dyeing applied to cloth?

(15) What species of great ape can only be found in the rainforests of Borneo and Sumatra?

(16) On which island was the famous Homo erectus found by the Dutch physician Eugene Dubois in 1889?

(17) What is the name of the strait between the island of Sumatra and the Malay Peninsula, one of the most important shipping lanes in the world?

(18) In which year did the devastating earthquake off the coast of Sumatra and the resulting tsunami which killed more than 300,000 people occur?

(19) Which 1982 film directed by Peter Weir and starring Mel Gibson, Sigourney Weaver and Linda Hunt takes place in Indonesia during the overthrow of President Sukarno?

(20) Gamelan, the traditional ensemble music of Java and Bali, is predominantly made up of what type of instruments?

INDONESIA ANSWERS

(1)   Java (c. 145 million)

(2)   Jakarta, the capital

(3)   False; it has borders with Papua New Guinea, East Timor and Malaysia

(4)   (b) 17,000 The actual number is not sure. Estimates range between 13,500 and 18,300.

(5)   Borneo

(6)   Sumatra

(7)   Krakatoa

(8)   Brunei and Malaysia

(9)   President Sukarno

(10) Red and white (horizontal bands) (Poland's flag is white and red horizontal bands).

(11) The Komodo dragon

(12) Sulawesi

(13) Bali

(14) Batik

(15) Orangutan

(16) Java ("Java Man")

(17) The Strait of Malacca

(18) 2004

(19) The Year of Living Dangerously

(20) Percussion

IRAN QUESTIONS

(1) Which sea borders Iran in the north?

(2) By what name is Iran also known?

(3) The Milad Tower, Golestan Palace and the National Museum of Iran can be seen in which Iranian city?

(4) Is the Persian cat long-haired or short-haired?

(5) Iranian director Asghar Farhadi has won two Oscars for his films A Separation (2012) and The Salesman (2016). In which category did he win?

(6) What are Mashhad and Isfahan?

(7) With which country did Iran go to war between 1980 and 1988?

(8) What is Farsi?

(9) A famous city in Iran has the same name as the alternative name for the syrah grape. What is it?

(10) Iran has borders with three -stan countries. Name two of them.

(11) What is the name of the strait between the Persian Gulf and the Gulf of Oman which is a highly important strategic location for international trade, especially oil and gas?

(12) Who was Mohammed Reza Pahlavi?

(13) What is the name of the Oscar-winning film directed by Ben Affleck which depicts the rescue of six US diplomats during the Iran hostage crisis under the guise of filming a science fiction film?

(14) Iran accounts for over half the world's production of what nut?

(15) Who became leader of Iran after the Shah was deposed in 1979?

(16) What is the name of the ancient Persian religion which may have originated about 4,000 years ago and is still practised as a minority religion in parts of Iran and India?

(17) What is the name of the archaeological site, the ceremonial capital of the Achaemenid Empire, situated 60 kilometres northeast of the city of Shiraz?

(18) The poetry of which Persian poet, mathematician, astronomer and philosopher became known to the English-speaking world through the translations of Edward Fitzgerald?

(19) Which King of Persia, son of Darius I, led a failed invasion of Greece in 480 BC?

(20) Ghali, Dozar, Kelleghi, Kenareh and Zaronim are all sizes used in what internationally known Iranian craft?

IRAN ANSWERS

(1) The Caspian Sea

(2) Persia

(3) Tehran, the capital

(4) Long-haired

(5) Best Foreign Language Film

(6) The second- and third-biggest cities in Iran

(7) Iraq

(8) Another name for the language Persian

(9) Shiraz

(10) Two from Afghanistan, Pakistan and Turkmenistan

(11) The Strait of Hormuz

(12) The last Shah of Iran

(13) Argo

(14) Pistachios

(15) Ayatollah Ruhollah Khomeini

(16) Zoroastrianism

(17) Persepolis

(18) Omar Khayyam

(19) Xerxes

(20) Rug or carpet making

IRAQ QUESTIONS

(1) The name of the currency of Iraq is derived from the Latin denarius. What is it?

(2) True or false: Iraq is a landlocked country.

(3) Name one of the two major rivers which runs through Iraq.

(4) Is the capital Baghdad on the Tigris or on the Euphrates?

(5) By what name is the region between the Tigris and Euphrates rivers historically known?

(6) What is the name of the city, the remains of which can be seen in Hillah, Iraq, which was capital of a kingdom in ancient Mesopotamia between the 18th and 6th centuries BC?

(7) Iraq has two official languages. Name one of them.

(8) Which country did Iraq invade in August 1990 triggering off the Gulf War?

(9) Which of the ancient Seven Wonders of the World was located in Iraq?

(10) Which location described in the Book of Genesis in the Bible is often thought to have been in Iraq by those who think the location is real rather than mythical?

(11) Which President of Iraq from 1979 to 2003 had two infamous sons called Uday and Qusay?

(12) Is Masgouf, often considered to be the national dish of Iraq, a meat dish or a fish dish?

(13) Which Biblical patriarch was born in the ancient Mesopotamian city of Ur?

(14) The motto of Iraq, which is written on the flag, is the phrase Allahu akbar. What does the motto mean in English?

(15) Which fictional sailor, born in Baghdad, often set sail from the Iraqi city of Basra?

(16) Which British actor portrayed Prince Faisal, who later became King Faisal I of Iraq, in the film Lawrence of Arabia?

(17) What ancient city on the banks of the Tigris near Mosul was the capital of the Neo- Assyrian Empire?

(18) Is Maqam al-iraqi a type of music or a type of bread?

(19) What is the Shatt-al-Arab?

(20) Which brothers, famous for their advertising agency which produced posters for the British Conservative Party for the 1979 general election, were born in Baghdad?

IRAQ ANSWERS

(1) The dinar

(2) False; Iraq has a 58-kilometre coastline on the Persian Gulf.

(3) Either the Tigris or the Euphrates

(4) On the Tigris

(5) Mesopotamia

(6) Babylon

(7) Either Arabic or Kurdish

(8) Kuwait

(9) The Hanging Gardens of Babylon

(10) The Garden of Eden

(11) Saddam Hussein

(12) Fish; it's a dish made from carp.

(13) Abraham

(14) Allah is the greatest.

(15) Sinbad

(16) Alec Guinness

(17) Nineveh

(18) A type of traditional Arab music in Iraq

(19) A river formed by the confluence of the Tigris and the Euphrates

(20) (Charles) Saatchi and (Maurice) Saatchi

IRELAND QUESTIONS

(1) What do the Irish call Ireland?

(2) Name one of the top three biggest selling Irish music acts of all time.

(3) Which actor of Irish descent holds the record of eight Oscar nominations without a win?

(4) Dublin is the capital, but what is Ireland's second-biggest city located in the province of Munster?

(5) What is the longest river in Ireland?

(6) What is the name of the Irish budget airline with its main bases at Dublin and Stansted airports?

(7) In which century was Guinness first brewed?

(8) Which city in the south-east of Ireland is particularly noted for its crystal?

(9) What name was given to Ireland when the state was established in 1922 under the Anglo-Irish Treaty?

(10) What is the rhyme scheme of the humorous verse known as a limerick?

(11) What office does the Taoiseach hold in Ireland?

(12) With which two other countries did Ireland join the EEC in 1973?

(13) In which building is the Book of Kells, an illuminated manuscript Gospel book in Latin, located?

(14) What is the name of the channel which separates the south-east of Ireland from South Wales?

(15) Which famous politician who had served as prime minister on a number of occasions became the third President of Ireland in 1959?

(16) Which of these Irish writers was not awarded the Nobel Prize for Literature: W.B. Yeats, James Joyce, George Bernard Shaw, Samuel Beckett and Seamus Heaney?

(17) What agricultural disaster between 1845 and 1849 led to a great emigration of Irish people to the USA?

(18) What is the name of the Irish sport where 15 team players use a stick to hit a ball called a sliotar between the opponents' goalposts?

(19) What is the name of Ireland's highest mountain range situated in County Kerry?

(20) What are the two main ingredients of the Irish dish colcannon?

IRELAND ANSWERS

(1) Eire

(2) One from U2, Enya or Westlife.

(3) Peter O'Toole

(4) Cork

(5) The River Shannon

(6) Ryanair

(7) The 18th century (1759)

(8) Waterford

(9) The Irish Free State

(10) AABBA

(11) The office of prime minister (The word Taoiseach means chief or leader in Irish.)

(12) The United Kingdom and Denmark

(13) The library of Trinity College, Dublin

(14) St. George's Channel

(15) Eamon de Valera

(16) James Joyce

(17) The Great Irish Potato Famine

(18) Hurling

(19) MacGillycuddy's Reeks

(20) Mashed potatoes and cabbage (or kale)

ISRAEL QUESTIONS

(1) What is the capital of Israel?

(2) What is the official language of Israel?

(3) What is the name of the river which flows through the Sea of Galilee into the Dead Sea?

(4) Was Jesus born in Bethlehem or Nazareth?

(5) In which year was the Declaration of the Establishment of the State of Israel proclaimed?

(6) What is the name of the city situated on the Mediterranean, the economic and technological centre of Israel, also known as a party capital?

(7) In which body of water is the world's lowest point situated?

(8) Which Israeli prime minister is considered to be the founder of the State of Israel?

(9) What name is given to the Israeli Parliament?

(10) Which transgender singer won the Eurovision Song Contest for Israel in 1998 with the song Diva?

(11) What name is given to food which has been prepared according to Jewish law?

(12) What name is given to the Islamic shrine located on the Temple Mount in the Old City of Jerusalem?

(13) Of which political party is Prime Minister Benjamin Netanyahu a member?

(14) What name is given to a collective community in Israel that was traditionally based on agriculture?

(15) With which musical instrument are Itzhak Perlman and Pinchas Zukerman associated?

(16) What name is often given to the ancient limestone wall in the Old City of Jerusalem which is considered to be one of the holiest places to pray?

(17) What name is usually given to the war fought between Israel and Egypt, Jordan and Syria in 1967?

(18) With whom did Prime Minister Menachim Begin share the 1978 Nobel Peace Prize?

(19) What is the name of the ancient fortification in south Israel situated on top of a rock plateau, the scene of a famous siege by Roman troops from 73 to 74 AD?

(20) On which gulf in the Red Sea is Israel's southernmost town Eilat situated?

ISRAEL ANSWERS

(1) Jerusalem

(2) Hebrew

(3) Jordan

(4) Bethlehem

(5) 1948

(6) Tel Aviv

(7) The Dead Sea

(8) David Ben-Gurion

(9) The Knesset

(10) Dana International

(11) Kosher

(12) The Dome of the Rock

(13) Likud

(14) A kibbutz

(15) The violin

(16) The Wailing Wall or Western Wall or the Buraq Wall

(17) The Six-Day War

(18) Anwar Sadat

(19) Masada

(20) The Gulf of Aqaba

ITALY QUESTIONS

(1) On which river is the capital Rome situated?

(2) In which city was the modern pizza invented?

(3) Which city, capital of Lombardy, is considered to be the fashion capital of Italy?

(4) Apart from Italian, which other language is an official language of the Italian province South Tyrol?

(5) Which Italian inventor, known for his work on long-distance radio transmission, is credited as the inventor of the radio?

(6) Who was the first Emperor of the Roman Empire?

(7) What is Italy's largest island?

(8) Name the three Italian volcanoes that have erupted in the last hundred years.

(9) Which Italian city is home to the oldest university in the world?

(10) Which famous Italian scientist argued that the earth revolved around the sun?

(11) What name is given to the waterbuses in Venice?

(12) Which famous gallery in Florence contains works by Michelangelo, Botticelli and Leonardo da Vinci?

(13) What name is given to the horse race which takes place around the Campo in Siena twice a year?

(14) In which year did Italy first win the FIFA World Cup?

(15) Which Italian Renaissance author's most important work was The Prince?

(16) Who directed the films Satyricon, Amarcord and La Strada?

(17) What grain is normally used to make polenta?

(18) Which of these operas did Puccini not compose: La Bohème, Tosca, Falstaff and Turandot?

(19) In which region of Italy is Chianti wine produced?

(20) What is the name of the 19th century Italian statesman, born in Turin, who was a leading figure in the movement towards Italian unification?

ITALY ANSWERS

(1) The River Tiber

(2) Naples

(3) Milan

(4) German

(5) Guglielmo Marconi

(6) Augustus

(7) Sicily

(8) Etna, Stromboli and Vesuvius

(9) Bologna

(10) Galileo Galilei

(11) Vaporetti

(12) The Uffizi

(13) The Palio

(14) 1934

(15) Machiavelli

(16) Federico Fellini

(17) (Yellow) maize

(18) Falstaff was composed by Verdi

(19) Tuscany

(20) Count of Cavour (Camillo Benso)

JAMAICA QUESTIONS

(1) Is the capital Kingston or Kingstown?

(2) True or false: Jamaica is the second-biggest island in the Caribbean after Cuba.

(3) Which world beauty pageant was won by Jamaicans Carole Crawford, Cindy Breakspeare, Lisa Hanna and Toni-Ann Singh?

(4) What is the name of the traditional Jamaican folk song best known from the 1956 Harry Belafonte version?

(5) True or false: The population of Kingston is over a million.

(6) What is the name of the Jamaican-born singer who had international hits with Oh Carolina and It Wasn't Me?

(7) True or false: Jamaica has never qualified for the finals of the FIFA World Cup.

(8) How many Olympic gold medals does Usain Bolt have?

(9) What style of music popularised, amongst others, by Bob Marley originated in Jamaica in the late 1960s?

(10) What is the name of the 1993 American comedy sports film loosely based on the Jamaica national bobsleigh team's appearance at the 1988 Winter Olympics?

(11) What is the name of the mountain range in the east of Jamaica famous for its coffee?

(12) Whose greatest hits album Legend is the best-selling reggae album of all-time?

(13) What is the most important meaning of the word jerk for Jamaicans?

(14) What was the name of the estate on Jamaica which the novelist Ian Fleming bought in 1946?

(15) Which Abrahamic religion developed in Jamaica in the 1930s?

(16) What sport is usually played at Sabina Park in Kingston?

(17) A National Hero of Jamaica, what is the name of the man who was premier from 1959 to 1962 and whose son became prime minister on two separate occasions?

(18) What is the name of the city, a popular tourist destination on the north coast, about which Bobby Bloom sang in his 1970 hit?

(19) Which infamous Welsh-born privateer, born in 1635, later became Lieutenant Governor of Jamaica?

(20) In Germany a coalition government of the political parties CDU, FDP and the Greens is sometimes called a Jamaica Coalition. Why?

JAMAICA ANSWERS

(1) Kingston

(2) False; it's the third-biggest. Hispaniola is second.

(3) Miss World

(4) Day-O (The Banana Boat Song)

(5) True; it's about 1.25 million

(6) Shaggy

(7) False: Jamaica qualified in 1998.

(8) Eight

(9) Reggae

(10) Cool Runnings

(11) The Blue Mountains

(12) Bob Marley

(13) Jerk is a style of Jamaican cooking. Meat is dry-rubbed, marinated in a hot spicy sauce and grilled.

(14) Goldeneye

(15) Rastafarianism

(16) Cricket

(17) Norman Manley

(18) Montego Bay

(19) Henry Morgan

(20) The colours of the three parties are the same as the colours on the Jamaican flag: CDU – black, FDP – yellow and the Greens – green.

JAPAN QUESTIONS

(1)   Which Japanese capital city was formerly known as Edo?

(2)   What is the meaning of Nihon or Nippon, the Japanese name for Japan?

(3)   Name the two main islands which begin with H.

(4)   Do they drive on the left or the right side of the road in Japan?

(5)   From which grain is sake made?

(6)   What is the name of the Japanese religion which has over 80,000 shrines in Japan?

(7)   In which sport are the terms rikishi and dohyo used?

(8)   What name is given to the Japanese art of arranging flowers?

(9)   Who succeeded Akihito as Emperor of Japan in May 2019?

(10) Which multinational consumer electronics, entertainment and financial conglomerate owns the publishing rights to the Lennon and McCartney catalogue?

(11) On which island is Mount Fuji located?

(12) What are the two famous styles of classical Japanese dance-drama, both of which are inscribed in the UNESCO Representative List of the Intangible Cultural Heritage of Humanity?

(13) What is the name of the monster which first appeared in Ishiro Honda's 1954 film?

(14) What is the literal meaning of the word Karaoke?

(15) What name, which when translated means whimsical drawings. is given to the comics or graphic novels which represent Japanese culture and history?

(16) What is the name of the island in the south of Japan, the scene of a bloody battle in the Second World War between April and June 1945?

(17) What is the common ingredient in all types of sushi?

(18) Who was the director of the Japanese films Rashomon, Seven Samurai, Kagemusha and Ran?

(19) Which martial art, developed in the Ryukyu Kingdom which Japan annexed in 1879, would have debuted at the 2020 Summer Olympics?

(20) The fifth-biggest city in Japan hosted the 1972 Winter Olympics. What is its name?

JAPAN ANSWERS

(1) Tokyo

(2) Land of the Rising Sun

(3) Hokkaido and Honshu

(4) On the left

(5) Rice

(6) Shinto

(7) Sumo; rikishi is a wrestler and dohyo is the circular ring.

(8) Ikebana

(9) Naruhito

(10) Sony

(11) Honshu

(12) Kabuki and Noh

(13) Godzilla

(14) Empty orchestra

(15) Manga

(16) Okinawa

(17) Vinegared rice

(18) Akira Kurosawa

(19) Karate

(20) Sapporo

JORDAN QUESTIONS

(1) What is the capital city?

(2) From what does the country take its name?

(3) True or false: Jordan has access to the Red Sea.

(4) With which country does Jordan have its longest border: Saudi Arabia, Syria or Iraq?

(5) Is the dominant religion Sunni Islam or Shia Islam?

(6) Who was King of Jordan from 1952 to 1999 whose fourth wife was Queen Noor?

(7) Who is the present King of Jordan?

(8) What is the name of the ancient Nabataean city rediscovered by Johann Ludwig Burckhardt in 1812?

(9) True or false: Petra is sometimes known as The Rose City.

(10) What is the name of Jordan's only seaport?

(11) The Emirate of Transjordan which existed between 1921 and 1946 was a protectorate of which country?

(12) What is the full name of the country of Jordan?

(13) To what does Hashemite refer?

(14) The archaeological World Heritage Site Al-Maghtas on the east bank of the River Jordan is considered to be the original location of the baptism of whom?

(15) In which Korean martial art did Jordan win a gold medal at the 2016 Rio Olympics?

(16) Which British archaeologist, army officer and diplomat, played by Peter O'Toole in a famous film, took part in the Battle of Aqaba in 1917?

(17) During the Hellenistic and Roman periods, the city of Amman was known by the same name as the capital of the US state Pennsylvania. What name?

(18) Why is the city of Jerash in the north of Jordan sometimes called "Pompeii of the East"?

(19) In which of the Indiana Jones' films is the ancient city of Petra briefly visited?

(20) The man who assassinated Robert Kennedy has Jordanian citizenship. What is his name?

JORDAN ANSWERS

(1) Amman

(2) The River Jordan which forms much of Jordan's north-western border.

(3) True; it has about 26 kilometres of shore along the Gulf of Aqaba.

(4) Saudi Arabia (731 km.), Syria (379 km.) and Iraq (179 km.)

(5) Sunni Islam

(6) King Hussein

(7) Abdullah II

(8) Petra

(9) True

(10) Aqaba

(11) The United Kingdom

(12) The Hashemite Kingdom of Jordan

(13) The Hashemites or House of Hashim are the royal family of Jordan

(14) The Baptism of Jesus

(15) Taekwondo – won by Ahmad Abu Ghaush. It was the first gold medal in any sport.

(16) T.E. Lawrence

(17) Philadelphia

(18) Because it is one of the best-preserved Greco-Roman cities.

(19) Indiana Jones and the Last Crusade

(20) Sirhan Sirhan

KAZAKHSTAN QUESTIONS

(1) What is the capital of Kazakhstan?

(2) What was the previous name of Nur-Sultan?

(3) After whom is the capital Nur-Sultan named?

(4) What is the largest city in Kazakhstan and capital from 1991 to 1997?

(5) What nationality was the architect Kisho Kurokawa who designed the master plan of Nur-Sultan?

(6) True or false: Kazakhstan is the world's largest landlocked country.

(7) Of which country was Kazakhstan a constituent republic from 1936 to 1991?

(8) With which large landlocked sea does Kazakhstan have a coastline in the west?

(9) What does the word -stan mean on the end of the country's name?

(10) True or false: Kazakhstan has territory in Asia and in Europe.

(11) What is pictured on the nation's flag, a sun or a moon?

(12) What is the name of the body of water shared with Uzbekistan which by 1997 had shrunk to 10% of its original size?

(13) What is the name of the town in Kazakhstan used as a launch site for human space flight by the Russians?

(14) Called alma by the locals, of which widely eaten fruit is Kazakhstan reckoned to be the original source?

(15) Who played Borat in the 2006 film Borat: Cultural Learnings of America for Make Benefit Glorious Nation of Kazakhstan?

(16) In which novel by Alexander Solzhenitsyn is the description of a Soviet labour camp based on a camp in northern Kazakhstan?

(17) The ancient sport of Berkutchi uses what sort of creature to hunt for rabbits, foxes and smaller birds?

(18) What is the name of the range of mountains in the eastern corner of Kazakhstan on the border with Russia and China, with Mount Belukha as its highest peak?

(19) Which famous Russian writer of Crime and Punishment spent five years' military service at the Semipalatinsk garrison in present-day Kazakhstan?

(20) How many tijn in a tenge?

KAZAKHSTAN ANSWERS

(1) Nur-Sultan

(2) Astana

(3) The former President of Kazakhstan, Nur-Sultan Nazarbayev who resigned as president in March 2019.

(4) Almaty

(5) Japanese

(6) True

(7) The USSR

(8) The Caspian Sea

(9) It's an ancient Persian word for land or nation.

(10) True; Kazakhstan has territory on both sides of the Ural River which is considered to be the boundary between Europe and Asia.

(11) A sun

(12) The Aral Sea

(13) Baikonur

(14) The apple

(15) Sacha Baron Cohen

(16) One Day in the Life of Ivan Denisovich

(17) Eagles or falcons

(18) The Altai Mountains

(19) Fyodor Dostoyevsky

(20) 100; the tenge is the currency of Kazakhstan, with the tijn as the subdivision.

KENYA QUESTIONS

(1) What is the capital city?

(2) Which country, which gained independence in 2011, borders Kenya to the northwest?

(3) The currency of Kenya has the same name as a pre-decimal British coin. What is it?

(4) Of which beverage is Kenya the third largest producer after China and India?

(5) True or false: The highest mountain in Kenya is called Mount Kenya.

(6) The official languages of Kenya are English and what language beginning with S or sometimes K?

(7) Who was the first President of Kenya who played a significant role in Kenya's independence from the UK?

(8) What is the name of Kenya's second-largest city and biggest port, situated on the Indian Ocean?

(9) True or false: The Big Five game animals of Africa, buffalo, elephant, leopard, lion and rhinoceros can all be found in Kenya.

(10) What name was given to the Kenya Land and Freedom Army which fought against the British between 1952 and 1960?

(11) Whose book Born Free describes the raising of a lion cub named Elsa in Kenya in the 1950s?

(12) Where were Princess Elizabeth and Prince Philip staying in Kenya when they received the news of King George VI's death?

(13) The second President of Kenya died in February 2020 at the age of 95. Who was he?

(14) What is the name of the game reserve in Narok County, Kenya, named in honour of the Maasai people?

(15) The father of which American President was born in Kenya?

(16) Name one of the other countries with which Kenya shares Lake Victoria.

(17) What diplomatic building was bombed in Nairobi in 1998 by Al-Qaeda operatives?

(18) Which is the largest ethnic group in Kenya: the Luhya, the Kamba or the Kikuyu?

(19) What is the name of the Kenyan paleoanthropologist and conservationist who became Chairman of the Board of the Kenya Wildlife Service in 2015?

(20) In which area of sport has Kenya won the most gold medals at the Summer Olympics: athletics, boxing, judo or weightlifting?

KENYA ANSWERS

(1) Nairobi

(2) South Sudan

(3) The (Kenyan) shilling

(4) Tea

(5) True

(6) Swahili or Kiswahili

(7) Jomo Kenyatta

(8) Mombasa

(9) True

(10) The Mau Mau

(11) Joy Adamson

(12) Treetops Hotel, Aberdare National Park

(13) Daniel arap Moi

(14) Maasai Mara

(15) Barack Obama

(16) Uganda or Tanzania. Kenya has only about 6% of the lake.

(17) The US embassy

(18) The Kikuyu (about 22%)

(19) Richard Leakey

(20) In athletics, by far!

KIRIBATI QUESTIONS

(1) In which ocean is Kiribati situated?

(2) How many island groups make up Kiribati, one, two or three?

(3) Is the capital of Kiribati Funafuti, Palikir or Tarawa?

(4) In which continent is Kiribati situated?

(5) Kiribati consists of 32 atolls. What is an atoll?

(6) From which country did Kiribati gain its independence in 1979?

(7) Kiribati was a part of which island group until 1976?

(8) Two separate countries were formed from the Gilbert and Ellice Islands. One was Kiribati. What was the other?

(9) True or false: Gilbertese exists as a language.

(10) Is Kiribati in Micronesia or Polynesia?

(11) True or false: Kiribati is the only country in the world to be situated in all four hemispheres.

(12) Which country's currency is often used as the currency of Kiribati: Australia, the UK or the USA?

(13) True or false: Christmas Island is part of Kiribati.

(14) What is the greatest danger facing Kiribati in the future?

(15) David Katoatau won a gold medal in weightlifting at the 2014 Commonwealth Games in Scotland. In which Scottish city did the games take place?

(16) What is the Kiribati's Internet country code top level domain?

(17) In what language is Kiribati pronounced Kiribas?

(18) What do the blue and white wavy bands on the Kiribati flag represent?

(19) Which country occupied the islands during World War II?

(20) What sort of creature is the bokikokiko which is only found on Kiribati?

KIRIBATI ANSWERS

(1) The Pacific Ocean

(2) Three: the Gilbert Islands, the Phoenix Islands and the Line Islands

(3) (South) Tarawa

(4) Oceania

(5) A ring-shaped coral reef

(6) The United Kingdom

(7) The Gilbert and Ellice Islands

(8) Tuvalu

(9) True; it is also known as Taetae ni Kiribati

(10) Micronesia

(11) True

(12) Australia

(13) True; it is also known as Kiritimati and is one of the Line Islands.

(14) Climate change leading to a rise in the level of the sea.

(15) Glasgow

(16) .ki

(17) Gilbertese; ti is pronounced like an s.

(18) The Pacific Ocean

(19) Japan

(20) A bird: the Kiritimati reed warbler

KOSOVO QUESTIONS

(1) What is the capital of Kosovo?

(2) Of which country was Kosovo a part until 1992?

(3) Which country claims Kosovo as the Autonomous Province of Kosovo and Metohija?

(4) Are the majority of the inhabitants Kosovo Albanians or Kosovo Serbs?

(5) True or false: Kosovo has a short coastline on the Adriatic.

(6) Pristina is the second-largest city in the world with a predominantly Albanian-speaking population. What is the largest city?

(7) As well as Kosovan, what other word is used to describe the inhabitants of Kosovo?

(8) The flag of Kosovo has a map of the country on it. Which is the only other country in the world to have a map of itself on its flag?

(9) True or false: The majority of Kosovans are Christian.

(10) With which sport is Kosovo-born Xherdan Shaqiri associated?

(11) Who was President of Serbia during the 1998 – 1999 Kosovo War?

(12) Which well-known singer who had hits with Anywhere and How We Do (Party) was born in Pristina in 1990?

(13) What international currency is used in Kosovo?

(14) The singer Dua Lipa's parents are Kosovo Albanians. What was the title of Dua Lipa's first solo number one single in the UK?

(15) Which country starting with the letter M borders Kosovo?

(16) Which 90s American president has a boulevard named after him in Pristina with a statue?

(17) What are the two official languages of Kosovo?

(18) Did Majlinda Kelmendi win a gold medal at the 2016 Rio Olympics in judo or karate?

(19) What is unusual about the national anthem of Kosovo?

(20) What do the six stars on the flag symbolise?

KOSOVO ANSWERS

(1) Pristina

(2) Yugoslavia

(3) Serbia

(4) Kosovo Albanians (about 81.6%)

(5) False; it is landlocked.

(6) Tirana, the capital of Albania

(7) Kosovar

(8) Cyprus

(9) False; the majority are Muslim.

(10) Football

(11) Slobodan Milosevic

(12) Rita Ora

(13) The euro

(14) New Rules

(15) Montenegro

(16) Bill Clinton

(17) Albanian and Serbian

(18) Judo

(19) It has no lyrics, so as not to offend the Serb minority living in Kosovo.

(20) The six major ethnic groups in Kosovo (Albanians, Serbs, Turks, Gorani, Romani and Bosniaks.)

KUWAIT QUESTIONS

(1) True or false: More expatriates live in Kuwait than Kuwaitis.

(2) Which country invaded Kuwait in 1990?

(3) Which commodity is most important for the Kuwaiti economy?

(4) True or false: Manama is the capital of Kuwait.

(5) Which two countries have a border with Kuwait?

(6) What is the official language of Kuwait?

(7) What body of water forms Kuwait's coastline?

(8) True or false: Kuwait is a member of OPEC.

(9) Of which country was Kuwait a protectorate from 1899 until 1961?

(10) What title does the monarch and head of state of Kuwait hold?

(11) Is the currency the Kuwaiti pound, the Kuwaiti dinar or the Kuwaiti dollar?

(12) Which bird of prey is the national animal of Kuwait?

(13) Which major desert covers most of Kuwait?

(14) A type of Arabian sailing ship appears on all Kuwaiti coins. What is it?

(15) Why is the Al-Sabah family important in Kuwait?

(16) True or false: Kuwait has never qualified for the finals of the FIFA World Cup.

(17) Failaka has a small number of inhabitants, Bubiyan is the biggest, but is uninhabited. What are they?

(18) What method of taking away certain mineral components from saline water does Kuwait use to produce its drinking water?

(19) Name two of the four colours which feature on the Kuwaiti flag.

(20) What is the name of the Queen Consort of Jordan who was born in Kuwait City in 1970?

KUWAIT ANSWERS

(1) True; about 70% of the population are expatriates.

(2) Iraq

(3) Oil

(4) False; Kuwait City is the capital. Manama is the capital of Bahrain.

(5) Iraq and Saudi Arabia

(6) Arabic

(7) The Persian Gulf

(8) True

(9) The United Kingdom

(10) Emir

(11) The Kuwaiti dinar

(12) The falcon

(13) The Arabian Desert

(14) A dhow

(15) It is the ruling family.

(16) False; it qualified for the 1982 finals in Spain. It scored one point, drawing 1-1 with Czechoslovakia.

(17) Kuwaiti islands

(18) Desalination

(19) Two out of black, green, red and white

(20) Rania Al-Abdullah

KYRGYZSTAN QUESTIONS

(1) Is the capital of Kyrgyzstan Ashgabat, Bishkek or Tashkent?

(2) With how many -stan countries does Kyrgyzstan have a border?

(3) True or false: Kyrgyzstan was never part of the Soviet Union.

(4) Are the colours of the flag red and yellow or blue and white?

(5) What is the dominant religion of the country?

(6) True or false: Kyrgyzstan has a Caspian Sea coastline.

(7) True or false: One of the routes of the Silk Road ran through Kyrgyzstan.

(8) Which city was formerly known by the names Pishpek and Frunze?

(9) What name is given to the portable, round tent covered with skins used as a dwelling by nomadic groups, the wooden crown of which (the tunduk) is featured in the middle of the flag?

(10) The sun on the flag has 40 rays. Does this represent the number of provinces in Kyrgyzstan or the number of tribes?

(11) The word Kyrgyz is thought to be derived from the Turkic word for which number?

(12) Is the Manas International Airport near Bishkek named after a former president or after a famous epic poem?

(13) The national drink of Kyrgyzstan is kumyz. From which animal does it come?

(14) The village of Barak is an exclave of Kyrgyzstan, completely surrounded by which country?

(15) With what sort of nut is the town of Arslanbob particularly associated: cashew nut, hazelnut or walnut?

(16) The Pamir-Alay and the Tian Shan extend through Kyrgyzstan. What are they?

(17) What would a Kyrgyz do with a komuz: eat it, wear it or play it?

(18) What is Issyk-Kul?

(19) Issyk-Kul is the world's second largest high-altitude lake. What is the name of the largest which is in South America?

(20) Kyrgyz is one official language of Kyrgyzstan. What is the other?

KYRGYZSTAN ANSWERS

(1) Bishkek

(2) Three: Kazakhstan, Uzbekistan and Tajikistan.

(3) False

(4) Red and yellow

(5) Islam (c. 89%)

(6) False

(7) True

(8) Bishkek

(9) A yurt

(10) The number of tribes

(11) Forty – a reference to the 40 clans

(12) A famous epic poem

(13) A mare

(14) Uzbekistan

(15) Walnut

(16) Mountain ranges

(17) Play it; it's an ancient fretless stringed instrument, one of Kyrgyzstan's national symbols.

(18) A large saline lake in eastern Kyrgyzstan, the second-largest saline lake in the world after the Caspian Sea.

(19) Lake Titicaca

(20) Russian

LAOS QUESTIONS

(1)   True or false: Laos is landlocked.

(2)   What is the capital city?

(3)   Laos was a protectorate of which European nation between 1893 and 1953?

(4)   Which river forms a large part of the western boundary with Thailand?

(5)   What is the English for a person from Laos?

(6)   What is the main religion?

(7)   The currency of Laos sounds like a colloquial English word for a short nap or a sleep. What is it?

(8)   Which part of the country is narrower, the top half or the bottom half?

(9)   The name of the official language of Laos is very similar to the name of the country. What is it?

(10) True or false: Laos does not have a border with China.

(11) Laos is sometimes known as the Land of a Million (a) Buffalo (b) Crocodiles (c) Elephants?

(12) The city of Vientiane is very close to the border with which country?

(13) What is the name of the trail on the Laos-Vietnam border which was heavily used by the North Vietnamese Army during the Vietnam War?

(14) What type of rice is particularly consumed in Laos?

(15) Which crop is important to Laos, coffee or tea?

(16) The Lao language is very similar to which neighbouring country's language?

(17) The Pha That Luang stupa in Vientiane is regarded as the most important national monument in Laos. What is a stupa?

(18) What shape is the sinh, a traditional skirt often worn by Laotian women?

(19) In which river is the Si Phan Don archipelago located?

(20) Is Laos a constitutional monarchy or a socialist state endorsing communism?

LAOS ANSWERS

(1) True

(2) Vientiane

(3) France

(4) The Mekong

(5) A Laotian

(6) (Theravada) Buddhism

(7) Kip

(8) The bottom half

(9) Lao

(10) False

(11) Elephants

(12) Thailand

(13) The Ho Chi Minh Trail

(14) Sticky rice

(15) Coffee

(16) Thailand

(17) A building with a dome that is a holy place for Buddhists

(18) Tube shape

(19) In the River Mekong in southern Laos. The name means 4,000 islands.

(20) A socialist state endorsing communism

LATVIA QUESTIONS

(1)   On which sea does Latvia have a coastline?

(2)   Is the capital Riga, Tallinn or Vilnius?

(3)   True or false: Latvia is situated between Estonia and Lithuania.

(4)   Which minority makes up about 30% of the population of Latvia?

(5)   The director of Battleship Potemkin and Alexander Nevsky was born in Riga in 1898. Who is he?

(6)   True or false: Riga is the biggest capital of the three Baltic states, Estonia, Latvia and Lithuania.

(7)   Which Nobel Prize did Riga-born Wilhelm Ostwald receive in 1909 for his work on catalysis, chemical equilibria and reaction velocities?

(8)   Latvian-born Jakobs Jufess partnered with Levi Strauss to produce what famous article of clothing?

(9)   In which year did Latvia join the EU?

(10) True or false: Latvia has never won the Eurovision Song Contest.

(11) What was the currency of Latvia before it changed to the euro in 2014?

(12) What is the connection between the flag of Latvia and the group that sang Moves Like Jagger and Girls Like You?

(13) The Latvian-born explorer Aleksandrs Laime was the first recorded human to reach which famous falls in Venezuela?

(14) Which of the four Grand Slam tennis championships did Latvian player Jelena Ostapenko win in 2017?

(15) Which former ballet dancer who appeared in the films The Turning Point and White Nights was born in Riga in 1948?

(16) More than 750 buildings in Riga are built in a style of architecture which was particularly popular between 1890 and 1910. What is the style?

(17) Which sport does Latvian Zemgus Girgensons play for the Buffalo Sabres in the USA?

(18) Governmentally speaking, what is the Saeima?

(19) What are Livonia and Courland?

(20) The play Red by John Logan, which won six Tony awards in 2010, was about which abstract expressionist painter who was born in Daugavpils, Latvia in 1903?

LATVIA ANSWERS

(1) The Baltic Sea

(2) Riga

(3) True

(4) The Russians

(5) Sergei Eisenstein

(6) True

(7) Chemistry

(8) Jeans

(9) 2004

(10) False; Latvia won in 2002 with Marie N singing the song I Wanna.

(11) The lats

(12) Maroon; the group is Maroon Five and the flag is coloured maroon and white.

(13) The Angel Falls

(14) The French Open

(15) Mikhail Baryshnikov

(16) Art Nouveau

(17) Ice hockey

(18) The Latvian parliament

(19) Historical names for various regions of Latvia (and other Baltic states).

(20) Mark Rothko

LEBANON QUESTIONS

(1) What is the capital city?

(2) Lebanon has borders with two countries. One is Syria, what is the other?

(3) Which island lies to the west of Lebanon in the Mediterranean Sea?

(4) What tree is pictured on the flag of Lebanon?

(5) The second-biggest city in Lebanon has the same name as the capital of Libya. What is its name?

(6) True or false: The currency is the Lebanese dollar.

(7) What is the international vehicle registration code for Lebanon?

(8) Which empire controlled Lebanon from 1516 to 1918?

(9) The parents of which Mexican multi-millionaire, from 2010 – 2013 the richest man in the world, originally came from Lebanon?

(10) Which two European languages are widely spoken in Lebanon?

(11) True or false: Lebanon has the largest population of Christians of any Middle Eastern country.

(12) The city of Baalbek contains two of the grandest Roman temple ruins, one to the god Bacchus and one to the king of the gods in Ancient Roman religion and mythology. Which god?

(13) Which envoy for the Church of England travelled to Lebanon to secure the release of four hostages and was himself kidnapped and held captive from 1987 to 1991?

(14) Of which ancient Semitic-speaking Mediterranean civilization was Lebanon the centre from 2500 BC to 539 BC?

(15) Which star of the films Speed and The Matrix was born in Beirut in 1964?

(16) In the Bible, of which Lebanese city was Sidon the mother city?

(17) What devastating occurrence took place in Lebanon between 1975 and 1990?

(18) Which British group had a top 20 hit in 1984 with a song called The Lebanon?

(19) True or false: There are no deserts in Lebanon.

(20) What is the name of the coastal city, one of the oldest continuously inhabited cities in the world, which is a UNESCO World Heritage Site?

LEBANON ANSWERS

(1) Beirut

(2) Israel

(3) Cyprus

(4) The cedar

(5) Tripoli

(6) False; it's the Lebanese pound.

(7) RL (République Libanaise)

(8) The Ottoman Empire

(9) Carlos Slim

(10) French and English

(11) True (about 40% of the population)

(12) Jupiter

(13) Terry Waite

(14) Phoenicia

(15) Keanu Reeves

(16) Tyre

(17) A civil war

(18) Human League

(19) True

(20) Byblos

LESOTHO QUESTIONS

(1)   By which country is Lesotho totally surrounded?

(2)   True or false: Lesotho is the only sovereign state completely surrounded by another country.

(3)   Is the capital Maseru or Mbabane?

(4)   True or false: Lesotho is the only country in the world which lies entirely above 1,000 metres.

(5)   By what name was Lesotho known until independence in 1966?

(6)   From which country did Basutoland gain independence in 1966?

(7)   Is Lesotho a kingdom or a republic?

(8)   Which famous range of mountains forms part of the border between Lesotho and the South African provinces of Eastern Cape and KwaZulu-Natal?

(9)   Which famous river, named in honour of the Dutch ruling family, rises in the Drakensberg mountains in Lesotho before flowing westwards through South Africa to the Atlantic Ocean?

(10) Apart from Sesotho, what is the other official language of Lesotho?

(11) True or false: Lesotho does not have its own currency, so uses South Africa's instead.

(12) Is Maseru situated in the centre of the country or on the western border to South Africa?

(13) True or false: A Mosotho is a citizen of Lesotho.

(14) Lesotho gained independence from the United Kingdom in the same year that England won the FIFA World Cup. Which year?

(15) Who are Moshoeshoe I and Letsie III?

(16) The mokorotlo, a type of straw hat, is the national symbol of Lesotho. What shape is it: (a) conical (b) triangular (c) square?

(17) Which of South Africa's three capitals, Bloemfontein, Cape Town and Pretoria, is closest to Lesotho?

(18) Is Thabana Ntlenyana (a) the prime minister of Lesotho (b) the longest river or (c) the highest mountain?

(19) The 1880-81 Gun War between British Cape Colony forces and rebellious Basotho chiefs was fought over the right of natives to bear what?

(20) What traditional colourful woollen garment is often worn in Lesotho?

LESOTHO ANSWERS

(1) South Africa

(2) False; both San Marino and the Vatican City are completely surrounded by Italy.

(3) Maseru; Mbabane is the capital of Eswatini.

(4) True; it's lowest point lies at 1,400 metres.

(5) Basutoland

(6) The United Kingdom

(7) A kingdom

(8) The Drakensberg

(9) The Orange River

(10) English

(11) False; Lesotho's currency is the loti and South Africa's the rand. The rand is used in Lesotho as well as the loti.

(12) On the western border to South Africa

(13) True; in the plural Basotho is used.

(14) 1966 (4th October)

(15) Kings of Lesotho

(16) (a) conical

(17) Bloemfontein

(18) The highest mountain (3,482 m.)

(19) Arms

(20) The Basotho blanket

LIBERIA QUESTIONS

(1) On which coast of Africa is Liberia situated, east or west?

(2) From which country did a number of black people come in the 19th century to settle in Liberia?

(3) What is the capital?

(4) Monrovia was named in honour of which US President?

(5) Only two world capitals are named after US Presidents. What is the other one?

(6) True or false: The descendants of the American slaves make up the majority of the population.

(7) The Liberian flag is very similar to the flag of the USA. How many white stars are there on the Liberian flag, 1, 2 or 50?

(8) The first devastating one was between 1989 and 1997, the second one between 1999 and 2003. The first and second what?

(9) True or false: Liberia has the largest maritime registry in the world due to its status as a shipping flag of convenience.

(10) With which of the Guinea countries does Liberia have a border?

(11) Which American singer recorded the song Liberian Girl in 1987?

(12) What is the name of the President from 1944 until 1977 who is regarded as "the father of modern Liberia"?

(13) Which former FIFA World Football Player of the Year became the 25th President of Liberia in 2018?

(14) What virus disease caused many deaths in Liberia between 2013 and 2016?

(15) Is the currency the Liberian dollar or the Liberian pound?

(16) Name one of the two English football clubs that George Weah briefly played for in 2000.

(17) Which endangered pygmy animal is native to the forests and swamps of Liberia?

(18) What is the name of the woman who served as the 24th President from 2006 - 18, the first elected female head of state in Africa?

(19) Liberia is one of three countries in the world founded by former slaves. Name one of the other two.

(20) Which famous American talk show host, actress and media executive traced her origins on her mother's side of the family to Liberia?

LIBERIA ANSWERS

(1) The west coast

(2) The USA; the American Colonisation Society assisted in the repatriation of former American slaves. Over the years there were often tensions between the indigenous people and the Americo-Liberians.

(3) Monrovia

(4) James Monroe

(5) Washington DC

(6) False; they account for about 5% of the population.

(7) One

(8) Civil war

(9) False; it is second to Panama.

(10) Guinea

(11) Michael Jackson

(12) William Tubman

(13) George Weah

(14) Ebola

(15) The Liberian dollar

(16) Chelsea or Manchester City

(17) The pygmy hippopotamus

(18) Ellen Johnson Sirleaf

(19) Haiti or Sierra Leone

(20) Oprah Winfrey

LIBYA QUESTIONS

(1) True or false: Libya has a border with Algeria.

(2) On which sea is the capital Tripoli situated?

(3) 95% of Libya is made up of which desert?

(4) What does the word Sahara mean?

(5) In what language does the name Tripoli mean three cities?

(6) What is the official language of Libya?

(7) Which ancient trading nation founded Tripoli?

(8) Who died of a gunshot wound to the head after being captured by rebel forces in his hometown of Sirte in October 2011?

(9) What colour was the flag of Libya during Gaddafi's Great Socialist People's Libyan Arab Jamahiriya?

(10) In which two cities do the two rival factions in the Second Libyan Civil War, which started in 2014, have their headquarters?

(11) Who was the last King of Libya who ruled from 1951 to 1969?

(12) The National Library of Libya is located in the second-biggest city. What is its name?

(13) Against which country's colonization of Libya did Omar al-Mukhtar lead the resistance for nearly twenty years from 1911?

(14) True or false: Simon of Cyrene, the man compelled by the Romans to carry the cross of Jesus as he was taken to his crucifixion, was born in Libya?

(15) Which port city on Libya's eastern Mediterranean coast was captured by the British in World War II, recaptured by the Germans under Rommel and then finally captured by the British again in 1942?

(16) Leptis Magna, the ruins of which can be visited on the Mediterranean coast, was a prominent Phoenician city which was later expanded by which great empire?

(17) Over which Scottish town did Pan Am Flight 103 explode in December 1988, believed to be the work of Libyan terrorists?

(18) Which tropic passes through the south of Libya?

(19) Who is the leader of the Libyan National Army which has been involved in the Second Libyan Civil War since 2014?

(20) What was the profession of Rossana Podesta who was born in Tripoli in 1934?

LIBYA ANSWERS

(1)   True

(2)   The Mediterranean Sea

(3)   The Sahara

(4)   Desert (sahra in Arabic)

(5)   Greek

(6)   Arabic

(7)   The Phoenicians

(8)   Muammar al-Gaddafi

(9)   Green

(10) Tripoli and Tobruk

(11) King Idris I

(12) Benghazi

(13) Against Italy

(14) True

(15) Tobruk

(16) The Roman Empire

(17) Lockerbie

(18) The Tropic of Cancer

(19) Khalifa Haftar

(20) Actress

LIECHTENSTEIN QUESTIONS

(1) What is the capital of Liechtenstein?

(2) Between which two countries is Liechtenstein situated?

(3) In which mountain range is it situated?

(4) True or false: Vaduz is the town with the biggest population.

(5) Is Liechtenstein a member of the EU?

(6) Which major river forms the entire border between Liechtenstein and Switzerland?

(7) Is the head of state a king, a president or a prince?

(8) Who is the current prince?

(9) Does the country have the Swiss franc or the euro as its official currency?

(10) What abbreviation is used for Liechtenstein on vehicle licence plates?

(11) What does FL mean?

(12) True or false: The Liechtenstein national anthem is sung to the same tune as the German national anthem.

(13) In which sport did the Wenzel family win a number of Olympic medals?

(14) True or false: Liechtenstein is the only country in the world which is landlocked by other landlocked countries.

(15) Liechtenstein was the last country in Europe to introduce the vote for women. Did they introduce the vote in (a) 1964 (b) 1974 or (c) 1984?

(16) With which country does Liechtenstein have its longest border, Austria or Switzerland?

(17) What nationality were the soldiers who sought asylum at Hinterschellenberg in May 1945?

(18) True or false: Liechtenstein is the largest exporter of false teeth.

(19) In which castle do the ruling prince's family live?

(20) True or false: The Liechtensteins originally bought the lands of present-day Liechtenstein so that they could have a direct connection to the Holy Roman Empire and therefore a seat in the Imperial Diet in Vienna.

LIECHTENSTEIN ANSWERS

(1) Vaduz

(2) Between Austria and Switzerland

(3) The Alps

(4) False; it's Schaan.

(5) No, although it participates in the Schengen Area and the European Economic Area.

(6) The Rhine

(7) A prince

(8) Hans Adam II

(9) The Swiss franc, although the euro is widely accepted.

(10) FL

(11) Fürstentum Liechtenstein (Principality of Liechtenstein)

(12) False; it's sung to the same tune as the British national anthem.

(13) Skiing (Hanni Wenzel, her brother Andreas and daughter Tina Weirather)

(14) False; Uzbekistan is landlocked by five landlocked countries, Kazakhstan, Kyrgyzstan, Tajikistan, Afghanistan and Turkmenistan. (The Caspian Sea is really a lake!)

(15) (c) 1984

(16) Switzerland (c. 41 km.); Austria (c. 35 km.)

(17) Russian; they were soldiers of the 1st Russian National Army of the German Wehrmacht.

(18) True (Vivadent AG, based in Schaan)

(19) Schloss Vaduz

(20) True

LITHUANIA QUESTIONS

(1) How many countries make up the Baltic states?

(2) With which of the two other Baltic states does Lithuania not have a border?

(3) In which language is Lithuania known as Lietuva?

(4) The capital is known as Wilno in Polish. By what name do we know it?

(5) True or false: Of the three Baltic states, Lithuania has the largest population.

(6) What is the unit of currency?

(7) The flag has three stripes of green, red and yellow. What is the correct order of the colours from the top?

(8) Which Russian exclave borders Lithuania to the southwest?

(9) Which famous film serial killer, played by Anthony Hopkins in The Silence of the Lambs, was born in Lithuania?

(10) Which large white bird, which is traditionally said to bring babies, is one of the national symbols of Lithuania?

(11) Sometimes known as the Neman, by what name do we normally know the major river which rises in Belarus and flows through Lithuania into the Curonian Lagoon and then into the Baltic Sea?

(12) Arvydas Sabonis played his sport for seven seasons in the NBA in the USA. What sport?

(13) Which of the following is the second-biggest city in Lithuania: Daugavpils, Kaunas or Tartu?

(14) Known as Baltic gold, which fossilized tree resin is particularly associated with Lithuania?

(15) Laruschka Mischa Skikne was born in Lithuania in 1928 and starred in the films Room at the Top and The Alamo. By what name is he better known?

(16) According to Lithuanian beliefs, on which holiday are animals able to speak?

(17) A tree in the village of Stelmuze is one of the oldest in Europe. Is it (a) a yew (b) an oak or (c) a birch?

(18) What is the Curonian Spit?

(19) The parents of the star of the Death Wish films were originally from Lithuania. What is the star's name?

(20) What is the name of the ice-free port on the Baltic, the third-largest city in Lithuania?

LITHUANIA ANSWERS

(1) Three: Estonia, Latvia and Lithuania

(2) Estonia

(3) Lithuanian

(4) Vilnius

(5) True, c. 2.8 million. (Latvia 1.9m and Estonia 1.3m)

(6) The euro

(7) Yellow, green, red

(8) Kaliningrad

(9) Hannibal Lecter

(10) The stork

(11) Memel

(12) Basketball; he is regarded as one of the best European players of all time.

(13) Kaunas; Tartu is the second-biggest city in Estonia and Daugavpils in Latvia.

(14) Amber

(15) Laurence Harvey

(16) Christmas Eve

(17) (b) an oak. It's about 1,500 years old.

(18) It's a 98 km. long, thin, curved sand-dune that separates the Curonian Lagoon from the Baltic Sea. It is shared by Lithuania and Kaliningrad.

(19) Charles Bronson

(20) Klaipeda

LUXEMBOURG QUESTIONS

(1) Is Luxembourg a kingdom, a principality or a grand duchy?

(2) True or false: Luxembourg has a border with the other two Benelux countries.

(3) What is the capital?

(4) True or false: The Luxembourg flag is identical to the flag of the Netherlands.

(5) What was the currency before the euro was introduced?

(6) What are the Sauer, the Our and the Alzette?

(7) Apart from Luxembourgish, what are the two other official languages?

(8) Which river, famous for its wine, forms the border with Germany for 39 km.?

(9) Which important EU legal institution has its seat in Luxembourg City?

(10) The production of what alloy, associated with the names ARBED and Arcelor, has always been important in Luxembourg?

(11) Which French singer won the Eurovision Song Contest for Luxembourg in 1965 with the song Poupée de cire, poupée de son?

(12) What is the name of the former Prime Minister of Luxembourg who was President of The European Commission from 2014 to 2019?

(13) What is the name of the town in Luxembourg after which the agreement abolishing internal border checks in the EU is named?

(14) With which Luxembourg radio station do you associate 208 and the name Barry Alldis?

(15) Luxembourg-born actress Vicky Krieps starred in the film Phantom Thread as a young waitress who becomes the muse of a couturier. Which actor was nominated for a Best Actor Oscar as the couturier in his final role before retirement?

(16) Which international telecommunications company famous for its video chat has one of its headquarters in Luxembourg City?

(17) Marc Girardelli, who won two silver medals for skiing at the 1992 Winter Olympics for Luxembourg, was actually born in which Alpine country?

(18) What nationality are the largest group of immigrants in Luxembourg?

(19) Which Luxembourg-born politician who was Prime Minister of France in 1947 and 1948 and President of the European Parliament from 1958 to 1960 is regarded as one of the founding fathers of the EU?

(20) The northern third of the country is called the Ösling. What is the name of the southern two-thirds, the English for which is "good country" or "good land"?

LUXEMBOURG ANSWERS

(1)   A grand duchy

(2)   False; it has a border with Belgium, but it doesn't have a border with the Netherlands.

(3)   Luxembourg City

(4)   False; the Luxembourg flag consists of three horizontal stripes of red, white and blue like the Netherlands flag, but it is longer and the blue and red stripe are of a lighter shade.

(5)   The Luxembourg franc

(6)   Rivers that flow through Luxembourg.

(7)   French and German

(8)   The Moselle

(9)   The European Court of Justice

(10)   Steel

(11)   France Gall

(12)   Jean-Claude Juncker

(13)   Schengen

(14)   Radio Luxembourg

(15)   Daniel Day-Lewis

(16)   Skype

(17)   Austria

(18)   Portuguese (over 100,000)

(19)   Robert Schuman

(20)   Gutland or Bon Pays

MADAGASCAR QUESTIONS

(1) Is the capital Antanarivo or Antananarivo?

(2) Why could the flag be described as the stop-go flag?

(3) True or false: Madagascar is the third-largest island country after Indonesia and the Philippines.

(4) In which ocean is Madagascar situated?

(5) Which country on the African mainland is closest to Madagascar?

(6) From which country did Madagascar gain independence?

(7) What is the name of the channel, named after an African country, which separates Madagascar from the African mainland?

(8) Which mammals with a pointed snout, large eyes and a bushy tail are only found on Madagascar?

(9) By what name was Madagascar known before it became the independent Republic of Madagascar?

(10) True or false: Rugby Union is very popular in Madagascar.

(11) Madagascar is one of the world's chief suppliers of which flavouring derived from orchids?

(12) True or false: Antananarivo is on the coast.

(13) Name one of the three islands in the world that is larger in area than Madagascar. (Australia is a continent and so not included.)

(14) Name two of the four Central Park animals unexpectedly shipwrecked on Madagascar in the 2005 DreamWorks animation film Madagascar.

(15) True or false: Madagascar was ruled by kings and queens in the 19th century.

(16) The island of Nosy Boraha, previously known as Ile Sainte-Marie, off the east coast of Madagascar, was often used as a base by people like William Kidd and Robert Culliford. In what criminal activities were they involved?

(17) What is the name of the nocturnal lemur noted for its thin middle finger?

(18) What is the name of the French writer, born in Antananarivo in 1913, who won the Nobel Prize for Literature in 1985?

(19) Madagascar is particularly known for Adansonia trees. By what name are the trees better known?

(20) What is Nosy Be: (a) an island (b) the national dish of Madagascar (c) the local beer?

MADAGASCAR ANSWERS

(1) Antananarivo

(2) The top half is red and the bottom half is green.

(3) False; Indonesia is bigger in area, but the Philippines smaller.

(4) In the Indian Ocean

(5) Mozambique

(6) France

(7) The Mozambique Channel

(8) Lemurs

(9) The Malagasy Republic

(10) True

(11) Vanilla

(12) False; it's in the centre of the country, in the Central Highlands region.

(13) Greenland, New Guinea or Borneo

(14) Two from lion, zebra, giraffe and hippo.

(15) True, the Merina kings and queens, e.g. Radama I and Ranavalona II.

(16) Piracy

(17) The aye-aye

(18) Claude Simon

(19) Baobabs

(20) (a) an island off the northwest coast. Nosy Be means big island in the Malagasy language and is an important tourist resort.

MALAWI QUESTIONS

(1)   True or false: The biggest lake in Malawi is called Lake Malawi.

(2)   Is the capital Lilongwe, Blantyre or Zomba?

(3)   Which of the two cities was the previous capital, Blantyre or Zomba?

(4)   What was the former name of Malawi?

(5)   Malawi is bordered by three countries with "z" in the name. Can you name them?

(6)   Between 1953 and 1963, Nyasaland was in a federation with the southern and northern part of which other country?

(7)   Which famous Scottish missionary and explorer reached Lake Malawi (then Lake Nyasa) in 1859?

(8)   The second-largest city in Malawi is named after the town in South Lanarkshire where Livingstone was born. What is its name?

(9)   True or false: Lilongwe is situated on the shores of Lake Malawi.

(10)   Which politician led Malawi to independence and was president from 1966 to 1994?

(11)   Two crops which are important for Malawi's exports both begin with the letter "T". What are they?

(12)   True or false: Lake Malawi is part of the Great Rift Valley.

(13)   Chichewa and Kwacha – which is the currency and which is one of the official languages?

(14)   The longest river in Malawi has the same name as an alternative word for county in Great Britain. What is its name?

(15)   Joyce Banda was President of Malawi from 2012 to 2014. Is she (a) Hastings Banda's wife (b) his daughter or (c) no relation to Hastings Banda at all?

(16)   Which large city in Malawi is also sometimes known as Mandala?

(17)   By what first name is Malawi-born musical performer Christopher Hesketh-Harvey better known?

(18)   True or false: Lake Malawi forms part of the border between Malawi and Zambia, and Tanzania and Mozambique.

(19)   In which aquatic sport have Blantyre-born sisters Cate and Bronte Campbell won Olympic medals for Australia?

(20)   True or false: Most of the ethnic groups in Malawi are of Bantu origin.

MALAWI ANSWERS

(1) True

(2) Lilongwe

(3) Zomba (until 1974)

(4) Nyasaland

(5) Zambia, Tanzania and Mozambique

(6) Rhodesia

(7) David Livingstone

(8) Blantyre

(9) False; it's situated on the Lilongwe River in the central region of Malawi.

(10) Hastings Banda

(11) Tea or tobacco

(12) True

(13) Chichewa is an official language (along with English) and kwacha is the currency.

(14) River Shire

(15) (c) No relation to Hastings Banda at all

(16) Blantyre

(17) Kit

(18) False; between Mozambique and Tanzania, but not Zambia.

(19) Swimming

(20) True

MALAYSIA QUESTIONS

(1) Is the capital Kuala Lumpur, Phnom Penh or Jakarta?

(2) True or false: Malaysia has mainland territory and island territory.

(3) With which country does Peninsular Malaysia share a land border?

(4) True or false: Singapore was once part of Malaysia.

(5) Which sea separates Peninsular Malaysia from East Malaysia?

(6) With which two countries does Malaysia share the island of Borneo?

(7) Which is bigger in area, Peninsular Malaysia or East Malaysia?

(8) How is Peninsular Malaysia linked to Singapore?

(9) True or false: Malaysia is a member of the Commonwealth of Nations.

(10) Which animal actually exists: the Malayan lion, the Malayan tiger or the Malayan leopard?

(11) What is the Sarawak Chamber?

(12) Pulau Langkawi is the biggest island of Malaysia. What does the word Pulau mean?

(13) The tallest twin towers in the world are in Kuala Lumpur. What is their name?

(14) Name one of the two Malaysian states on the island of Borneo.

(15) What is the name of the stretch of water which separates Peninsular Malaysia from the island of Sumatra?

(16) What is the ringgit?

(17) In which racket sport has Malaysia been most successful at the Olympic Games?

(18) What does the word nasi mean in dishes such as nasi goreng and nasi lemak, the Malaysian national dish?

(19) Which Malaysian politician, born in 1903, was the first prime minister of independent Malaysia and is regarded as the country's founding father?

(20) Which British author, famous for the novel A Clockwork Orange, wrote The Malayan Trilogy which takes place during the Malayan Emergency (1948 – 60)?

MALAYSIA ANSWERS

(1) Kuala Lumpur

(2) True: Peninsular Malaysia and East Malaysia (Malaysian Borneo)

(3) Thailand

(4) True, until Singapore was expelled from the federation in 1965.

(5) The South China Sea

(6) Brunei and Indonesia

(7) East Malaysia

(8) By a causeway and a bridge

(9) True

(10) The Malayan tiger

(11) One of the biggest cave chambers in the world.

(12) Island

(13) The Petronas Towers

(14) Sabah or Sarawak

(15) The Strait of Malacca

(16) Malaysia's currency

(17) Badminton

(18) Rice

(19) Tunku Abdul Rahman

(20) Anthony Burgess

MALDIVES QUESTIONS

(1) In which ocean are the Maldives situated?

(2) True or false: The Republic of Maldives is the smallest Asian country by land area and by population.

(3) What is the capital?

(4) From which country did the Maldives gain independence in 1965?

(5) Which is correct: (a) Dhivehi is the official language (2) English is the official language (c) Both are official languages?

(6) The closest island country to the Maldives has Sri Jayawardenepura.Kotte as its capital. What is it?

(7) True or false: The Maldives is the lowest country in the world.

(8) Is the currency the rupee or the rufiyaa?

(9) What natural disaster devastated the islands in 2004?

(10) Is a dhoni a multi-purpose sailboat used in the Maldives or the traditional garment worn by men?

(11) What colour is the crescent on the flag of the Maldives?

(12) What is the Internet country code top level domain?

(13) What is the main climate risk for the Maldives in the future?

(14) What is the name of the shells which are abundant on the islands and which were once used as currency?

(15) True or false: The word atoll originally comes from the Maldivian language Dhivehi.

(16) What is the main religion of the Maldives?

(17) What sort of a percussion instrument called a bodu beru is used to accompany a dance of the same name?

(18) Before the advent of tourism in the 1970s, what was the mainstay of the island economy?

(19) The UK had an RAF base on Gan Island, the southernmost island of Addu Atoll, from 1957 to 1976. By what name was the base known?

(20) What politically speaking is the People's Majlis?

MALDIVES ANSWERS

(1)   The Indian Ocean

(2)   True

(3)   Malé

(4)   The United Kingdom

(5)   (a) is correct.

(6)   Sri Lanka (c. 766 km. away)

(7)   True (average elevation: 1.5 metres above sea level.)

(8)   The rufiyaa

(9)   A tsunami, the aftermath of the earthquake in the Indian Ocean.

(10) It's a multi-purpose sailboat.

(11) White

(12) .mv

(13) Rising sea levels (global warming)

(14) Cowry shells

(15) True

(16) (Sunni) Islam

(17) A drum

(18) Fishing

(19) RAF Gan

(20) It's the unicameral legislative body of the Maldives.

MALI QUESTIONS

(1) True or false: The city of Timbuktu is in Mali.

(2) Is the capital city Bamako situated on the River Niger or the River Congo?

(3) The main language of Mali is Bambara, but what is the official language?

(4) Mali has borders with seven countries. Name two of them.

(5) A large portion of the country lies within which famous desert?

(6) What is the predominant religion in Mali?

(7) Seydou Keita is the most capped national player for which sport?

(8) Mali is Africa's third-biggest producer after South Africa and Ghana of what precious metal?

(9) By what name was Mali known as a French colonial territory from 1880 until 1960, French Sudan or French Guinea?

(10) The motto of the country is "Un peuple, un but, une foi", meaning "One people, one goal, one what"?

(11) Which river, named after a West African country, forms parts of the border between Mali and Guinea and Mali and Mauritania?

(12) Which other West African country joined with Mali to achieve independence in 1960 as the Mali Federation?

(13) One of the national symbols of Mali is the Great Mosque of Djenné, a large adobe building. What does adobe mean?

(14) With which Welsh town on the river Wye, famous for books, is Timbuktu twinned?

(15) In what field is Mali-born Salif Keita famous?

(16) What Berber people started a rebellion in 2012 against the Mali government with the goal of attaining independence for the northern region of Mali, known as Azawad?

(17) The flag of Mali has the same three colours as the flag of Senegal. Two of the colours are red and green. What is the third?

(18) For which international music award was the album Welcome to Mali by Amadou and Mariam nominated in 2010?

(19) In 2013 the French launched an operation named after an African wild cat species beginning with S to oust Islamic militants from the north of Mali. What is the cat's name?

(20) Mali was once part of three West African empires that controlled trans-Saharan trade: the Ghana Empire, the Songhai Empire and what is the third empire?

MALI ANSWERS

(1) True

(2) On the River Niger

(3) French

(4) Two from Algeria, Burkina Faso, Guinea, Ivory Coast, Mauritania, Niger and Senegal.

(5) The Sahara Desert

(6) Islam

(7) Football (102 caps)

(8) Gold

(9) French Sudan

(10) Faith

(11) The Senegal River

(12) Senegal (which later withdrew from the federation.)

(13) Adobe is a building material made from earth and organic materials, a type of mudbrick.

(14) Hay-on-Wye

(15) He is an afro-pop singer-songwriter, "The Golden Voice of Africa".

(16) The Tuaregs

(17) Yellow is the middle colour

(18) The Grammy (Best Contemporary World Music Album)

(19) The serval

(20) The Mali Empire

MALTA QUESTIONS

(1) In which sea is Malta situated?

(2) What cross which was awarded to Malta by George VI in 1942 features on the flag of the country?

(3) Which mainland country is closest to Malta?

(4) What are the two official languages of Malta?

(5) True or false: The euro is the unit of currency of Malta.

(6) What is the capital of Malta?

(7) Only the three largest islands are inhabited. One is Malta, name one of the other two.

(8) What is the name of the national airline?

(9) What political office did both Dom Mintoff and George Borg Olivier hold in Malta?

(10) From which country do more tourists come than from any other?

(11) Which Catholic military order controlled Malta from 1530 until 1798?

(12) To which language is Maltese closely related?

(13) Which 2000 film directed by Ridley Scott and starring Russell Crowe was partly shot on Malta?

(14) What was the profession of Daphne Caruana Galizia who was murdered in a car bomb explosion in October 2017?

(15) What is the nickname of the city of Mdina which was once the capital of Malta, the Holy City or the Silent City?

(16) On which of the islands is the famous Blue Lagoon?

(17) Which biblical character was shipwrecked on Malta while on his way to Rome?

(18) Is Kinnie a Maltese soft drink, a type of sausage or the Maltese for rabbit?

(19) Ursula, the wife of which English composer, famous for Fantasia on a Theme by Thomas Tallis and The Lark Ascending was born in Valletta in 1911?

(20) Maltese-born actor Joseph Calleia appeared in the film Touch of Evil. Who directed and starred in it?

MALTA ANSWERS

(1) The Mediterranean Sea

(2) The George Cross

(3) Italy (80 km)

(4) Maltese and English

(5) True

(6) Valletta

(7) Gozo or Comino

(8) Air Malta

(9) Prime minister

(10) From the United Kingdom

(11) The Order of Knights of the Hospital of Saint John of Jerusalem

(12) Arabic

(13) Gladiator

(14) Journalist

(15) The Silent City

(16) Comino

(17) St. Paul

(18) It's a soft drink brewed from bitter oranges and extracts of wormwood.

(19) Ralph Vaughan Williams

(20) Orson Welles

MARSHALL ISLANDS QUESTIONS

(1) In which ocean are the Marshall Islands located?

(2) What is the capital?

(3) What nationality was the explorer after whom the islands are named?

(4) With which country are the Marshall Islands now particularly associated?

(5) Which major currency is also the currency of the islands?

(6) Does the language Marshallese exist?

(7) True or false: The flag of the Marshall Islands is the American stars and stripes.

(8) Are the Marshall Islands part of Micronesia or Polynesia?

(9) The country is often abbreviated to RMI. What does this mean?

(10) One of the following nations has never occupied the islands: USA, France, Germany, Japan. Which one?

(11) Which famous atoll in the Marshall Islands was used to test nuclear bombs by the USA between 1946 and 1958?

(12) The dried meat or kernel of the coconut from which coconut oil can be extracted is the most important commercial crop on the Marshall Islands. What is its name?

(13) The Marshall Islands are one of the four atoll nations. Can you name one of the other three?

(14) Is Majuro north or south of the Equator?

(15) Which international institution did the islands join in 1991?

(16) True or false: The Marshall Islands have a population of over 100,000.

(17) Which fish is particularly important to the economy of the islands?

(18) With which city are the D-U-D communities, the islets of Delap-Uliga-Djarrit, connected?

(19) The actress Lisa Loring was born in the Marshall Islands in 1958. In which horror/black comedy sitcom did she play the daughter Wednesday from 1964 to 1966?

(20) The islands consist of two parallel island groups, the Ratak Chain and the Ralik Chain. The name Ratak means sunrise, what does Ralik mean?

MARSHALL ISLANDS ANSWERS

(1)   The Pacific Ocean

(2)   Majuro

(3)   British; John Marshall (1748 – 1819)

(4)   The USA

(5)   The US dollar

(6)   Yes, it is an official language along with English.

(7)   False

(8)   Micronesia

(9)   Republic of the Marshall Islands

(10) France has never occupied the islands.

(11) Bikini Atoll

(12) Copra

(13) One from Kiribati, the Maldives or Tuvalu.

(14) North

(15) The United Nations

(16) False; the population is well under 100,000.

(17) Tuna

(18) Majuro; they are the main population centres of the capital.

(19) The Addams Family

(20) Sunset

MAURITANIA QUESTIONS

(1)   Is Mauritania on the Atlantic or the Indian Ocean?

(2)   Large parts of the country lie within which desert?

(3)   What is the capital?

(4)   Which disputed territory lies to the north of Mauritania?

(5)   What is the official language of Mauritania?

(6)   True or false: The country's full name is The Islamic Republic of Mauritania.

(7)   Which colonial power ruled the country until independence in 1960?

(8)   True or false: Mauritania is not included as one of the Maghreb countries.

(9)   Which name used in English to refer to the Muslim inhabitants of the Maghreb, the Iberian Peninsula, Sicily and Malta during the Middle Ages, comes from the name Mauritania?

(10) With which of its neighbours did Mauritania fight a border war between 1989 and 1991?

(11) Lack of what essential commodity is a problem for Mauritania?

(12) True or false: The unit of currency, the ouguiya, is not a decimal currency.

(13) One of the main streets in Nouakchott was named after Egypt's second president. What is his name?

(14) Which river forms the border between Mauritania and Senegal?

(15) True or false: Leblouh, the practice of force-feeding young girls to increase their chance of marriage because high body volume used to be a sign of wealth, is still prevalent in Mauritania.

(16) Is the population of Mauritania under (a) 5 million (b) 5 – 10 million or (c) 20 million?

(17) Rising 633m above the desert floor, Ben Amera is the world's second-largest monolith. The largest is in Australia. What is its name?

(18) The Richat Structure, a prominent circular feature of exposed sedimentary rock 40 kilometres in diameter, is sometimes known as (a) the eye of Africa or (b) the mouth of Africa?

(19) The holy city of Chinguetti has a 13th century minaret and is a UNESCO World Heritage Site. What offshore discovery in 2001, which might make a major contribution to the country's economy, has been named after it?

(20) What did Mauritania abolish in 1981: (a) death penalty (b) slavery (c) nomadic life?

MAURITANIA ANSWERS

(1)   The Atlantic Ocean

(2)   The Sahara Desert

(3)   Nouakchott

(4)   Western Sahara

(5)   Arabic

(6)   True

(7)   France

(8)   False; it is included along with Algeria, Libya, Morocco, Tunisia and Western Sahara.

(9)   The Moors

(10) Senegal

(11) Water

(12) True; there are five khoums in one ouguiya. (The only other non-decimal currency is the Malagasy ariary from Madagascar.)

(13) Gamal Abdel Nasser

(14) The Senegal River

(15) True

(16) (a) under 5 million

(17) Uluru (Ayers Rock)

(18) The Eye of Africa

(19) The Chinguetti oil field

(20) (b) Slavery

MAURITIUS QUESTIONS

(1) True or false: Mauritius consists of only one island.

(2) Is Mauritius in the Atlantic, Indian or Pacific Ocean?

(3) Known as Les Quatre Bandes in French, how many stripes are there in the Mauritius flag?

(4) Is the capital (a) Port Moresby (b) Port-au-Prince or (c) Port Louis?

(5) Altogether there are six capitals with Port or Porto in their name, Three were mentioned in the previous question. Can you name two of the remaining three?

(6) Which country ceded Mauritius to the United Kingdom in 1814 through the Treaty of Paris?

(7) Is Mauritius considered to be part of Africa or Asia?

(8) True or false: About two-thirds of the population is of Indo-Pakistani origin.

(9) What is the name of the flightless bird endemic to Mauritius which became extinct at the end of the 17th century?

(10) Which work by Lewis Carroll helped to make the dodo famous?

(11) The name of the currency is the same as in India. What is it?

(12) Which island, 175 km. southwest of Mauritius, is an overseas department and region of France?

(13) With which aquatic mammal is it possible to swim in Tamarin Bay?

(14) Among the rarest postage stamps in the world, the Mauritius orange-red one penny and deep blue two pence were issued in September 1847. Who is pictured on them?

(15) Put the three religions Christianity, Hindu and Islam in order of popularity on Mauritius.

(16) Which country disputes Mauritius's claim over the Chagos Archipelago including the island of Diego Garcia, some 2,000 km. to the northeast?

(17) The popular tourist attraction Sir Seewoosagur Ramgoolam Botanical Garden is often known by the name of the district in which it is situated whose name means grapefruits in French. What is the name of the district?

(18) Mauritius was named after Maurice, Prince of Orange. What nationality was he?

(19) What is the name of the 1788 novel by Jacques-Henri Bernardin de Saint-Pierre set on Mauritius under French rule which helped to make the island known to the world?

(20) What is Sega: (a) one of the major music genres of Mauritius (b) the most grown crop or (c) a traditional drink made from rum?

MAURITIUS ANSWERS

(1) False; there are several including Rodrigues, Agaléga and St. Brandon.

(2) Indian Ocean

(3) Four: horizontal bands of red, blue, yellow and green.

(4) Port Louis (Port Moresby is the capital of Papua-New Guinea and Port-au-Prince of Haiti.)

(5) Two from Port of Spain (Trinidad and Tobago), Port Vila (Vanuatu) and Porto Novo (Benin)

(6) France

(7) Africa

(8) True

(9) The dodo

(10) Alice's Adventures in Wonderland

(11) The (Mauritian) rupee

(12) Réunion

(13) Dolphin

(14) Queen Victoria

(15) Hindu 48.5% (2) Christianity (32.7%) (3) Islam (17.2%)

(16) The United Kingdom (The island of Diego Garcia was cleared of its inhabitants by the British, so that the USA could establish a military base on the island.)

(17) Pamplemousses

(18) Dutch

(19) Paul et Virginie

(20) (a) One of the major music genres of Mauritius

MEXICO QUESTIONS

(1) Name one of the two Central American countries with which Mexico has a border.

(2) What is the unit of currency?

(3) True or false: The border between Mexico and the USA is the longest border in the world.

(4) In what field are Alfonso Cuarón and Alejandro González Inárritu well known?

(5) In which year were the Summer Olympics held in Mexico City, 1964, 1968 or 1972?

(6) Which river rises in Colorado, later forming part of the border between the USA and Mexico, before it flows into the Gulf of Mexico?

(7) Which city on the Pacific coast is noted for its cliff divers?

(8) Which Mexican state shares its name with a small dog?

(9) Chichen Itza is one of the most visited archaeological sites in Mexico. Which civilization built it?

(10) What is the name of the peninsula in south-eastern Mexico with the capital Merida which separates the Gulf of Mexico from the Caribbean?

(11) The Mexicans call this holiday in November Dia de Muertos. What is it in English?

(12) What name is given to the traditional Mexican dish consisting of a small tortilla with a filling?

(13) Name one of the animals featured on the Mexican flag.

(14) Which Mexican actress played the part of the artist Frida Kahlo in the 2002 film Frida?

(15) What is Mariachi?

(16) What is the name of the peninsula to the west of mainland Mexico, famous for its cacti?

(17) What was the name of the Mexican general born in 1878 who was one of the major figures of the Mexican Revolution between 1910 and 1920?

(18) What is the name of the active volcano in central Mexico, the country's second-highest peak?

(19) Which Mexican-born actor won two Best Supporting Actor Oscars for Viva Zapata! and Lust for Life?

(20) From which plant is tequila made?

(1) Belize or Guatemala

(2) The peso

(3) False; it is ninth-longest. The USA-Canada border is the longest.

(4) Film directing

(5) 1968

(6) The Rio Grande (Spanish: Rio Bravo del Norte)

(7) Acapulco

(8) Chihuahua

(9) The Mayans

(10) The Yucatan Peninsula

(11) Day of the Dead

(12) A taco

(13) Either an eagle or a snake

(14) Salma Hayek

(15) A style of Mexican music played by groups with violins, trumpets and guitars.

(16) Baja California

(17) Pancho Villa

(18) Popocatépetl

(19) Anthony Quinn

(20) The (blue) agave

MOLDOVA QUESTIONS

(1) In which continent is the Republic of Moldova?

(2) To which country did Moldova belong until independence in 1991?

(3) Moldova used to be part of the historical region Bessarabia along with part of one of its neighbouring countries. Which one?

(4) Apart from the Ukraine, which other country does Moldova have a border with?

(5) On which sea does Moldova have a coast?

(6) True or false: The River Danube briefly flows through Moldova.

(7) What is the capital of Moldova?

(8) True or false: Chisinau has a wide trolleybus network.

(9) Which Moldovan group had an international hit with the song Dragostea Din Tei in 2004?

(10) True or false: The language Moldovan is very different from Romanian.

(11) True or false: Moldova is the poorest country in Europe.

(12) The currency has the same name as the Romanian currency. What is it?

(13) A traditional dish of Moldova is a porridge made out of yellow maize flour. Which Italian dish is very similar to it?

(14) True or false: The colours of the Moldovan flag are identical to those of the Romanian flag.

(15) The Prut forms much of the border between Romania and Moldova. Into which great river does it eventually flow?

(16) With what alcoholic beverage is the name Milesti Mici associated?

(17) Chisinau-born director Lewis Milestone won two Best Director Oscars. One was for the film Two Arabian Nights in 1927. What was the name of the famous anti-war film of 1930 for which he won an Oscar?

(18) What is the name of the disputed territory between the River Dniester and the Ukrainian border which claims independence from Moldova?

(19) What is the name of the second-largest city in Moldova, which is also the capital of Transnistria, Tiraspol or Balti?

(20) Do the Gagauz minority, a Turkic people who speak their own language Gagauz, live in the north or south of Moldova?

MOLDOVA ANSWERS

(1) In Europe

(2) The Soviet Union

(3) Ukraine

(4) Romania

(5) None, it is landlocked.

(6) True; Moldova has access to the Danube for about 480 metres at the port of Giurgiulesti.

(7) Chisinau

(8) True

(9) O-Zone

(10) False; the two languages are very similar. Moldovan was written in Cyrillic script until 1989, but now uses Latin script.

(11) True

(12) The (Moldovan) leu (100 bani = 1 leu)

(13) Polenta

(14) True; vertical stripes of blue, yellow and red. The Moldovan flag, however, also shows the Moldovan coat of arms.

(15) Into the Danube

(16) Wine; the wine producer has the biggest wine collection in the world in the cellars which extend for 200 kilometres, although only 55 kms are currently in use.

(17) All Quiet on the Western Front

(18) Transnistria or Transdniestria

(19) Tiraspol

(20) In the south

MONACO QUESTIONS

(1) True or false: Monaco is the world's smallest country.

(2) With how many countries does Monaco share a border?

(3) What is the capital?

(4) What is the name of the royal family which has ruled Monaco since 1297?

(5) Who is the current prince?

(6) In which sport did Albert's wife Charlene represent South Africa at the 2000 Sydney Olympics?

(7) What is the unit of currency?

(8) What is a native of Monaco called?

(9) What is the nearest international airport to Monaco?

(10) Which German city do the Italians call Monaco di Baviera?

(11) What sort of festival is held in January every year in Monaco with Princess Stéphanie as President?

(12) Which famous Brazilian driver won the Monaco Grand Prix a record six times?

(13) The flag of which Asian island country is almost identical to Monaco's flag?

(14) Which top football club that competes in the French Ligue 1 plays its home matches at the Stade Louis II in Fontvieille, Monaco?

(15) In which film did Grace Kelly make her last appearance before marrying Prince Rainier in 1956?

(16) Which automobile event was first organised in 1911 by the Automobile Club de Monaco?

(17) Which film starring Tony Curtis and Terry-Thomas was known in America by the title Those Daring Young Men in their Jaunty Jalopies?

(18) Which famous oceanographer, filmmaker and explorer was director of the Oceanographic Museum of Monaco from 1957 to 1988?

(19) Which ethnic group is the largest in Monaco: Monégasque, French or Italian?

(20) Which famous music hall song of the late 19th century referring to Monaco featured in the films The Magnificent Ambersons and Lawrence of Arabia?

MONACO ANSWERS

(1) False; the Vatican City is the smallest.

(2) Only one: France

(3) Monaco-Ville

(4) Grimaldi

(5) Prince Albert II

(6) Swimming

(7) The euro

(8) Monégasque

(9) Nice Cote d'Azur Airport

(10) Munich

(11) The International Circus Festival of Monte-Carlo

(12) Ayrton Senna

(13) Indonesia, the flags are both horizontal stripes, one red, one white. The Indonesian flag is longer.

(14) AS Monaco

(15) High Society

(16) The Monte Carlo Rally

(17) Monte Carlo or Bust!

(18) Jacques-Yves Cousteau

(19) French (c. 28.4%), then Monégasque (21.6%) and then Italian (18.7%).

(20) The Man Who Broke the Bank at Monte Carlo

MONGOLIA QUESTIONS

(1)   Between which two powerful countries is Mongolia sandwiched?

(2)   What is the capital?

(3)   Was the historic name for the country Inner Mongolia or Outer Mongolia?

(4)   What relation was Kublai Khan to Genghis Khan: (a) grandson (b) son (c) no relation?

(5)   What is the tögrög or tugrik?

(6)   What is the predominant religion?

(7)   What is the name of the desert which covers parts of southern Mongolia?

(8)   From which country did Mongolia gain independence in the 1920s?

(9)   How many countries are more sparsely populated than Mongolia: none, one or two?

(10) Which American actor, famous for his roles in westerns, played the Mongol conqueror Genghis Khan in the 1956 film The Conqueror?

(11) Because it has so many sunny days per year, the country is known as "The Land of the Eternal Blue what"?

(12) Name one of the three traditional Mongolian sports celebrated at the main national festival of Naadam.

(13) In Mongolia it is known as a ger, but what is the more usual name for the round tent covered with skins or felt which is used by nomadic groups?

(14) A horseback statue to which great conqueror and founding father of Mongolia can be found on the banks of the River Tuul near Ulaanbaatar?

(15) Which Mongolian city was formerly known as Urga?

(16) What sort of musical instrument is the traditional Mongolian morin khuur?

(17) How many humps has the Bactrian camel which is native to Mongolia?

(18) What method of transport connects Ulan-Ude in Russia to Jining in China via Ulaanbaatar?

(19) Is airag, Mongolia's national drink, fermented mare's milk or fermented camel milk?

(20) What is the name of the range of mountains that stretch into south-west Mongolia: (a) the Himalayas (b) the Carpathians (c) the Altai?

MONGOLIA ANSWERS

(1) Between China and Russia

(2) Ulaanbaatar

(3) Outer Mongolia

(4) Grandson

(5) The currency

(6) Buddhism

(7) The Gobi Desert

(8) China

(9) None

(10) John Wayne

(11) Sky

(12) One from: archery, horse racing and wrestling

(13) A yurt

(14) Genghis Khan

(15) Ulaanbaatar

(16) A stringed instrument

(17) Two

(18) The Trans-Mongolian Railway

(19) Fermented mare's milk

(20) The Altai

MONTENEGRO QUESTIONS

(1)   From which country did Montenegro declare independence in 2006?

(2)   What does the name Montenegro mean in English?

(3)   What adjective or noun can be formed from Montenegro to describe the people or the language?

(4)   Is the capital Cetinje or Podgorica?

(5)   By what name was Podgorica known between 1946 and 1992?

(6)   Are the borders of the flag of Montenegro gold or silver?

(7)   True or false: The population of Montenegro is over one million.

(8)   What major currency is used in Montenegro?

(9)   True or false: Montenegro is a member of NATO.

(10) On which sea does Montenegro have a coast?

(11) A pedestrian bridge over the River Moraca in Podgorica is named after the city in Russia which gave it as a gift to the people of Montenegro. Which Russian city was it?

(12) What is most important for the country's economy: agriculture, industry or the service sector?

(13) The President of Montenegro has his official residence in the town of Cetinje. Is the palace known as the (a) yellow (b) blue or (c) green palace?

(14) In which 2006 James Bond movie does the hero play a high-stake poker tournament in Montenegro?

(15) Which home country topped the qualifying group for the UEFA Euro 2020 in which Montenegro came last?

(16) The largest lake in Montenegro is Lake Skadar. Two-thirds of it lies in Montenegro. In which country does the other third lie?

(17) What is the name of the long bay, similar to a fjord, in the south-west of Montenegro, popular with cruise ships?

(18) Which Canadian tennis player, who reached the Wimbledon finals in 2016, was born in Titograd in 1990?

(19) Montenegro-born director Veljko Bulajic directed the 1969 film The Battle of Neretva. Which actor, famous for playing the King of Siam, starred in it?

(20) What is the name of the small islet and 5-star hotel resort on the Adriatic coast, whose name means Saint Stephen in English?

MONTENEGRO ANSWERS

(1)   Serbia

(2)   Black Mountain

(3)   Montenegrin

(4)   Podgorica (Cetinje is the Old Royal Capital of Montenegro).

(5)   Titograd

(6)   Gold; the flag is red with golden borders and the coat of arms in the middle.

(7)   False; it's about 630,000.

(8)   The euro

(9)   True; the country joined in 2017.

(10) On the Adriatic

(11) Moscow, hence the Moscow Bridge

(12) The service sector

(13) The blue palace, because of the colour of its exterior walls.

(14) Casino Royale (It was not filmed in Montenegro, but in the Czech Republic.)

(15) England

(16) In Albania

(17) The Bay of Kotor

(18) Milos Raonic

(19) Yul Brynner

(20) Sveti Stefan

MOROCCO QUESTIONS

(1) Morocco has a coast on a sea and an ocean. What are they?

(2) Which are the only two other countries to have both a Mediterranean and Atlantic coast?

(3) What is the capital?

(4) What is the largest city: Casablanca, Fes, Marrakesh or Rabat?

(5) In which city on the Atlantic coast is the Hassan II Mosque situated, the second-largest In Africa?

(6) Is Morocco a republic or a constitutional monarchy?

(7) What is the name of the current king?

(8) Change one letter of the English city of Durham and you have got the currency! What is it?

(9) To which country do the disputed enclaves of Ceuta, Melilla and Penon de Vélez de la Gomera belong?

(10) What is the Rif?

(11) What sort of tea is particularly popular in Morocco?

(12) What word can be used for a Moroccan city and a type of cylindrical headwear?

(13) Which city more or less had to be rebuilt after a disastrous earthquake in 1960?

(14) The Jemaa el-Fnaa is perhaps one of the best-known squares in Africa. In which city is it located?

(15) With which sport are Said Aouita and Hicham El Guerrouj associated?

(16) True or false: Part of the film Casablanca was shot in Morocco.

(17) To which territory to its south does Morocco lay claim?

(18) Which city located at the western entrance to the Strait of Gibraltar was a popular residence for many writers including Paul Bowles, Tennessee Williams and Joe Orton?

(19) What is the name of the earthenware pot with a dome- or cone-shaped cover that is often used in Moroccan cuisine?

(20) At the 1986 UEFA World Cup, Morocco shared a group with England, Poland and Portugal. What amazing feat did they achieve in the group?

MOROCCO ANSWERS

(1)   The Mediterranean Sea and the Atlantic Ocean

(2)   France and Spain

(3)   Rabat

(4)   Casablanca

(5)   Casablanca

(6)   A constitutional monarchy

(7)   Mohammed VI

(8)   Dirham

(9)   Spain

(10) A mountainous region in the northern part of Morocco

(11) Green mint tea

(12) Fez or Fes

(13) Agadir

(14) Marrakesh

(15) Athletics, running

(16) False; the entire film was shot in California.

(17) To Western Sahara

(18) Tangier

(19) A tajine or tagine

(20) They won it with 4 points. They were knocked out in the Round of 16 by West Germany.

MOZAMBIQUE QUESTIONS

(1)   Is the capital Dodoma or Maputo?

(2)   What was the former name of Maputo from 1876 to 1976?

(3)   Which European nation colonized Mozambique?

(4)   True or false: Mozambique is not a member of the Commonwealth of Nations.

(5)   Which major river, the fourth-longest in Africa, flows through Mozambique into the Indian Ocean?

(6)   Which large island is separated from Mozambique by the Mozambique Channel?

(7)   True or false: There is also an Island of Mozambique off the north coast of the country.

(8)   What is the official language of Mozambique?

(9)   With which country apart from Tanzania does Mozambique share Lake Malawi?

(10) One of the most dangerous snakes in Africa is called the Mozambique spitting what?

(11) Which famous South African national park lies on the border to Mozambique?

(12) What Russian weapon is pictured on the Mozambique flag?

(13) True or false: The River Limpopo flows into the sea in Mozambique.

(14) Which famous footballer, who played for Portugal in the 1966 UEFA World Cup, was born in Lourenco Marques in 1942?

(15) What is the Mozambican metical: (a) a type of monkey (b) the currency (c) the correct name for the flag?

(16) Which large city on the Indian Ocean in the central region of Mozambique was particularly badly hit by the 2019 Cyclone Idai?

(17) In which running distance did Olympic champion Maria Mutola specialize?

(18) Which Mozambique-born vocalist and jazz guitarist was popular in England during the 1930s, singing songs such as Goodnight, Sweetheart and The Very Thought of You?

(19) Which military commander and first President of Mozambique after independence died in a plane crash in 1986?

(20) Which famous South African leader did Graca Machel, Samora Machel's widow, marry in 1998?

(1)   Maputo (Dodoma is the capital of Tanzania.)

(2)   Lourenco Marques

(3)   Portugal

(4)   False; Mozambique joined in 1995, the first country without any former colonial or constitutional links with the UK to do so.

(5)   The Zambezi

(6)   Madagascar

(7)   True

(8)   Portuguese

(9)   Malawi

(10) Mozambique spitting cobra

(11) The Kruger National Park

(12) An AK-47, a Kalashnikov rifle

(13) True

(14) Eusebio

(15) The Mozambican currency

(16) Beira

(17) 800 metres

(18) Al Bowlly

(19) Samora Machel

(20) Nelson Mandela

MYANMAR QUESTIONS

(1) By what name is Myanmar also known?

(2) What is the capital?

(3) What is the largest city?

(4) What was the previous name of Yangon?

(5) On which bay does Myanmar have a coastline?

(6) What is the main religion of Myanmar?

(7) What is the name of the 1957 film starring Alec Guinness about the building of a bridge on the Burma Railway during the Second World War?

(8) Which important river flows through Burma from the north to the south?

(9) What is the name of the Nobel Peace Prize winner who became State Counsellor of Myanmar, the equivalent of prime minister, in 2016?

(10) What is the name of the stateless Indo-Aryan ethnic group which predominantly follows Islam which was driven out of Myanmar in 2017 - 2018?

(11) What was the name of the Burmese diplomat who was the third Secretary-General of the United Nations from 1961 to 1971?

(12) What does Naypidaw have in common with other capital cities like Canberra and Brasilia?

(13) The second city of Myanmar suffered badly during the Second World War and was occupied by the Japanese from 1942 to 1945. What is its name?

(14) Which India-born British author wrote the poem Mandalay which is the origin of the phrase "on the road to Mandalay", which was later set to music?

(15) Down which peninsula does southern Myanmar stretch?

(16) Of which drug is Myanmar one of the largest producers in the world?

(17) What sort of government was in power when Ne Win was president from 1962 to 1988: (a) a constitutional monarchy (b) a military dictatorship (c) a welfare state?

(18) Is Shwedagon Paya (a) a Buddhist pagoda in Yangon (b) the national dish of Myanmar or (c) the President of Myanmar?

(19) Of which group, which had a Top Ten UK hit with Go Wild in the Country, was Rangoon-born Annabella Lwin the lead singer?

(20) At which meal is Mohinga, a rice noodle and fish soup considered to be the national dish of Myanmar, traditionally eaten?

MYANMAR ANSWERS

(1)   Burma

(2)   Naypidaw

(3)   Yangon

(4)   Rangoon

(5)   The Bay of Bengal

(6)   Buddhism

(7)   The Bridge on the River Kwai (The River Kwai is actually in Thailand.)

(8)   The Irrawaddy River

(9)   Aung San Suu Kyi

(10) Rohingya people

(11) U Thant

(12) It is also a planned city.

(13) Mandalay

(14) Rudyard Kipling

(15) The Malay Peninsula

(16) Opium

(17) (b) a military dictatorship

(18) A Buddhist pagoda in Yangon

(19) Bow Wow Wow

(20) At breakfast

NAMIBIA QUESTIONS

(1) Is Namibia located in south-east or south-west Africa?

(2) From which country did Namibia gain independence on 21 March 1990?

(3) Which European country colonized the region from 1884 until 1919?

(4) Name one of the countries with which Namibia shares a border.

(5) What is the capital?

(6) What is the official language?

(7) Which language is spoken by about 60% of the white population: Afrikaans, English or German?

(8) True or false: Namibia plays football, rugby and cricket internationally.

(9) What is the name of the desert that stretches along the coast of Namibia and into Angola and South Africa?

(10) Apart from the Namib, which other desert covers parts of Namibia?

(11) What is the name of one of the two Bantu peoples who were victims of genocide by the Germans in 1904?

(12) True or false: The towns of Swakopmund, Walvis Bay and Lüderitz are all on the Atlantic coast.

(13) Whose daughter Shiloh was born in Namibia in 2006?

(14) Is the town of Lüderitz named after the German founder of South West Africa or a town in Germany?

(15) With which sport is Windhoek-born Frankie Fredericks associated?

(16) What other name is given to the hunter-gatherer people known as the San?

(17) Deriving its name from the whale and seal bones that once littered the shore and the many shipwrecks, what bony name is given to the northern part of the Atlantic coast of Namibia and the southern coast of Angola?

(18) Named after a German chancellor, what is the name of the narrow strip of land which juts out from the north-eastern corner of Namibia into Angola, Zambia and Botswana?

(19) Namibia has the second-lowest population density of any sovereign country apart from which Asian country sandwiched between Russia and China?

(20) What is the name of the national park situated in the north-west of Namibia which includes the Etosha salt pan?

NAMIBIA ANSWERS

(1) In south-west Africa

(2) South Africa

(3) Germany (It was known as German South West Africa).

(4) One from Angola, Botswana, South Africa and Zambia

(5) Windhoek

(6) English

(7) Afrikaans

(8) True

(9) The Namib Desert

(10) The Kalahari Desert

(11) The Herero or the Nama

(12) True

(13) The daughter of Angelina Jolie and Brad Pitt

(14) It's named after the founder, Adolf Lüderitz, a German merchant.

(15) Athletics - sprinting

(16) Bushmen

(17) The Skeleton Coast

(18) The Caprivi Strip; Chancellor Leo von Caprivi negotiated the acquisition of the land in 1890 in an exchange with the UK. German South West Africa wanted access to the River Zambezi and thus to German East Africa (now Tanzania) and the Indian Ocean. The river later proved unnavigable because of the Victoria Falls.

(19) Mongolia

(20) The Etosha National Park

NAURU QUESTIONS

(1) In which ocean is Nauru situated?

(2) True or false: Nauru was formerly known as Pheasant Island.

(3) Which is the nearest neighbour to Nauru: Kiribati, Tuvalu or Vanuatu?

(4) True or false: Nauru is the smallest island nation in the world.

(5) What does Nauru use as its currency: the US dollar, the Australian dollar or the Hong Kong dollar?

(6) What is the capital?

(7) Is Nauru north or south of the Equator?

(8) Which European country annexed Nauru in 1888 after an agreement with Great Britain?

(9) What mineral rock was mined on Nauru which harmed the island's environment?

(10) Off which eastern Australian state is Curtis Island where it was proposed to relocate the population of Nauru in 1964 because of the damage done to the island by the mining?

(11) What percentage of the island has been devastated by the mining: 40%, 60% or 80%?

(12) Does Nauru have a problem with obesity or malnutrition?

(13) True or false: Nauruan and English are the official languages.

(14) For which country did Nauru house an offshore immigration detention facility until 2008, which then re-opened in 2012?

(15) What nationality was John Fearn, the first European to report sighting Nauru in 1798?

(16) Nauru became independent in the year Martin Luther King was assassinated and the Russians invaded Czechoslovakia. Which year?

(17) Is Nauru in Melanesia, Micronesia or Polynesia?

(18) What shape best describes the outline of the island: oval, round or square?

(19) The blue of the Nauru flag represents the Pacific, the star the 12 indigenous tribes of Nauru. What imaginary geographical line does the thin gold horizontal stripe in the middle represent?

(20) Which Australian sport is considered to be the national sport of Nauru?

NAURU ANSWERS

(1) In the Pacific Ocean

(2) False; it was formerly known as Pleasant Island.

(3) Kiribati (about 300 km. east)

(4) True; it is third-smallest nation after the Vatican City and Monaco.

(5) The Australian dollar

(6) Nauru doesn't really have a capital, although the government offices are located in Yaren District.

(7) South of the Equator

(8) Germany

(9) Phosphate

(10) Queensland; the people of Nauru did not want to become Australian citizens, so rejected the proposal. Nauru chose to become independent.

(11) About 80%

(12) Obesity

(13) True

(14) Australia

(15) English

(16) 1968

(17) In Micronesia

(18) Oval

(19) The Equator

(20) Australian rules football

NEPAL QUESTIONS

(1) In which mountain range is Nepal mainly situated?

(2) Between which two great nations is Nepal sandwiched?

(3) How many of the world's ten tallest mountains are situated in Nepal: six, eight or all ten?

(4) What is the capital?

(5) What is unusual about the flag of Nepal?

(6) The currency has the same name as the Indian currency. What is it?

(7) The international border between Nepal and which other country runs across the Summit of Mount Everest?

(8) What is the name of the Nepalese soldiers who have a reputation for fearless military prowess and whose settlement rights in the UK were championed by the actress Joanna Lumley?

(9) Which Chinese autonomous region borders on Nepal to the north?

(10) What title did Gyanendra Shah hold from 2001 to 2008?

(11) Which part of the body do the Nepali consider to be sacred and therefore must not be touched by another person: (a) the left hand (b) the head (c) the back?

(12) Which religious leader is said to have been born in the holy Nepalese pilgrimage site of Lumbini?

(13) What is the name of the Sherpa mountaineer who accompanied Sir Edmund Hillary to the top of Everest in May 1953?

(14) What dramatic event took place in Nepal on April 25th 2015?

(15) On which side of the road do they drive in Nepal?

(16) What is the national flower of Nepal: the rose, the rhododendron or the ranunculus?

(17) What is the name of the second-biggest city of Nepal, often considered to be its tourist capital?

(18) Which singer, famous for Matthew and Son, recorded a song called Katmandu on his third album Mona Bone Jakon?

(19) The only living member of the genus Ailurus, what is the name of the endangered animal with reddish-brown fur and a long, shaggy tail that lives in the mountains of Nepal?

(20) Who was Everest after whom the mountain is named?

NEPAL ANSWERS

(1) The Himalayas

(2) China and India

(3) Eight

(4) Kathmandu

(5) It is the world's only non-quadrilateral flag. It is a combination of two single pennants.

(6) The (Nepalese) rupee

(7) China

(8) The Gurkhas

(9) Tibet

(10) King of Nepal

(11) The head

(12) Siddhartha Gautama (Buddha)

(13) Tenzing Norgay

(14) An earthquake (7.9 on the Richter scale).

(15) On the left

(16) The rhododendron

(17) Pokhara

(18) Cat Stevens

(19) The red panda

(20) Sir George Everest, a British surveyor and geographer, who was Surveyor General of India from 1830 to 1843. He had no direct connection with the mountain and never saw it, although he hired people to make formal observations of the mountain and calculate its height.

NETHERLANDS QUESTIONS

(1) Which city is the seat of government of the Netherlands?

(2) What is the Netherlands' second city, the largest seaport in Europe?

(3) What is the Dutch national colour?

(4) Which large Australian island is named after a Dutch seafarer and explorer?

(5) With what sort of market is the town of Alkmaar particularly associated?

(6) Born in Leiden in 1606, which artist painted the famous Night Watch?

(7) In which Dutch city do Europol and the International Court of Justice have their headquarters?

(8) What is the name of Amsterdam airport?

(9) What is the name of the Anglo-Dutch oil and gas company with its Dutch HQ in the Hague?

(10) What is the name of the current King of the Netherlands?

(11) Which city in the province of North Holland is the principal centre for radio and television in the Netherlands?

(12) Name one of the Netherlands' Caribbean islands.

(13) Which two bodies of water does the Afsluitdijk separate?

(14) Which southern Dutch city is particularly known for DAF Trucks and Philips?

(15) In which sport have the Netherlands won by far the most Winter Olympic medals?

(16) How did Vincent van Gogh die?

(17) Which two other major rivers contribute to the Rhine delta in the Netherlands?

(18) As what are Martin Garrix, Oliver Heldens and Armin van Buuren well known?

(19) What name is given to the youngest province of the Netherlands, created in 1986, which was formed from land reclaimed from the Zuiderzee?

(20) Which English comedian and singer first recorded the song Tulips from Amsterdam in English?

NETHERLANDS ANSWERS

(1)   The Hague

(2)   Rotterdam

(3)   Orange

(4)   Tasmania, named after Abel Tasman

(5)   A cheese market

(6)   Rembrandt van Rijn

(7)   The Hague

(8)   Schipol

(9)   Royal Dutch Shell

(10) Willem Alexander

(11) Hilversum

(12) One from Curacao, Aruba, Sint Maarten, Bonaire, Saba or Sint Eustatius

(13) The North Sea and the Ijsselmeer (previously Zuiderzee)

(14) Eindhoven

(15) Speed skating

(16) He shot himself

(17) The Meuse and the Scheldt

(18) DJs

(19) Flevoland

(20) Max Bygraves

NEW ZEALAND QUESTIONS

(1) True or false: Wellington is the capital and biggest city of New Zealand.

(2) What are the names of the two main islands of New Zealand?

(3) What bird nickname is often given to New Zealanders?

(4) From where does the country get its name?

(5) What name is given to the mountain range that extends along much of the length of the South Island?

(6) True or false: New Zealand was the first country in the world to give women the vote.

(7) What is the name of the singer who had hits in the UK and USA with the songs Royals and Green Light?

(8) Which epic monster film did Wellington-born film director Peter Jackson remake in 2005?

(9) The largest city in the South Island suffered from a series of earthquakes between 2010 and 2012. What is its name?

(10) True or false: Auckland-born Sir Edmund Hillary led the expedition to conquer Mount Everest in 1953.

(11) What is Aotearoa?

(12) Which Gisborne-born opera singer sang at the wedding of Prince Charles and Lady Diana in 1981?

(13) What is New Zealand's highest mountain?

(14) Which film starring Holly Hunter as a psychologically mute young woman was set on the west coast of New Zealand?

(15) For which white wine is New Zealand particularly famous?

(16) Which New Zealand-born physicist who died in 1937 is often known as the father of nuclear physics?

(17) What is the name of the traditional dance of the Maori people which the rugby union team, the All Blacks, perform before their international matches?

(18) What is the name of the city in the North Island famous for its geysers and geothermal activity?

(19) What is the name of the famous fjord on the south-west coast of the South Island, named after a town in Wales?

(20) What is the name of the short story writer and poet, friend of D.H. Lawrence and Virginia Woolf, who died in 1923 at the age of 34?

NEW ZEALAND ANSWERS

(1) False: it is the capital, but Auckland is the biggest city.

(2) North Island and South Island

(3) Kiwis

(4) From the Dutch province of Zeeland; the country was first sighted by Dutchman Abel Tasman and named Nova Zeelandia by Dutch cartographers. James Cook anglicised the name.

(5) The Southern Alps

(6) True (in 1893)

(7) Lorde

(8) King Kong

(9) Christchurch

(10) False; the expedition was led by John Hunt.

(11) The Maori name for New Zealand, usually translated as "the land of the long white cloud".

(12) Kiri Te Kanawa

(13) Mount Cook

(14) The Piano

(15) Sauvignon blanc

(16) Ernest Rutherford

(17) The haka

(18) Rotorua

(19) Milford Sound

(20) Katherine Mansfield

NICARAGUA QUESTIONS

(1) Is the capital Managua situated on the Pacific, the Caribbean or on Lake Managua?

(2) Does Nicaragua share a border with Mexico?

(3) Is Spanish or English the official language?

(4) In which month is the popular Palo de Mayo festival celebrated?

(5) What is the most important sport in Nicaragua: football, baseball or basketball?

(6) Who became President of Nicaragua in 2007: Daniel Ortega, Nicolas Maduro or Raul Castro?

(7) The Mosquito Coast stretches along the Caribbean coast of Nicaragua. Is it named after (a) the insect (b) an indigenous ethnic group of people (c) the capital of Ecuador?

(8) The currency of Nicaragua has the same name as a city in Andalusia, Spain, famous for many notable pieces of Moorish architecture such as The Mezquita. Which city?

(9) Which family more or less ruled Nicaragua as a military dictatorship for 43 years from 1927 to 1979?

(10) What is the name of the National Liberation Front which toppled the Somoza regime?

(11) In the Contra War did the USA back the Sandinistas or the Contras?

(12) What is the name of the city situated on the shores of Lake Nicaragua which has the same name as an Andalusian city and an ITV regional television company?

(13) Which is the biggest lake in Central America, Lake Nicaragua or Lake Managua?

(14) What engineering project, making use of Lake Nicaragua and the San Juan River which flows into the Caribbean, was scheduled to begin in 2014 but has not yet started?

(15) To which famous rock star was Managua-born Bianca Pérez-Mora Macias married?

(16) True or false: Nicaragua has no active volcanoes.

(17) Who directed the film Carla's Song which follows the relationship between a Scottish bus driver and a Nicaraguan refugee from the Contra War?

(18) What is the name of the second city of Nicaragua, the cultural and religious centre, which has the same name as the capital of the province of León in Spain?

(19) In which James Bond film did Nicaraguan-born actress Barbara Carrera play Fatima Blush?

(20) What is the name of the Nicaraguan poet who initiated the Spanish-American literary movement known as modernism that flourished at the end of the 19th century?

NICARAGUA ANSWERS

(1) On Lake Managua

(2) No, it shares a border with Honduras and Costa Rica.

(3) Spanish

(4) In May

(5) Baseball

(6) Daniel Ortega (Maduro – Venezuela, Castro – Cuba)

(7) (b) An indigenous ethnic group of people, the Miskito

(8) Cordoba (Oro)

(9) The Somoza family

(10) The Sandinista National Liberation Front

(11) The USA backed the right-wing rebel group the Contras who opposed the socialist Sandinistas.

(12) Granada

(13) Lake Nicaragua (8,157 sq. km.) (Lake Managua: 1,042 sq. km.)

(14) A canal joining the Pacific and the Caribbean to rival the Panama Canal, a project which has often been suggested.

(15) Mick Jagger (from 1971 - 78)

(16) False; it has several active volcanoes.

(17) Ken Loach

(18) León

(19) Never Say Never Again

(20) Rubén Darío

NIGER QUESTIONS

(1) From what does the country take its name?

(2) True or false: Niger does not share a border with Nigeria.

(3) What is in the centre of the flag: a red star, a red cross or a red circle?

(4) True or false: The capital Niamey is situated on the River Niger.

(5) Is Niger a secular state or a theocratic state?

(6) What is the predominant religion?

(7) True or false: Niger was a part of French West Africa.

(8) What is the adjective from Niger?

(9) With which country, capital Abuja, does Niger share its longest border?

(10) What is the name of the large, shallow lake on the border between Niger, Nigeria and Chad?

(11) True or false: Niger has the largest population of the Hausa ethnic group in Africa.

(12) Which chemical element with the symbol U is an important export for the country?

(13) Which cereal crop is the main staple food of Niger?

(14) Which famous Scottish explorer explored the country in the 19th century when looking for the mouth of the River Niger?

(15) Which nomadic ethnic group living in the Sahara region of Niger has repeatedly rebelled against the government of Niger?

(16) What is the Internet country code top level domain for Niger?

(17) What was the nationality of the explorer Heinrich Barth who visited Niger in 1850 and whose house can be visited in the town of Agadez?

(18) Name two of the five African countries which are bigger in area than Niger.

(19) La Cure Salée is an annual festival of Tuareg and Wodaabe nomads to celebrate the end of the rainy season. What does the name mean?

(20) True or false: Niger has never won an Olympic medal.

NIGER ANSWERS

(1) From the Niger River

(2) False; Nigeria is to the south of Niger.

(3) A red circle

(4) True

(5) A secular state, the separation of religion and state is guaranteed in the constitution.

(6) Islam

(7) True

(8) Nigerien

(9) With Nigeria (1,608 km.)

(10) Lake Chad

(11) False; Nigeria is first with 61m Hausa and Niger second with about 11m.

(12) Uranium

(13) Millet

(14) Mungo Park

(15) The Tuaregs

(16) .ne

(17) German

(18) Two from: Algeria, Democratic Republic of the Congo, Sudan, Libya and Chad.

(19) Salt Cure

(20) False; Issaka Daborg won a bronze medal in boxing in 1972 and Abdoul Razak Issoufou won a silver medal in Taekwondo in 2016.

NIGERIA QUESTIONS

(1) What is Nigeria's biggest city?

(2) Which country has a bigger population, Egypt or Nigeria?

(3) What is the name of the jihadist terrorist organisation based in north-eastern Nigeria?

(4) What is the second biggest city after Lagos: Ibadan, Kano, Abuja or Benin City?

(5) Paul McCartney's most successful album was largely recorded at the EMI studio in Lagos in 1973. What is its name?

(6) True or false: Christianity and Islam are the most widely practised religions in Nigeria.

(7) Is the capital Abuja situated in the north, the centre or the south of the country?

(8) What was the name of the secessionist state in the south-east of Nigeria which went to war with the government of Nigeria from 1967 to 1970?

(9) Nigeria is sometimes referred to as one of the MINT countries. Can you name one of the other three MINT countries?

(10) Nigeria has never gone beyond Round 2 of the FIFA World Cup. Can you name one of the three African teams that has reached the quarter-finals?

(11) Which Nigerian-born singer recorded the albums Diamond Life and Stronger Than Pride?

(12) Into which river does the River Benue flow?

(13) Actor Chiwetel Ejiofor is of Nigerian descent. In which film did he play Solomon Northup?

(14) Of which two important energy commodities is Nigeria the largest producer in Africa?

(15) In which field are Wole Soyinka and Chinua Achebe well known?

(16) Was Fela Kuti (a) a politician (b) an influential Nigerian musician or (c) a President of Nigeria?

(17) Which politician with the fortunate name was President of Nigeria from 2010 to 2015?

(18) What is known as Nollywood?

(19) The three largest ethnic groups in Nigeria are the Hausa, the Igbo and which group beginning with Y?

(20) Which Port Harcourt-born singer and songwriter was nominated for the International Male Solo Artist Award at the 2020 Brit Awards?

NIGERIA ANSWERS

(1)   Lagos

(2)   Nigeria (Egypt's population is half that of Nigeria.)

(3)   Boko Haram

(4)   Kano

(5)   Band on the Run

(6)   True; (Islam c. 51.6%, Christianity c 47%)

(7)   In the centre

(8)   Biafra

(9)   One from Mexico, Indonesia and Turkey

(10) Cameroon (1990), Ghana (2010) and Senegal (2002)

(11) Sade

(12) The River Niger

(13) 12 Years a Slave

(14) Oil and gas

(15) Literature (Soyinka was the first African to win the Nobel Prize for Literature in 1986).

(16) (b) An influential Nigerian musician, pioneer of the Afrobeat music genre.

(17) Goodluck Jonathan

(18) The Nigerian film industry

(19) Yoruba

(20) Burna Boy

NORTH KOREA QUESTIONS

(1) What is the capital?

(2) True or false: The North Korean flag uses the same colours as the British flag.

(3) Does North Korea have borders with both China and Russia?

(4) The country is sometimes referred to as DPR Korea. What does DPR mean?

(5) What is the number of the parallel along which the border between North and South Korea runs?

(6) What name is usually given to the strip of land which separates North and South Korea?

(7) In what years did the Korean War take place?

(8) Put these North Korean leaders in the correct order: grandfather, son, grandson, Kim Jong-il, Kim Il-sung and Kim Jong-un.

(9) Explain this sentence: The North Koreans have won when they have money in their pockets.

(10) Which of the two Koreas has the biggest population, North or South?

(11) Named after a colour, what is the sea off the west coast of North Korea?

(12) True or false: The second-biggest city of North Korea is called Hamhung.

(13) Where did US President Donald Trump and Kim Jong-un meet for the first time on June 12, 2018: (a) Hanoi (b) Singapore or (c) the Demilitarized Zone?

(14) What was the name of the US navy ship which was seized by North Korea in 1968, allegedly having entered North Korean territorial waters?

(15) What name is given to the period of famine and economic crisis in North Korea from 1994 to 1998?

(16) What was the name of the 2014 film starring James Franco and Seth Rogen in which journalists interviewing Kim Jong-un are recruited by the CIA to assassinate him?

(17) Which European country with Eusebio as its star player defeated North Korea in the quarter final of the 1966 FIFA World Cup 3 – 5?

(18) What celestial name does the famous crater lake at the top of the highest mountain Paektu have?

(19) What was the name of the American student who was imprisoned in North Korea in 2016 and who died shortly after being released in a comatose state?

(20) What is the meaning of the Korean word juche, the official state ideology of North Korea: (a) Communism (b) Control (c) Self-reliance?

NORTH KOREA ANSWERS

(1)   Pyongyang

(2)   True: red, white and blue

(3)   Yes

(4)   The Democratic People's Republic (of Korea)

(5)   The 38th Parallel

(6)   The Demilitarized Zone

(7)   1950 – 53

(8)   Grandfather: Kim Il-Sung (Leader: 1972-94), Father: Kim Jong-il (Leader: 1994 – 2011)

(9)   The North Korean currency is called the won, so the sentence is true!

(10) South Korea (c. 51m) is twice as populated as North Korea (c25m).

(11) The Yellow Sea

(12) True

(13) Singapore

(14) USS Pueblo; the US insisted that the ship was in international waters.

(15) The Arduous March or the March of Suffering

(16) The Interview; the film greatly angered the North Korean government.

(17) Portugal

(18) Heaven Lake

(19) Otto Warmbier

(20) (c) Self-reliance

NORTH MACEDONIA QUESTIONS

(1) In which year was the country renamed the Republic of North Macedonia?

(2) Prior to 2019, the country was known as FYR Macedonia. What did the FYR stand for?

(3) With which country did the country have problems over the name Macedonia?

(4) The agreement with Greece over the name change was called after a lake in North Macedonia. Is it Lake Ohrid, Lake Prespa or Doiran Lake?

(5) The capital of North Macedonia was hit by a disastrous earthquake in 1963. What is the city's name?

(6) On which sea does the country have a coast?

(7) After Macedonians, the largest ethnic group comes from the country which has Tirana as its capital. Which country?

(8) True or false: Alexander the Great was born in present-day North Macedonia.

(9) Which famous Albanian-Indian Roman Catholic nun and missionary was born in Skopje in 1910?

(10) The moon or the sun, which of the two appears on the flag?

(11) Is the Macedonian language written in Cyrillic script?

(12) What is the unit of currency?

(13) True or false: North Macedonia has never qualified for the FIFA World Cup finals.

(14) Tikves, a plain in the centre of the country, is famous for producing what alcoholic beverage?

(15) Alexander the Great's father founded the city of Bitola as Heraclea Lyncestis in the middle of the 4th century BC. What was the father's name?

(16) Pristina is the closest capital city to Skopje. Of which country is it the capital?

(17) Is the town of Struga, situated in the south-west of the country, famous for rock concerts or poetry evenings?

(18) What is the occupation of Hatidze Muratova, whose life is portrayed in the documentary film Honeyland which was the first film to receive an Oscar nomination for both Best International Feature Film and Best Documentary Feature at the 92nd Academy Awards in 2020?

(19) With which other country does North Macedonia share Lake Ohrid?

(20) From which transcontinental country do the most tourists come to North Macedonia?

NORTH MACEDONIA ANSWERS

(1) 2019

(2) Former Yugoslav Republic

(3) With Greece

(4) Lake Prespa (The Prespa Agreement)

(5) Skopje

(6) It doesn't have a coast. It's landlocked.

(7) Albania (about 25% of the population)

(8) False; he was born in Pella in Central Macedonia in Greece.

(9) Mother Teresa

(10) The (golden yellow) sun on a red background

(11) Yes

(12) The Macedonian denar

(13) True

(14) Wine

(15) Philip II of Macedon

(16) Kosovo

(17) Poetry evenings. The festival awards a prestigious prize, the Golden Wreath, to living poets (e.g. W.H. Auden, Ted Hughes, Seamus Heaney etc.)

(18) A beekeeper

(19) Albania

(20) Turkey

NORWAY QUESTIONS

(1) True or false: Norway is the only European country whose capital, Oslo, has four letters.

(2) What is the Norwegian for Norway?

(3) Magnus Carlsen is a world champion in what?

(4) Which Nobel Prize is awarded in Norway?

(5) Who is the present king of Norway?

(6) True or false: Norway has a border with Russia.

(7) Which was Norwegian group a-ha's only number one hit in the UK, Take On Me or The Sun Always Shines on TV?

(8) Which playwright, famous for Peer Gynt, A Doll's House and Hedda Gabler was born in Norway in 1828?

(9) True or false: Norway is the most successful nation at the Winter Olympics.

(10) What is the name of the longest fjord in Norway, which is the third-longest in the world?

(11) What is the name of the Norwegian archipelago situated in the Arctic Ocean about midway between Norway and the North Pole?

(12) By what name are the Sámi people often known in English?

(13) What is the name of the archipelago in the north of Norway with the main town of Leknes?

(14) What post did Oslo-born politician Jens Stoltenberg take over in 2014?

(15) How many versions of his famous painting The Scream did Edvard Munch create?

(16) Which Norwegian explorer led the first expedition to reach the South Pole in 1911?

(17) What is the name of the Norwegian politician who became the first Secretary-General of the United Nations?

(18) Why did Larvik-born Thor Heyerdahl undertake his Kon-Tiki raft voyage across the Pacific in 1947?

(19) From which work by Bergen-born composer Edvard Grieg do Anitra's Dance and The Death of Ase come?

(20) What name is given to the strait running between the south coast of Norway, the west coast of Sweden and the Jutland peninsula of Denmark?

(1) False; Bern, Kiev, Riga and Rome have four letters.

(2) Norge

(3) In chess

(4) The Nobel Peace Prize

(5) Harald V

(6) True

(7) The Sun Always Shines on TV; Take On Me got to number 2.

(8) Henrik Ibsen

(9) True

(10) Sognefjord

(11) Svalbard (formerly Spitzbergen)

(12) The Lapps or Laplanders

(13) The Lofoten Islands

(14) Secretary-General of NATO

(15) Four. two versions in paint and two in pastels. He also produced a lithograph stone from which several prints survive.

(16) Roald Amundsen

(17) Trygve Lie

(18) To show that ancient peoples could have made long sea voyages and thus contact other cultures.

(19) Peer Gynt

(20) The Skaggerak

OMAN QUESTIONS

(1)   What is the official name of Oman?

(2)   Is Oman located on the south-eastern or south-western coast of the Arabian peninsula?

(3)   What is the capital?

(4)   What is the adjective from Oman which is also used to describe the people?

(5)   Is the currency the dinar or the rial?

(6)   Qaboos bin Said was Sultan of Oman for almost 50 years from 1970 until which year?

(7)   Which European country occupied Muscat for 140 years from 1508 to 1648?

(8)   What is the name of the gulf off the north-east of Oman?

(9)   What is the name of the sea in the south-east of Oman?

(10) True or false: Oman is one of the founder members of the Arab League.

(11) Historically, the region of Dhofar in southern Oman was the chief source of what aromatic resin associated with the Three Wise Men?

(12) The Musandam Peninsula located between the Persian Gulf and Gulf of Oman is governed by Oman, but surrounded by which other country?

(13) True or false: Oman is a member of OPEC.

(14) Which Swedish DJ with hits such as Hey Brother and Wake Me Up died in Muscat in 2018?

(15) Which African island, famous for spices, came under the influence of the Sultanate of Oman in 1698?

(16) What is a khanjar: (a) a traditional Omani dagger (b) an earthenware cooking pot or (c) a pair of loose-fitting trousers?

(17) Mountain Dew is very popular in Oman. What is it?

(18) Speleologists would marvel at Majlis al Jinn, 100 km south-east from Muscat. What is it?

(19) Muscat-born actress Isla Fisher is married to which English actor and comedian?

(20) True or false: Oman is the only sovereign state in the world beginning with the letter O.

OMAN ANSWERS

(1) The Sultanate of Oman

(2) On the south-eastern coast

(3) Muscat

(4) Omani

(5) The rial

(6) 2020; he was Sultan from 23 July 1970 until his death on 10 January 2020.

(7) Portugal

(8) The Gulf of Oman

(9) The Arabian Sea

(10) False; the league was formed in 1945 and Oman joined in 1971.

(11) Frankincense

(12) The United Arab Emirates

(13) False; it is an observer, but not a member.

(14) Avicii

(15) Zanzibar

(16) (a) A traditional Omani dagger

(17) A carbonated soft drink produced by Pepsi

(18) The second-largest known cave chamber in the world.

(19) Sacha Baron Cohen

(20) True

PAKISTAN QUESTIONS

(1) True or false: the population of Pakistan exceeds two hundred million.

(2) Which of these cities has never been capital of Pakistan: Islamabad, Karachi, Lahore, Rawalpindi?

(3) What is the current capital?

(4) What is the biggest city?

(5) In which year did the Partition of India into the Union of India and the Dominion of Pakistan take place?

(6) By what name was Bangladesh known between 1955 and 1971 before independence?

(7) What is the name of the ex-cricketer who became Prime Minister of Pakistan in 2018?

(8) True or false: Pakistan is a nuclear power.

(9) The father served as President of Pakistan from 1971 to 1973 and Prime Minister from 1973 to 1977 and the daughter was Prime Minister twice. What is the family's name?

(10) Which two internationally played team sports are the most popular games in Pakistan?

(11) The second-highest mountain in the world is situated on the border between China and Pakistan. What is its name?

(12) As well as English, one of the following languages is an official language: Pashto, Punjabi or Urdu. Which language?

(13) What is the name of the great river which rises in Tibet and flows into the Arabian Sea near Karachi?

(14) What is the name of the famous pass in the north-west of Pakistan, on the border with Afghanistan, which appeared in the title of one of the Carry On films?

(15) Who was killed by US special forces in Abbotabad, Pakistan on May 2, 2011?

(16) For what reason was Malala Yousafzai awarded the Nobel Peace Prize in 2014?

(17) What is the name of the highway, a popular tourist attraction, which passes through the mountain range of the same name before crossing into China?

(18) Is Shalwar Kameez (a) a famous Pakistani pop singer (b) the traditional Pakistani dress or (c) the national dish of Pakistani?

(19) The markhor is the national animal of Pakistan. Is it (a) a goat (b) a monkey or (c) an antelope?

(20) Which Pakistan-born actor starred in The Jewel in the Crown on ITV and appeared in the films A Passage to India and The Living Daylights?

PAKISTAN ANSWERS

(1) True (c. 210m)

(2) Lahore has never been the capital.

(3) Islamabad

(4) Karachi

(5) 1947

(6) East Pakistan

(7) Imran Khan

(8) True

(9) Bhutto (Father: Zulfikar Ali Bhutto; daughter: Benazir Bhutto)

(10) Cricket and field hockey

(11) K2

(12) Urdu

(13) The Indus

(14) The Khyber Pass

(15) Osama bin Laden

(16) For her struggle against the suppression of children and for the right of all children to education.

(17) The Karakoram Highway

(18) (b) The traditional Pakistani dress

(19) (a) A goat

(20) Art Malik

PALAU QUESTIONS

(1)   Is Palau situated in the Atlantic, the Pacific or the Indian Ocean?

(2)   Is the capital Melekeok or Ngerulmud?

(3)   Were the islands part of the Spanish East Indies or the Dutch East Indies from 1574 to 1898?

(4)   Which major currency is also used by Palau?

(5)   Palau is part of the Caroline Islands. Which nation makes up the other part of the islands?

(6)   Is the flag a blue disk on a yellow background or a yellow disk on a blue background?

(7)   Does the yellow disk on the flag represent the sun or a full moon?

(8)   Which town became the capital when Palau gained independence in 1994, Koror or Melekeok?

(9)   True or false: The population of Palau is less than 20,000.

(10)   Do most of the population live on Koror Island or Babeldoab Island?

(11)   What aquatic pastime is the main tourist activity on Palau?

(12)   For what type of fish did Palau create a sanctuary in 2009?

(13)   Is Palau a male dominated society or a female dominated one?

(14)   Which European nation ruled Palau from 1899 to 1919?

(15)   From which language do the words Ungil tutau meaning good morning come?

(16)   Which 1968 World War II film starring Lee Marvin and Toshiro Mifune was shot in the Rock Islands of Palau?

(17)   A famous lake for snorkelling on Palau's Eil Malk Island is named after a gelatinous free-swimming marine animal with umbrella-shaped bells and trailing tentacles, millions of which migrate across the lake every day. What is its name?

(18)   What title did the Rock Islands of Palau, a collection of 250 to 300 small limestone or coral islands in Palau's Southern Lagoon, receive from UNESCO in 2012?

(19)   Which island country in Asia, capital Taipei, gave a $20 million dollar loan to Palau to help finance the new government buildings in Ngerulmud to secure Palau's diplomatic recognition?

(20)   Does Palau have a unicameral or a bicameral legislature?

PALAU ANSWERS

(1)   In the Pacific Ocean

(2)   Ngerulmud

(3)   The Spanish East Indies

(4)   The US dollar

(5)   The Federated States of Micronesia

(6)   A yellow disk on a blue background

(7)   A full moon

(8)   Koror

(9)   False; it's about 21,000.

(10)   On Koror Island (about 70% of the population)

(11)   Diving and snorkeling

(12)   The shark

(13)   A female dominated one: women are the ones who lead.

(14)   Germany

(15)   Palauan

(16)   Hell in the Pacific

(17)   Jellyfish (the lake is called Jellyfish Lake).

(18)   UNESCO World Heritage Site

(19)   Taiwan

(20)   Bicameral; the National Congress has a House of Delegates and a Senate.

PALESTINE QUESTIONS

(1) Is the State of Palestine officially recognized by the United Nations?

(2) Most sovereign states are de jure and de facto states, but Palestine is seen to be only a de jure state. What does this mean?

(3) Name two of the three pieces of territory Palestine claims.

(4) Although Palestine claims Jerusalem as its capital, which West Bank city is de facto the administrative centre of the state?

(5) Which famous Palestine leader proclaimed the establishment of the State of Palestine in1988?

(6) What is the name of the fundamentalist militant organization, founded in 1987, which controls the Gaza Strip?

(7) On which sea does the Gaza Strip have a coastline?

(8) True or false: The biggest city in the Gaza Strip is Gaza City.

(9) Who became President of the State of Palestine in 2005?

(10) Name two of the four colours that feature on the flag of Palestine.

(11) What is the official language?

(12) True or false: The West Bank does not contain any of the Dead Sea.

(13) What bird features on the coat of arms of the State of Palestine?

(14) Of which organization was Yasser Arafat chairman from 1969 to 2004?

(15) Yasser Arafat was born and spent most of his youth in an African capital city. Was it Cairo, Tripoli, Tunis or Rabat?

(16) What is Fatah?

(17) Name one of the two Israelis who was awarded the Nobel Peace Prize in 1994 along with Yasser Arafat.

(18) What is the name of the American DJ who had international hits with Wild Thoughts and I'm the One whose parents originally came from Palestine?

(19) What is the Internet country code top level domain for Palestine?

(20) Palestine first competed at the Summer Olympics in 1996. In which city were the games held?

PALESTINE ANSWERS

(1) Yes (and recognized by about 138 UN member states)

(2) It's a state in law (de jure), but the territory it claims is de facto under the control of Israel.

(3) The West Bank (bordering Israel and Jordan), the Gaza Strip and East Jerusalem

(4) Ramallah

(5) Yasser Arafat

(6) Hamas

(7) The Mediterranean

(8) True

(9) Mahmoud Abbas

(10) Two from red, black, white and green

(11) Arabic

(12) False; it has a shoreline in the south-east.

(13) An eagle (The Eagle of Saladin)

(14) The PLO (Palestine Liberation Organization)

(15) Cairo

(16) A Palestinian nationalist social democratic political party connected with the PLO

(17) Yitzhak Rabin or Shimon Peres

(18) DJ Khaled

(19) .ps

(20) Atlanta

PANAMA QUESTIONS

(1) True or false: The only South American country with which Panama has a border is Venezuela.

(2) What feat of engineering was completed between 1904 and 1914 in Panama?

(3) True or false: Panama has the largest ship registry in the world.

(4) Which country borders Panama to the north?

(5) What name beginning with the letter I is given to a narrow strip of land, like Panama, connecting two masses of land that would otherwise be separated by water?

(6) The currency of Panama is the same word as the surname of Sylvester Stallone's Rocky character. What is it?

(7) Which other currency is legal tender in Panama?

(8) True or false: The Panama hat originally comes from Panama.

(9) Is Panama City located on the Pacific side of the Panama Canal or the Caribbean side?

(10) With which sport do you associate Roberto Durán and Eusebio Pedroza?

(11) Which city near the Atlantic entrance to the Panama Canal sounds like a piece of punctuation?

(12) Which ruler of Panama was deposed during the United States invasion of Panama between 1989 and 1990?

(13) What is the name of the artificial lake to the south of Colón which forms a major part of the Panama Canal?

(14) The Darien Scheme, an unsuccessful attempt to establish a colony called Caledonia on the Isthmus of Panama in the late 1690s, was carried out by which European country?

(15) What are the Panama Papers?

(16) In which year did Panama take over control of the Panama Canal: 1989, 1999 or 2009?

(17) Which French diplomat and developer of the Suez Canal also tried to build a Panama canal?

(18) Which famous English ballerina was married to the Panamanian lawyer, diplomat and journalist Roberto Arias?

(19) What does the motto of Panama Pro Mundi Beneficio mean?

(20) Which Grammy award winning singer, songwriter and actor was appointed minister of tourism in Panama in 2004?

PANAMA ANSWERS

(1) False; it's Colombia.

(2) The Panama Canal

(3) True

(4) Costa Rica

(5) Isthmus

(6) Balboa

(7) The US dollar

(8) False; it originally comes from Ecuador.

(9) On the Pacific side

(10) Boxing

(11) Colón

(12) Manuel Noriega

(13) The Gatun Lake

(14) Scotland

(15) 11.5 million leaked documents detailing financial information about offshore entities, some of which were used for illegal purposes, e.g. tax evasion.

(16) 1999

(17) Ferdinand de Lesseps

(18) Dame Margot Fonteyn

(19) For the Benefit of the World

(20) Rubén Blades

PAPUA NEW GUINEA QUESTIONS

(1) In which continent is Papua New Guinea located?

(2) With which country does Papua New Guinea share the island of New Guinea?

(3) The capital is sometimes nicknamed Pom City. What is its correct name?

(4) Which country administered Papua New Guinea from World War I until 1975?

(5) True or false: New Guinea is the world's second-largest island.

(6) Who is the head of state?

(7) The Torres Strait is situated between Papua New Guinea and which other country?

(8) True or false: Papua New Guinea is part of Melanesia.

(9) Is the Internet country code top level domain .pg or .png?

(10) Which multi-sport event, much like the Olympic Games, has Papua New Guinea hosted three times?

(11) How many known languages are there in Papua New Guinea: about 250, 550 or more than 800?

(12) Which sport played by two teams of 13 players is by far the most popular sport in Papua New Guinea?

(13) What is Tok Pisin?

(14) What is the name of the archipelago, named after a German chancellor, which includes the islands New Britain and New Ireland?

(15) What colourful sort of bird features on the country's flag?

(16) Which sea, which contains the Great Barrier Reef off Queensland, lies to the south-east of Papua New Guinea?

(17) Why did Spanish explorer Inigo Ortiz de Retes name the island New Guinea?

(18) Which part of Papua New Guinea voted overwhelmingly in 2019 for independence?

(19) Mount Wilhelm is the highest mountain in Papua New Guinea. After which 19th century German Chancellor's son is it named?

(20) What sort of creature is a pitohui, a species endemic to New Guinea, which is the only known poisonous one of its type?

PAPUA NEW GUINEA ANSWERS

(1)   Oceania

(2)   Indonesia

(3)   Port Moresby

(4)   Australia

(5)   True

(6)   The British monarch

(7)   Australia

(8)   True

(9)   .pg

(10) The Pacific Games

(11) More than 800

(12) Rugby League

(13) A creole language spoken throughout Papua New Guinea

(14) The Bismarck Archipelago

(15) The (Raggiana) bird-of-paradise

(16) The Coral Sea

(17) Because the islanders resembled the people of Guinea in Africa.

(18) Bougainville

(19) Bismarck's son Wilhelm

(20) A bird

PARAGUAY QUESTIONS

(1) On which sea does Paraguay have a coast?

(2) What is the capital city?

(3) With which other landlocked South American country does Paraguay have a border?

(4) Is the Internet country code top level domain .pa, .pg or .py?

(5) The national musical instrument of Paraguay is an instrument also associated with Ireland. What is it?

(6) Paraguay is sometimes called the "Corazón de América". What does this mean?

(7) The two official languages are Guarani and which European language?

(8) What is the name of the second-longest river in South America which flows through Paraguay, as well as Argentina and Brazil?

(9) With which sport is Luque-born José Luis Chilavert associated?

(10) The currency has the same name as one of the official languages. What is it?

(11) What is the name of the army officer who served as a repressive President of Paraguay from 1954 to 1989?

(12) True or false: Although landlocked, Paraguay has a navy.

(13) For which German team did Asuncion-born footballer Roque Santa Cruz play between 1999 and 2007?

(14) The Itaipu Dam on the Parana River which provides most of the electricity for Paraguay is on the border with which other country?

(15) The right-wing political party which ruled Paraguay continuously for 61 years from 1947 has the same name as an American state, capital Denver. What is the party's name?

(16) By what name beginning with the letter C is Western Paraguay often known?

(17) What important South American football competition did Paraguay win in 1953 and 1979?

(18) The country's coat of arms and treasury seal make the Paraguayan flag unique. In what way?

(19) What would a Paraguayan do with a chipa: (a) drink it (b) eat it or (c) wear it?

(20) The Paraguayan War or War of the Triple Alliance (1864 – 1870) was the deadliest interstate war in Latin American history, which devastated Paraguay. The war was between Paraguay and three other countries. Name two of them.

PARAGUAY ANSWERS

(1) It doesn't have a coast, it's landlocked.

(2) Asuncion

(3) Bolivia

(4) .py

(5) The (Paraguayan) harp

(6) The heart of America, because it's located in the centre of the South American continent.

(7) Spanish

(8) The Parana

(9) Football; he played as goalkeeper.

(10) Guarani

(11) Alfredo Stroessner

(12) True; Paraguay has access to the Atlantic through the Paraguay and Parana rivers and has the largest navy of any landlocked country.

(13) Bayern Munich

(14) Brazil

(15) The Colorado Party

(16) The Chaco

(17) Copa America

(18) It's the only national flag in the world to have different emblems on each side – i.e. the coat of arms on one side and the treasury seal on the other.

(19) (b) Eat it, it's a popular type of small, baked, cheese-flavoured roll.

(20) Two from Argentina, Brazil and Uruguay. The war ended with the defeat of Paraguay.

PERU QUESTIONS

(1) What is the capital city?

(2) Is the currency the peso or the sol?

(3) True or false: Peru took part in the first FIFA World Cup in 1930.

(4) With which country does Peru share Lake Titicaca?

(5) What two colours make up Peru's flag and are also used in the national football team's strip?

(6) True or false: The source of the Amazon is in Peru.

(7) What is the name of the warm water current which arrives on the coast of Peru and Ecuador every year around Christmas?

(8) What is the national animal of Peru: the alpaca, the llama or the vicuna?

(9) Which empire located its administrative, political and military centre in the city of Cusco?

(10) Which language was the main language of the Inca people and is still widely spoken in Peru today?

(11) Which Peruvian of Japanese descent was President of Peru from 1990 to 2000 and was charged with corruption and human rights violations?

(12) What name is given to the 15th century Inca citadel situated 80 kms. northwest of Cusco at a height of about 2,430 metres, discovered by Hiram Bingham in 1911?

(13) Which Peruvian who lived to be 100 was the fifth Secretary-General of the United Nations?

(14) Which member of the Goons had a Peruvian father?

(15) What is pisco?

(16) Which Nobel Prize winning author was born in Arequipa in 1936 and wrote The Green House and Aunt Julia and the Scriptwriter?

(17) What name is given to the collection of geoglyphs in the desert, comprising more than 70 human figures and animals and 10,000 lines, which still remain an archaeological mystery?

(18) The dish ceviche originated in Peru. What is the main ingredient of it?

(19) Who wrote the play The Royal Hunt of the Sun which depicts the conflict between the Inca emperor Atahualpa and the conquistador Francisco Pizarro?

(20) Which everyday vegetable was cultivated by the Incas in Peru and found its way into Europe in the 15th and 16th centuries?

PERU ANSWERS

(1) Lima

(2) The sol

(3) True

(4) Bolivia

(5) Red and white

(6) True; the sources are considered to be the Mantaro and Apurimac Rivers.

(7) El Nino

(8) The vicuna

(9) The Incan Empire

(10) Quechua

(11) Alberto Fujimori

(12) Machu Picchu

(13) Javier Pérez de Cuéllar

(14) Michael Bentine

(15) A type of brandy produced in the winemaking regions of Peru – and also Chile. (Both countries claim that pisco is their national drink.)

(16) Mario Vargas Llosa

(17) The Nazca Lines

(18) Fresh raw fish

(19) Peter Shaffer

(20) The potato

PHILIPPINES QUESTIONS

(1)   What is the capital?

(2)   How many islands make up the Philippines: more than (a) 5,500 (b) 7,500 or (c) 9,500?

(3)   What word beginning with the letter F is used to describe the people?

(4)   True or false: The predominant religion is Islam.

(5)   Which island nation with the capital Taipei lies north of the Philippines?

(6)   True or false: The population of the Philippines is more than 100 million.

(7)   Which wife of a President of the Philippines was famous for her collection of shoes?

(8)   The Philippines were named in honour of King Philip II. Of which country was he king?

(9)   Metropolitan Manila is made up of 16 cities and the population is about 13 million. Manila itself is not the biggest city in the metropolitan area. Which city with the initials QC is?

(10) Which famous Portuguese explorer discovered the Philippines in 1521 and was killed there in the same year at the Battle of Mactan?

(11) What is a jeepney: (a) a species of snake endemic to the Philippines or (b) colourful buses originally based on US military jeeps?

(12) What are the two largest islands of the Philippines?

(13) With which sport do you associate Manny Pacquiao?

(14) What is the name of the volcano which erupted violently in 1991 on the island of Luzon?

(15) To which country did Spain cede the Philippines in 1898?

(16) In which musical did Manila-born Lea Salonga star as Kim, becoming the first Asian woman to win a Tony award?

(17) Which popular spinning toy was popularized in the USA by Filipino businessman Pedro Flores?

(18) Where was politician and Marcos critic Benigno Aquino assassinated in 1983?

(19) What is Tagalog?

(20) The sea located to the south-west of the Philippines has the same name as the character played by George Takei in the TV series Star Trek. What is the name?

PHILIPPINES ANSWERS

(1) Manila

(2) (b) More than 7,500. Some previously unknown islands have recently increased the number to 7,641 islands.

(3) Filipino

(4) False; 80% of its population are Roman Catholic.

(5) Taiwan

(6) True

(7) Imelda Marcos

(8) Spain (King from 1556 – 1598)

(9) Quezon City

(10) Ferdinand Magellan

(11) (b) Colourful buses

(12) Luzon and Mindanao

(13) Boxing

(14) Mount Pinatubo

(15) The USA

(16) Miss Saigon

(17) The yo-yo

(18) At Manila International Airport

(19) One of the main languages of the Philippines, officially called Filipino.

(20) Sulu (Sea)

POLAND QUESTIONS

(1)   What is the Polish for Poland?

(2)   Is the capital Warsaw on the River Oder or the River Vistula?

(3)   Who directed the 2002 film The Pianist based on Wladyslaw Szpilman's experiences in the Warsaw Ghetto during World War II?

(4)   What is the name of the area in north-eastern Poland which has more than 2,000 lakes?

(5)   What is the name of the artificial language invented by Polish ophthalmologist Ludwik Zamenhof in 1873?

(6)   Born in Krakow, with what do you associate the name Helena Rubinstein?

(7)   What is the Sejm?

(8)   What city is known as Breslau by the Germans?

(9)   Which member of Solidarnósc became President of Poland in 1990?

(10) Which river forms the border between Poland and Germany for 187 kilometres?

(11) The first woman to win the Nobel Prize, who in fact won it twice, was born in Warsaw. What is her name?

(12) For which musical instrument did Frédéric Chopin write most of his compositions?

(13) The Polish dish bigos is made from various kinds of chopped meat and white cabbage together with what other pickled vegetable?

(14) Which former Prime Minister of Poland was chosen as President of the European Council in 2014?

(15) For which German team did Robert Lewandowski, the captain of the Polish national team, start to play from 2014?

(16) Which count was one of the leaders of the group which failed to assassinate Adolf Hitler at the Wolf's Lair in Gierloz, Poland, in 1944?

(17) Which Polish astronomer, born in 1473, formulated the heliocentric model of the solar system, placing the Sun rather than the Earth at the centre?

(18) By what three letter name is the national Polish airline usually known?

(19) Considered to be one of Europe's most beautiful cities, which city on the River Vistula was European Capital of Culture in 2000 and the archbishopric of Pope John Paul II from 1964 – 78?

(20) What notable achievement do the writers Henryk Sienkiewicz, Wladyslaw Reymont, Czeslaw Milosz, Wislawa Szymborska and Olga Tokarczuk all have in common?

POLAND ANSWERS

(1)   Polska

(2)   On the River Vistula

(3)   Roman Polanski

(4)   The Masurian Lake District

(5)   Esperanto

(6)   Cosmetics

(7)   The lower house of the Polish parliament

(8)   Wroclaw

(9)   Lech Walesa

(10) The Oder

(11) Marie Curie

(12) The piano

(13) Sauerkraut (pickled cabbage)

(14) Donald Tusk

(15) FC Bayern Munich

(16) Claus Graf (Count) von Stauffenberg

(17) Nicolaus Copernicus

(18) LOT

(19) Krakow

(20) They have all won the Nobel Prize for Literature.

PORTUGAL QUESTIONS

(1) What is the Portuguese name for Lisbon, the capital?

(2) What name is given to the holiday region in the south of Portugal, with the capital Faro?

(3) Name one of the British football teams that Setúbal-born José Mourinho has managed.

(4) Which river in Northern Portugal is particularly famous for the production of port?

(5) Portuguese is the official language in six African countries. Can you name three of them?

(6) Who was the Portuguese explorer who was the first European to reach India by sea?

(7) Which former Portuguese colony was handed back to China on 20 December 1999?

(8) In which century was Henry the Navigator active, a central figure in the early days of the Portuguese Empire and the main initiator of the Age of Discovery?

(9) Which archipelago of nine volcanic islands in the North Atlantic Ocean belongs to Portugal?

(10) On which Portuguese island was footballer Cristiano Ronaldo born in 1985?

(11) What is bacalhau?

(12) What catastrophic event took place in Portugal on 1 November 1755?

(13) Situated on the estuary of the River Douro, what is Portugal's second-biggest city?

(14) What name is given to the mournful style of music which can be traced back to the 1820s in Lisbon, of which Amália Rodrigues was one of the foremost artists?

(15) Who ruled Portugal as a dictator from 1932 until 1968?

(16) Named after a flower, what is the name given to the revolution in 1974 which overthrew the authoritarian Estado Novo regime?

(17) What city in Central Portugal where three little shepherds saw apparitions of the Virgin Mary is famous as a pilgrimage destination?

(18) Which Portuguese navigator and explorer is regarded as the European discoverer of Brazil?

(19) How did Salvador Sobral shoot to fame in 2017?

(20) Which Portuguese writer, born in c. 1524 and best remembered for his epic work Os Lusiadas, is considered to be Portugal's greatest poet?

PORTUGAL ANSWERS

(1) Lisboa

(2) The Algarve

(3) One from Chelsea, Manchester United and Tottenham Hotspur

(4) The River Douro

(5) Three from: Angola, Cape Verde, Guinea-Bissau, Mozambique, Sao Tomé and Principe and since 2011 Equatorial Guinea.

(6) Vasco da Gama

(7) Macau

(8) The 15th century

(9) The Azores

(10) Madeira

(11) Cod – usually dried and salted

(12) The Great Lisbon earthquake

(13) Porto

(14) Fado

(15) Antonio Salazar

(16) The Carnation Revolution

(17) Fátima

(18) Pedro Cabral

(19) He won the Eurovision Song Contest for Portugal with the song Amar pelos dois.

(20) Luís de Camoes

QATAR QUESTIONS

(1) True or false: Qatar is an island.

(2) With which country does Qatar have a land border?

(3) On which major gulf is Qatar situated?

(4) True or false: More expatriates live in Qatar than Qataris.

(5) The flag of Qatar is similar to which close island nation?

(6) Of which country was Qatar a protectorate until 1971?

(7) Is the capital of Qatar Doha, Manama or Sana'a?

(8) Which major sporting event will be held in Qatar in 2022?

(9) Which family is the ruling family of Qatar, Al-Masud or Al Thani?

(10) The name of the Qatari currency is the same as the Saudi Arabian. What is it?

(11) Which global media conglomerate has its headquarters in Doha?

(12) Is Doha situated on the east or the west coast of Qatar?

(13) If it's noon in London, what time is it in Qatar?

(14) Why did a number of Arab countries, including Saudi Arabia, the United Arab Emirates and Egypt, sever diplomatic relations with Qatar in 2017?

(15) Many Qataris once earned their living by diving for what?

(16) True or false: The population of Qatar is below one million.

(17) What title is given to the ruler of Qatar: emir, king or sheik?

(18) What gulf separates Qatar from Bahrain, the Gulf of Qatar or the Gulf of Bahrain?

(19) Which species of antelope with straight long horns is the national animal of Qatar?

(20) What percentage of Qatar's population are women: (a) 25% (b) 45% (c) 55%?

QATAR ANSWERS

(1) False; it is located on the Qatar Peninsula.

(2) Saudi Arabia

(3) The Persian Gulf

(4) True; about 88% of the population are expatriates.

(5) Bahrain; the Qatari flag is maroon and white and has nine points, the flag of Bahrain red and white with five points.

(6) The United Kingdom

(7) Doha

(8) The FIFA World Cup

(9) Al Thani

(10) The riyal

(11) Al Jazeera

(12) On the east coast

(13) 3 pm

(14) They accused Qatar of supporting terrorism.

(15) Pearls

(16) False; it's 2.65 million

(17) Emir

(18) The Gulf of Bahrain

(19) The oryx

(20) (a) 25%

REPUBLIC OF THE CONGO QUESTIONS

(1) Which country is bigger in area, the Republic of the Congo or the Democratic Republic of the Congo?

(2) Was the country a Belgian or a French colony?

(3) In which year did the country gain independence from France: (a) 1960 (b) 1970 or (c) 1980?

(4) What word was added to the front of the country's name when it was a Marxist-Leninist state between 1969 and 1992?

(5) What is the capital?

(6) On which river is Brazzaville situated?

(7) Which city in Saxony, Germany is twinned with Brazzaville?

(8) True or false: Oil is an important factor in the country's economy.

(9) The second city is an important port on the Atlantic and means Black Point when translated into English. What is its French name?

(10) True or false: The Equator runs through the country.

(11) What nationality was the explorer Pietro Savorgnan di Brazza, after whom the capital is named?

(12) What adjective, which can also be used to describe the people, can be formed from the word Congo?

(13) What exploded in Brazzaville in 2012 killing 282 people and injuring more than 2,300?

(14) Does the Republic of the Congo have its longest border with DR Congo or Gabon?

(15) In which area of the country do most people live: north, south, east or west?

(16) Is the country a kingdom or a presidential republic?

(17) Are the stripes on the flag of the country (a) vertical (b) horizontal or (c) diagonal?

(18) Which Asian country is the Republic of Congo's main export/import partner?

(19) The country almost won its first medal at the 2016 Olympic Games when Franck Elemba was placed fourth behind Ryan Crouser, Joe Kovacs and Tomas Walsh in what throwing event?

(20) What is unusual about the country's border with Angola?

REPUBLIC OF THE CONGO ANSWERS

(1)   The DR Congo (2,345,409 km²). The Republic of the Congo is 342,000 km².

(2)   A French colony

(3)   (a) 1960

(4)   People's (Republic of the Congo)

(5)   Brazzaville

(6)   On the Congo

(7)   Dresden

(8)   True

(9)   Pointe-Noire

(10) True

(11) French

(12) Congolese

(13) An ammunition dump

(14) Gabon (2,567 km.); DR Congo (1,229 km.)

(15) In the south

(16) It's a presidential republic.

(17) (c) diagonal (Colours: green, yellow, red)

(18) China

(19) The shot put

(20) The border is with the Angolan enclave of Cabinda and not with the main Angola.

ROMANIA QUESTIONS

(1) What is the capital?

(2) On which sea does Romania have a coast, the Caspian Sea or the Black Sea?

(3) Which great river's delta lies largely in Romania?

(4) Is Romanian a Romance language or a Slavic language?

(5) With which sport do you associate Ilie Nastase and Simona Halep?

(6) For what sort of film was Lugoj-born actor Bela Lugosi particularly famous?

(7) The name Romania is derived from the Latin romanus meaning citizen of which city?

(8) Which historical region in central Romania is particularly associated with Dracula?

(9) Which range of mountains crosses Romania from the north to the southwest?

(10) The three main regions of Romania are Moldavia, Transylvania and which third region?

(11) Which dictator ruled Romania from 1965 until his execution in December 1989?

(12) What is the name of the Romanian gymnast who, at the age of 14, was the first to be awarded a perfect score of 10.0 at the Montreal Olympic Games in 1976?

(13) Which Romanian-born playwright, one of the foremost figures of the French avant-garde theatre, wrote Rhinocéros, Tueur sans Gages and La Cantatrice Chauve?

(14) Which Romanian city is the largest port on the Black Sea?

(15) From which fruit is the traditional Romanian spirit Tuica made?

(16) Which Romanian football club was the first Eastern European team to win the European Cup, now known as the Champions League, in 1986?

(17) Which Romanian car manufacturer, named after a Roman province which included present-day Romania, has been a subsidiary of Renault since 1999?

(18) Of what material are the famous churches of Maramures in northern Transylvania made?

(19) What was the name of the last King of the Romanians: Carol, Ferdinand or Mihai?

(20) Which city do the Germans call Hermannstadt: Cluj, Sibiu or Timisoara?

ROMANIA ANSWERS

(1)   Bucharest

(2)   On the Black Sea

(3)   The Danube

(4)   A Romance language

(5)   Tennis

(6)   Horror films

(7)   Citizen of Rome

(8)   Transylvania

(9)   The Carpathian Mountains

(10) Wallachia

(11) Nicolae Ceausescu

(12) Nadia Comaneci

(13) Eugène Ionesco

(14) Constanta

(15) Plums

(16) Steaua Bucuresti

(17) Dacia

(18) Wood

(19) Mihai (Michael I)

(20) Sibiu

RUSSIA QUESTIONS

(1)   On which river is Moscow situated?

(2)   In which city would you find the Hermitage Museum and the Winter Palace?

(3)   By what name is Tsar Ivan IV often known?

(4)   What was the name of the famous city on the Neva River when Vladimir Putin was born in it: Petrograd, Leningrad or St. Petersburg?

(5)   The longest river in Europe flows through Russia into the Caspian Sea. What is its name?

(6)   What is the Russian rouble divided into?

(7)   What is the name of the lake in southern Siberia which is the world's deepest?

(8)   Who was the last tsar of Russia?

(9)   What is the name of the cathedral situated in Red Square, Moscow?

(10) What is the present name of the city formerly known as Stalingrad?

(11) Which Russian composer is famous for the opera Eugene Onegin and the 1812 Overture, among other compositions?

(12) What is the name of the strait which separates Russia from Alaska, USA?

(13) What name is given to the traditional Russian pancakes, often served with caviar?

(14) Who directed the famous films Alexander Nevsky and Battleship Potemkin?

(15) What is the basic meaning of the word glasnost, used by Mikhail Gorbachev as a political slogan?

(16) In which city were the 2014 Winter Olympics held?

(17) Who was the First Secretary of the Communist Party of the Soviet Union from 1953 to 1964, responsible for the de-Stalinization of the country?

(18) What name is given to the sprawling pine forests which occupy large parts of Siberia?

(19) Who wrote the novels The Idiot and The Brothers Karamazov?

(20) What is the name of the multinational energy corporation famous for its Nord Stream and Turk Stream pipelines to Western Europe?

RUSSIA ANSWERS

(1) On the River Moskva

(2) St. Petersburg

(3) Ivan the Terrible

(4) Leningrad; Putin was born in 1952.

(5) The Volga

(6) Kopeks

(7) Lake Baikal

(8) Nicholas II

(9) St. Basil's Cathedral

(10) Volgograd

(11) Tchaikovsky

(12) The Bering Strait

(13) Blini

(14) Sergei Eisenstein

(15) Openness and transparency

(16) Sochi

(17) Nikita Khrushchev

(18) Taiga

(19) Fyodor Dostoevsky

(20) Gazprom

RWANDA QUESTIONS

(1) What is the capital of Rwanda?

(2) Which two European languages are official languages of Rwanda?

(3) True or false: Rwanda is largely a flat country.

(4) What shining symbol represents enlightenment on the Rwandan flag?

(5) Is the currency the Rwandan franc or the Rwandan pound?

(6) Rwanda is sometimes called Le pays des Mille Collines in French. What does it mean?

(7) How many times has the Rwandan national football team qualified for the finals of the FIFA World Cup?

(8) Kigali-born actress Sonia Rolland appeared in the 2011 film Midnight in Paris as Josephine Baker. Who directed the film?

(9) The Rwandan genocide of 1994, during the Rwandan Civil War, saw a mass slaughter of moderate Hutu and which other ethnic group?

(10) Germany colonized Rwanda in 1884, but which country took over control in 1916?

(11) With which other present-day African country was Rwanda ruled as Ruanda-Urundi by the Belgians?

(12) Volcanoes National Park in Rwanda was the base of primatologist Dian Fossey. Which animal was she particularly interested in?

(13) Who played Dian Fossey in the 1985 film Gorillas in the Mist?

(14) What does the Kigali Memorial Centre commemorate?

(15) The Belgians named the city of Butare in southern Rwanda Astrida in honour of whom?

(16) Rwanda shares its biggest lake, Lake Kivu, with which large country with the capital Kinshasa?

(17) What is the international vehicle registration code for Rwanda?

(18) What is the name of the 2004 film based on the Rwandan genocide starring Don Cheadle and Sophie Okonedo which was nominated for three Oscars?

(19) What is the name of the real-life hotel manager that Don Cheadle played in the film. Is it Paul Kagame or Paul Rusesabagina?

(20) Is the population of Rwanda over (a) 2 million (b) 12 million or (c) 22 million?

RWANDA ANSWERS

(1) Kigali

(2) English and French

(3) False; the lowest point is 950 metres above sea level.

(4) The sun

(5) The Rwandan franc

(6) The Land of a Thousand Hills

(7) They have never qualified for the finals.

(8) Woody Allen

(9) The Tutsi

(10) Belgium

(11) With Burundi

(12) Mountain gorillas

(13) Sigourney Weaver

(14) The 1994 genocide

(15) Queen Astrid of Belgium, the first wife of King Leopold II, who died in a car accident in 1935 at the age of 29.

(16) The Democratic Republic of the Congo

(17) RWA

(18) Hotel Rwanda

(19) Paul Rusesabagina, who hid and protected 1,268 refugees during the genocide. Paul Kagame is the President of Rwanda.

(20) (b) Over 12 million

SAMOA QUESTIONS

(1) True or false: Until July 1997 Samoa was known as Western Samoa.

(2) True or false: Samoa is also sometimes known as American Samoa.

(3) Is the capital Apia or Pago Pago?

(4) The two main islands of Samoa are Savai'I and Upolu. On which island is Apia located?

(5) Which country in Oceania administered Samoa until 1962?

(6) True or false: Samoa is a member of the Commonwealth of Nations.

(7) In which ocean is Samoa situated?

(8) The writer of the novels Treasure Island and Kidnapped is buried near Apia on Samoa. Who is he?

(9) From 1900 to 1914 was Samoa known as British, French or German Samoa?

(10) Of what popular English sport is Kilikiti a form?

(11) As well as English, which other language is widely spoken in Samoa?

(12) What sort of epidemic killed one fifth of the population in 1918 – 19?

(13) In 2009 did Samoa switch to driving on the left or on the right?

(14) Which Samoan sport team, which performs a traditional Samoan challenge called siva tau before every game, is known as Manu Samoa?

(15) What disaster struck Samoa in September 2009?

(16) Is the currency (a) the Australian dollar (b) the New Zealand dollar or (c) the tala?

(17) What do Samoan houses not possess which most other houses do?

(18) What position did Malietoa Tanumafili II hold from 1962 until his death in 2007?

(19) When Samoans talk about Pe'a and Malu on their bodies, what are they talking about?

(20) Why did Samoa move to the west of the International Date Line in 2011?

SAMOA ANSWERS

(1) True

(2) False; American Samoa is an unincorporated territory of the USA.

(3) Apia (Pago Pago is the capital of American Samoa).

(4) Upolu

(5) New Zealand

(6) True; it joined in August 1970.

(7) In the South Pacific Ocean

(8) Robert Louis Stevenson

(9) German Samoa

(10) Cricket

(11) Samoan

(12) Influenza

(13) It switched to the left, to fit in with other Commonwealth countries.

(14) The Samoa national rugby union team

(15) A tsunami

(16) The tala

(17) Walls

(18) He was head of state or King of Samoa.

(19) Tattooing

(20) To help business with Australia and New Zealand which are now closer in time.

SAN MARINO QUESTIONS

(1) True or false: The capital of San Marino is San Marino.

(2) Which country completely surrounds San Marino?

(3) What is the official language?

(4) True or false: The capital city is the biggest settlement in San Marino.

(5) Which range of mountains runs through San Marino?

(6) True or false: San Marino still uses the Italian lira as its currency.

(7) How many captains regent are elected every six months as heads of state?

(8) Which famous resort on the Adriatic coast is only about 22 kilometres from San Marino?

(9) In Italian the country is sometimes known as Serenissima Repubblica di San Marino. What does the word Serenissima mean?

(10) From which modern-day country on the other side of the Adriatic did the founder of San Marino, Saint Martinus, come?

(11) Name one of the other two countries in the world which is completely surrounded by another country.

(12) What is the international vehicle identification code for San Marino?

(13) The nearest international airport is at Rimini and is named after a famous Italian film director who was born there. What is his name?

(14) True or false: San Marino does not have a university.

(15) The Gualta, the Cesta and the Montale located on the three peaks of Monte Titano near the capital are what sort of building?

(16) What name is given to the citizens of San Marino?

(17) The San Marino Grand Prix, a Formula One championship race run between 1981 and 2006, was not held in San Marino. In which Italian town was it held?

(18) Which 19th century American President was granted honorary citizenship after writing an admiring letter to San Marino in 1861?

(19) What was the name of the Sammarinese singer who achieved some success in Britain in the late 1950s and early 1960s, appearing on the TV show Boy Meets Girl and having a top 20 hit with the song Too Good?

(20) What name is given in Italian to the municipalities into which San Marino is divided?

SAN MARINO ANSWERS

(1)   True

(2)   Italy

(3)   Italian

(4)   False; the biggest settlement is Dogana.

(5)   The Apennines

(6)   False; it uses the euro.

(7)   Two

(8)   Rimini

(9)   Most serene: Most Serene Republic of San Marino

(10) From Croatia (the island of Rab)

(11) Lesotho (surrounded by South Africa) or Vatican City (surrounded by Italy)

(12) RSM

(13) Federico Fellini

(14) False; the University of the Republic of San Marino was established in 1985.

(15) Towers; they are known as the Three Towers of San Marino.

(16) The Sammarinese

(17) Imola

(18) Abraham Lincoln

(19) Little Tony (born in Italy, but his parents were Sammarinese and he never took on Italian nationality.)

(20) Castelli (singular: castello)

SAO TOMÈ & PRINCIPE QUESTIONS

(1) True or false: Sao Tomé & Principe is an island country in Africa.

(2) In which ocean is it situated?

(3) What is the name of the gulf in which the islands are situated?

(4) Which European nation discovered the islands in the 15th century?

(5) True or false: Sao Tomé & Principe is the smallest African nation in area.

(6) Is the capital Sao Tomé or Principe?

(7) What is the English equivalent of the name Sao Tomé & Principe?

(8) Which of the islands is bigger in area?

(9) How far apart are the two islands: about (a) 100 km. (b) 120 km. or (c) 140 km.?

(10) Which crop represents about 95% of the islands' exports?

(11) Which other African island nation speaks Portuguese?

(12) Is the currency the dobra, the escudo or the euro?

(13) From what commodity discovered in the Gulf of Guinea are the islands hoping to profit?

(14) Are most of the inhabitants Christian or Muslim?

(15) Which of the two islands has about 96% of the population?

(16) Which African mainland nation is the closest to the island of Sao Tomé?

(17) The country achieved independence the year after the Carnation Revolution took place in Portugal. What year?

(18) Sao Tomé and Principe has taken part in the Lusophony Games. What sort of countries take part in the games: (a) island countries (b) Portuguese-speaking countries (c) West African countries?

(19) Why did the Portuguese choose to name the island Sao Tomé after St. Thomas the Apostle?

(20) Four colours feature on the country's flag. Give two of them.

SAO TOMÈ & PRINCIPE ANSWERS

(1) True

(2) The Atlantic Ocean

(3) The Gulf of Guinea

(4) Portugal

(5) False; the Seychelles is smaller.

(6) Sao Tomé

(7) Saint Thomas and Prince

(8) Sao Tomé (c 854 sq. km.); Principe (c. 136 sq. km.)

(9) (c) About 140 km.

(10) Cocoa

(11) Cape Verde

(12) The dobra (which is linked to the euro)

(13) Oil

(14) Christian

(15) Sao Tomé

(16) Gabon

(17) 1975

(18) (b) Portuguese-speaking countries

(19) Because they discovered the island on the saint's feast day, 21st December.

(20) Two from red, green, yellow and black

SAUDI ARABIA QUESTIONS

(1)   Which is correct: The Kingdom of Saudi Arabia or the Republic of Saudi Arabia?

(2)   True or false: Saudi Arabia is the only country with a Red Sea and Persian Gulf coast.

(3)   In which city was the prophet Muhammad born?

(4)   In which holy city was Muhammad buried?

(5)   What is the capital of Saudi Arabia?

(6)   What is the predominant colour of the Saudi flag?

(7)   What is Saudi Arabia's main export?

(8)   What is the family name of all the Kings of Saudi Arabia so far?

(9)   What name is given to the annual Islamic pilgrimage to Mecca which must be carried outat least once by all able-bodied and financially capable adults?

(10) Saudi businessman Adnan Khashoggi, known for his lavish business deals and lifestyle, was the uncle of which film producer and businessman who was killed in the same car crash as Princess Diana?

(11) Who was the first founder and monarch of the Saudi state in 1932?

(12) Which famous terrorist who was born in Riyadh was killed by the US in Pakistan in 2011?

(13) Saudi Arabia does not have any permanent rivers, but what name is given to the riverbeds which are either permanently or intermittently dry?

(14) In which city is the Kingdom Tower, planned to be the world's first one-kilometre-high building, being built?

(15) Is a thawb worn by men or by women?

(16) Which other nation is connected to Saudi Arabia by the King Fahd Causeway?

(17) What name is given to the building at the centre of the Great Mosque of Mecca, which is the most sacred site in Islam?

(18) Judoka Wojdan Shaherkani and runner Sarah Attar were the first to do what in London in 2012?

(19) Which Saudi oil company, one of the largest companies in the world, started trading on the Saudi Tadawul stock exchange in December 2019?

(20) What was the name of the Saudi journalist who was killed in the Saudi consulate in Istanbul in October 2018?

SAUDI ARABIA ANSWERS

(1)   The Kingdom of Saudi Arabia

(2)   True

(3)   Mecca

(4)   Medina

(5)   Riyadh

(6)   Green (with a white Arabic inscription and a white sword)

(7)   Crude oil

(8)   Saud

(9)   The Hajj

(10) Dodi Fayed

(11) Ibn Saud

(12) Osama bin Laden

(13) Wadis

(14) Jeddah (It is now known as the Jeddah Tower.)

(15) By men. It's an ankle-length garment similar to a kaftan.

(16) Bahrain

(17) The Kaaba

(18) They were the first Saudi women to compete in an Olympic Games.

(19) Saudi Aramco

(20) Jamal Khashoggi

SENEGAL QUESTIONS

(1)   Which country is largely surrounded by Senegal?

(2)   True or false: The capital city Dakar is the westernmost city on the African mainland.

(3)   Which country gave Senegal independence in 1960?

(4)   Which great river forms the border between Senegal and Mauritania?

(5)   True or false: The flag of Senegal is a tricolour.

(6)   Is the African Renaissance Monument near Dakar the oldest statue in Africa or the tallest statue?

(7)   True or false: The predominant religion in the country is Christianity.

(8)   Which king of the jungle is the national animal of Senegal?

(9)   Which African island country lies some 560 kilometres off the coast of Senegal?

(10)   True or false: The singer Akon was born in Senegal.

(11)   The first President of Senegal, Léopold Sédar Senghor, a poet and politician, was the first African to be elected to which pre-eminent French council for matters pertaining to the French language?

(12)   With which Swedish singer-songwriter did Dakar-born Youssou N'Dour collaborate on the song 7 Seconds?

(13)   For which British football team did Senegalese Sadio Mané start playing in 2016?

(14)   What colour are the waters of Lake Retba, often known as Lac Rose?

(15)   Which city on the northwest coast of Senegal, near the mouth of the Senegal River, has the same name as the city situated on the western bank of the Mississippi River in Missouri?

(16)   Which famous rally used to finish in Senegal between 1979 and 2007, but is now located in other parts of the world, e.g. South America?

(17)   What sort of musical instrument is a sabar?

(18)   For what sort of cross-Atlantic trade was Senegal particularly famous in the 18th and 19th centuries?

(19)   Which river flows from Guinea through Senegal and on to Gambia where it enters the sea?

(20)   Of which Famous French politician was Dakar-born Ségolène Royal the partner between 1978 and 2007?

SENEGAL ANSWERS

(1) Gambia

(2) True

(3) France

(4) The Senegal River

(5) True; the colours are green, yellow and red with a green star in the centre.

(6) The tallest statue

(7) False; it's Islam.

(8) The lion

(9) Cape Verde

(10) False; he was born in the USA but spent a significant part of his childhood in Senegal.

(11) The Académie Francaise

(12) Neneh Cherry

(13) Liverpool

(14) Pink (caused by algae)

(15) Saint Louis

(16) The Paris-Dakar Rally

(17) A drum (The music played on the drum and the dancing is also called sabar.)

(18) The slave trade

(19) The Gambia River

(20) Francois Hollande

SERBIA QUESTIONS

(1) True or false: Serbia has an Adriatic coast.

(2) What is the capital?

(3) Belgrade is situated at the confluence of the River Sava with which great European river?

(4) Which state unilaterally declared its independence from Serbia in 2008?

(5) What is the currency of Serbia: (a) the dinar (b) the euro (c) the leu?

(6) True or false: Josip Broz Tito, President of Yugoslavia from 1953 until 1980, was born in present-day Serbia.

(7) Is the national fruit of Serbia the apple, the plum or the raspberry?

(8) What was the first name of the politician Milosevic who served as President of Serbia?

(9) With which other Balkan state did Serbia form a union which was dissolved in 2006?

(10) Which of the Grand Slam tennis tournaments has Serbian tennis star Novak Djokovic won the most times?

(11) In what two letters of the alphabet do many Serbian surnames end?

(12) The father of actor Karl Malden came from Serbia. For which 1954 film did Karl Malden win Best Supporting Actor Oscar?

(13) In which sport has Serbia won two World Championships, three European Championships and two Olympic silver medals?

(14) The Serbian language is the only European language with active digraphia. What does that mean?

(15) What did Kragujevac-born Marija Serifovic win in 2007?

(16) Serbia is one of the largest producers in the world of which popular berry?

(17) Which German footballer, who played for FC Bayern Munich, did Belgrade-born tennis player Ana Ivanovic marry in 2016?

(18) Although born in present-day Bosnia and Herzegovina, the man who assassinated Franz Ferdinand in Sarajevo in 1914 came from a Serb family. What is his name?

(19) Which Serbian-American inventor, best known for his contributions to the design of the modern alternating current electricity supply system, was played by David Bowie in the film The Prestige?

(20) Serbia's second city is famous for its music festival EXIT. Its name translated from Serbian means 'new orchard'. What is its name?

SERBIA ANSWERS

(1) False; it is landlocked.

(2) Belgrade

(3) The Danube

(4) Kosovo

(5) (a) The dinar

(6) False; he was born in Kumrovec in present-day Croatia.

(7) The plum

(8) Slobodan

(9) Montenegro

(10) The Australian Open (8 times up to 2020)

(11) ic

(12) On the Waterfront

(13) Basketball

(14) The Serbian language uses both the Cyrillic and the Latin alphabets. (Digraphia is the use of more than one writing system for the same language.)

(15) The Eurovision Song Contest with the song Molitva (Prayer).

(16) The raspberry

(17) Bastian Schweinsteiger

(18) Gavrilo Princip

(19) Nikola Tesla

(20) Novi Sad

SEYCHELLES QUESTIONS

(1) In which ocean would you find the Seychelles?

(2) The capital is named after a 19ᵗʰ century British monarch. What is its name?

(3) Do the Seychelles belong to Africa or Asia?

(4) From which country did the Seychelles proclaim independence in 1976?

(5) The Seychelles have three official languages. Name two of them.

(6) Are the Seychelles a kingdom, a republic or a dictatorship?

(7) Are there more than a hundred Seychelles islands or fewer than a hundred?

(8) What nationality were the first people to settle on the islands in the 18ᵗʰ century?

(9) True or false: of the African nations only Djibouti has a smaller population.

(10) Which Portuguese explorer, the first European to reach India by sea, spotted the Seychelles in the 15ᵗʰ century?

(11) Which country on the African mainland with the capital Mogadishu is the closest to the Seychelles?

(12) Big Ben and Little Ben can be seen in London. Which of the two can be seen in Victoria, the capital of the Seychelles?

(13) Are the Seychelles named after a French finance minister or a type of mollusc only found on the islands?

(14) Can you name one of the four biggest Seychelles islands?

(15) The Seychelles parrot is the national bird of the Seychelles. Is it known as the red parrot, the brown parrot or the black parrot?

(16) On which island is the capital Victoria situated?

(17) What is the name of the rare species of palm tree native to the Seychelles, the nut of which is noted for its odd shape?

(18) What did Mad Mike Hoare, a British mercenary, attempt to do in the Seychelles in 1981?

(19) Which members of the British royal family spent their honeymoon on the Seychelles?

(20) The Aldabra giant what is a reptile which is endemic to the Seychelles?

303

SEYCHELLES ANSWERS

(1) The Indian Ocean

(2) Victoria

(3) Africa

(4) The United Kingdom

(5) Two from English, French and Seychellois Creole

(6) A republic

(7) More than a hundred (115)

(8) French

(9) False; the Seychelles have the smallest population of any African country (c. 97,000)

(10) Vasco da Gama

(11) Somalia

(12) Little Ben

(13) An 18th century French finance minister, Jean Moreau de Séchelles

(14) One from Mahé, Praslin, Silhouette Island and La Digue

(15) The black parrot, although it is grey-brown in colour.

(16) On Mahé

(17) The coco de mer

(18) He attempted a coup d'état.

(19) William and Kate

(20) Tortoise

SIERRA LEONE QUESTIONS

(1) On which ocean is Sierra Leone situated?

(2) Sierra Leone has two neighbouring countries with the capitals Conakry and Monrovia. Name one of them.

(3) True or false: Sierra Leone has had a fairly peaceful existence since it gained independence from the UK in 1961.

(4) What is the capital?

(5) In which century was Freetown founded by freed African-American slaves, the 18th or the 19th ?

(6) The outbreak of what disease in 2014 killed more than 3,000 people in the country?

(7) Is it the dry season in Sierra Leone from May to November or the rainy season?

(8) True or false: The flag of Sierra Leone only consists of the colours green and blue.

(9) What is the literal meaning of Sierra Leone?

(10) What is a staple food in Sierra Leone: rice, potatoes or noodles?

(11) After which 20th century English monarch is the large deepwater quay in Freetown named?

(12) Is the currency (a) the sierra (b) the leone or (c) the sierra leone?

(13) What do locals mean when they refer to Salone?

(14) What is the name of the film set during the 1991-2002 Sierra Leone Civil War starring Leonardo DiCaprio and Djimon Hounsou, whose title refers to precious stones mined in war zones and used to finance conflicts?

(15) What is the Star of Sierra Leone?

(16) The second city of Sierra Leone has the same name as Barack Obama's Portuguese Water Dog and Mr. Diddley. What is it?

(17) Sometimes known as a kapok tree and now a famous symbol of Freetown, what name is given to the tree where the slaves who arrived in the area in the 18th century first held a Thanksgiving Service?

(18) Which sport did Mohamed Kallon, Rodney Strasser and Komba Yomba play for Sierra Leone?

(19) The father of the star of the BBC One series Luther was from Sierra Leone. Who is the the star?

(20) What nationality was the explorer who originally gave the country the name Serra Leoa?

SIERRA LEONE ANSWERS

(1) On the Atlantic

(2) Guinea (Conakry) or Liberia (Monrovia)

(3) False; it has a history of military coups and civil war.

(4) Freetown

(5) The 18th century (1787 - 1792)

(6) Ebola

(7) The rainy season

(8) False; the flag is a horizontal tricolour of green, white and blue.

(9) Lion(ess) Mountains

(10) Rice

(11) Queen Elizabeth II

(12) (b) The leone

(13) They mean Sierra Leone

(14) Blood Diamond

(15) One of the biggest diamonds ever discovered

(16) Bo

(17) A cotton tree

(18) Football

(19) Idris Elba

(20) Portuguese

SINGAPORE QUESTIONS

(1)   On the southern tip of which peninsula is Singapore situated?

(2)   Is Singapore north or south of the Equator?

(3)   True or false: Singapore is an island country.

(4)   Of the four official languages, English, Malay, Mandarin and Tamil, which one is the main language used in business, government, law and education?

(5)   Is Singapore known as the lion city, the tiger city or the monkey city?

(6)   True or false: Singapore consists of only one island.

(7)   How is Singapore connected to Malaysia: (a) by a bridge (b) by a causeway (c) by a bridge and a causeway?

(8)   In what year did Singapore gain independence: 1945, 1955 or 1965?

(9)   What is the name of the hotel in Singapore which is named after the British coloniser of the country?

(10)   What name is given to the official mascot of Singapore, depicted as a mythical creature with a lion's head and the body of a fish?

(11)   Which nation triumphed in the Battle of Singapore in February 1942?

(12)   What is the name of the main shopping street in Singapore which reminds one of fruit trees?

(13)   Who was the first Prime Minister of Singapore who served from 1959 to 1990?

(14)   Which German driver won the Singapore Grand Prix for the fifth time in 2019?

(15)   Singapore is one of only three city-states in the world. Can you name one of the other ones?

(16)   Which Norwegian DJ who had hits with Stole the Show and Higher Love was born in Singapore on 11 September 1991?

(17)   Which two statesmen met on Sentosa Island, Singapore on June 12, 2018?

(18)   With which sport is Joseph Schooling associated: swimming, boxing or athletics?

(19)   Which charming antihero played on television by Roger Moore did Singapore-born Leslie Charteris create?

(20)   What is Singlish?

SINGAPORE ANSWERS

(1) The Malay Peninsula

(2) About one degree north of the Equator

(3) True

(4) English

(5) The lion city

(6) False; it consists of about 64 islands, many of which are small.

(7) (c) By a bridge and a causeway

(8) 1965

(9) The Raffles Hotel (named after the British statesman Sir Thomas Stamford Raffles)

(10) The merlion

(11) Japan

(12) Orchard Road

(13) Lee Kuan Yew

(14) Sebastian Vettel

(15) Monaco or the Vatican City

(16) Kygo

(17) Donald Trump and Kim Jong-un

(18) Swimming (He won the gold medal in the 100m butterfly at the 2016 Rio Olympics).

(19) Simon Templar, alias The Saint

(20) An English-based Creole language spoken in Singapore

SLOVAKIA QUESTIONS

(1)   What is the capital city?

(2)   On which river is Bratislava?

(3)   The Velvet Divorce of 1993 saw the peaceful dissolution of which country into the Czech Republic and Slovakia?

(4)   True or false: The official language is Czech.

(5)   About 8.5% of the population have their roots in the country situated to the south of Slovakia. Which country?

(6)   Which other capital city on the Danube is only 60 kilometres away from Bratislava?

(7)   What was the name of the Slovak-born leader of Czechoslovakia who attempted to reform the communist government during the Prague Spring in 1968?

(8)   What building directly above the Danube, sometimes called the upturned table, is a dominant feature of Bratislava?

(9)   At which winter sport has the Slovak national team been most successful?

(10) Which Swiss tennis player who won five Grand Slam titles was born in the Slovak city of Kosice in 1980?

(11) Is the currency the Slovak koruna or the euro?

(12) Is Gerlachovský stít the highest mountain or the name of a daily newspaper?

(13) The Visegrád Group is a cultural and political alliance of four Central European EU member countries, including Slovakia, to promote co-operation and further integration in the EU. Name two of the other countries.

(14) The parents of which American pop artist and film director known for his Campbell's Soup Cans and Marilyn Diptych originally came from present-day Slovakia?

(15) What is the name of the chain of mountains, the highest range in the Carpathian Mountains, which forms the border between Poland and Slovakia?

(16) In what field of the arts was Slovak-born Lucia Popp well known?

(17) Václav Klaus and Vladimír Meciar were the first Prime Ministers of the independent countries the Czech Republic and Slovakia. Which of the two was the Slovak PM?

(18) What name did the Germans give to Bratislava?

(19) With which two countries does Bratislava have direct borders?

(20) What was the profession of Ján Kuciak who was shot dead together with his fiancée in February 2018?

SLOVAKIA ANSWERS

(1)   Bratislava

(2)   On the Danube

(3)   Czechoslovakia

(4)   False; it's Slovak, a language closely related to Czech.

(5)   Hungary

(6)   Vienna

(7)   Alexander Dubcek

(8)   Bratislava Castle

(9)   Ice hockey

(10) Martina Hingis

(11) The euro; the country adopted it in 2009.

(12) The highest mountain (2,655m.)

(13) Two from the Czech Republic, Hungary and Poland

(14) Andy Warhol

(15) The Tatra Mountains

(16) Opera

(17) Vladimír Meciar

(18) Pressburg

(19) Austria and Hungary

(20) An investigative journalist, particularly investigating tax fraud

SLOVENIA QUESTIONS

(1)   On which sea does Slovenia have a coast?

(2)   True or false: Slovenia was never part of Yugoslavia.

(3)   Is the capital Ljubljana or Maribor?

(4)   What mythical fire-breathing beast is the symbol of Ljubljana?

(5)   True or false: The only ex-Yugoslav country with which Slovenia has a border is Croatia.

(6)   The wife of which American President was born in Novo Mesto in 1970?

(7)   With what winter sport is Planica particularly associated?

(8)   Is 75% of the country's wine production white wine or red wine?

(9)   With which winter sport do you associate Tina Maze?

(10)   Which city do Germans sometimes call Marburg an der Drau?

(11)   How many days did the Slovenian War of Independence in 1991 last: 7, 10 or 14?

(12)   What breed of horse originating in Slovenia is closely associated with the Spanish Riding School of Vienna?

(13)   What is the name of the town and lake in north-western Slovenia, a famous tourist attraction?

(14)   The largest park in Ljubljana has the same name as an amusement park in Copenhagen. What is its name?

(15)   Slovene ski jumper Peter Prevc won the 2015-16 Four Hills Ski Jumping Tournament. Name one of the four towns at which the competition takes place.

(16)   With which two other countries does Slovenia share the peninsula of Istria?

(17)   What is a kozolec which can be found throughout Slovenia: (a) a beehive (b) a hayrack (c) a winepress?

(18)   Why is Slovenia a delightful country for speleologists?

(19)   What is the name of the highest mountain, a national symbol, the shape of which is featured on the coat of arms of Slovenia?

(20)   Which female Jamaican sprinter, who holds the record for the most Olympic appearances of any track and field athlete, represented Slovenia between 2002 and 2012?

SLOVENIA ANSWERS

(1)   The Adriatic Sea

(2)   False

(3)   Ljubljana

(4)   The dragon

(5)   True

(6)   Donald Trump (Wife: Melania)

(7)   Ski jumping

(8)   White wine

(9)   Skiing

(10)   Maribor (on the River Drava)

(11)   Ten days

(12)   Lippizaner, originally from Lipica in Slovenia

(13)   Bled

(14)   Tivoli (City Park)

(15)   One from Oberstdorf, Garmisch-Partenkirchen (both Germany), Innsbruck or Bischofshofen (both Austria)

(16)   Croatia and Italy

(17)   A hayrack

(18)   It has so many caves, over 13,150. Postojna Cave is the biggest.

(19)   Mount Triglav

(20)   Merlene Ottey

SOLOMON ISLANDS QUESTIONS

(1) Are Solomon Islands in Africa, Asia or Oceania?

(2) In which ocean are they situated?

(3) Which large country is situated about 2,000 kilometres south-west of Solomon Islands?

(4) What is the official language?

(5) What is the capital?

(6) On which island is Honiara situated: Malaita, Guadalcanal or New Georgia?

(7) After whom are the islands named?

(8) Is the currency the Australian dollar or the Solomon Islands dollar?

(9) Are most of the population Melanesian, Polynesian or Micronesian?

(10) Which island was the scene of bitter fighting between Japanese and American forces between August 1942 and February 1943?

(11) True or false: Rugby union is a popular sport on the islands.

(12) Bougainville is geographically part of Solomon Islands archipelago, but is politically part of which country?

(13) What is Solomon Islands pijin: (a) a bird (b) a language (c) a weapon?

(14) The Pijin word wantok meaning people who speak the same language, who belong to the same culture and who are friends and help one another out is important for the islands' culture. On what two English words is the word wantok based?

(15) How many stars are on the flag: one, three or five?

(16) Is the sea between Papua New Guinea and Solomon Islands called the Papua Sea or the Solomon Sea?

(17) True or false: Solomon Islands suffered from ethnic tensions in the last years of the 1990s and the early years of the 2000s.

(18) Which American President has an uninhabited island in Solomon Islands named after him, the island which the crew of the PT-109 swam to after their craft was wrecked by the Japanese destroyer Amagiri?

(19) What is Walkabout long Chinatown?

(20) Which members of the British Royal Family visited Solomon Islands in 2012 to mark the 60th anniversary of the accession of Queen Elizabeth II?

SOLOMON ISLANDS ANSWERS

(1) Oceania

(2) The Pacific Ocean

(3) Australia

(4) English

(5) Honiara

(6) Guadalcanal

(7) The wealthy biblical King Solomon

(8) The Solomon Islands dollar

(9) Melanesian (c. 95%) (Polynesian c. 3% and Micronesian just over 1%)

(10) Guadalcanal

(11) True

(12) Papua New Guinea

(13) (b) The language that is mostly spoken on the islands.

(14) One talk

(15) Five (white stars)

(16) The Solomon Sea

(17) True; in 2003 the Regional Assistance Mission to Solomon Islands was created as an answer to the Governor-General's request for international aid.

(18) John F. Kennedy; the island was originally called Plum Pudding Island.

(19) A popular folksong from Solomon Islands, often described as the national song of the islands and of Melanesia as a whole.

(20) The Duke and Duchess of Cambridge

SOMALIA QUESTIONS

(1) What is the capital?

(2) Apart from Somali, which other language is an official language of the country?

(3) True or false: Somalia has the longest coastline of any African country.

(4) Is the currency the Somali pound, shilling or penny?

(5) On which ocean is the capital city located?

(6) What name is given to the part of Africa in which Somalia is located?

(7) Does the flag consist of a white star on a blue background or a blue star on a white background?

(8) Which Somalia-born British distance runner is the 2012 and 2016 Olympic gold medallist in the 5000m and the 10000m?

(9) Which rock star did Mogadishu-born Iman marry in 1992?

(10) What name is given to the region in the north which declared itself an independent republic in 1991, but which is unrecognised by any country or international organisation?

(11) In which decade did Puntland declare itself to be an autonomous state?

(12) Garowe and Hargeisa: which is the capital of Somaliland and which of Puntland?

(13) Germany abandoned its efforts to colonize Somalia in 1890, but which other two European nations did establish colonies?

(14) What is the name of the 2001 film directed by Ridley Scott about the US military's 1993 raid in Mogadishu?

(15) What is the Internet country code for Somalia?

(16) What role has been assigned to the Combined Task Force 150, a multinational coalition naval task force, off the coast of Somalia?

(17) What was the name of the 2013 film about Somali piracy which starred Tom Hanks and Mogadishu-born Barkhad Abdi?

(18) For which running event did athlete Abdi Bile win the gold medal at the 1987 Rome World Championships?

(19) With which African country did Somalia fight the Ogaden War between July 1977 and March 1978?

(20) The father of the lead singer of the British punk rock band X-Ray Spex was born in Somalia. By what name was she known?

SOMALIA ANSWERS

(1)   Mogadishu

(2)   Arabic

(3)   False; Madagascar comes first, then Somalia and then South Africa.

(4)   The Somali shilling

(5)   On the Indian Ocean

(6)   The Horn of Africa

(7)   A white star on a blue background

(8)   Sir Mo Farah

(9)   David Bowie

(10) The Republic of Somaliland

(11) In the 1990s (1998)

(12) Garowe: Puntland and Hargeisa: Somaliland

(13) Britain and Italy

(14) Black Hawk Down

(15) .so

(16) To control piracy and terrorism in the Horn of Africa region.

(17) Captain Phillips

(18) 1500 metres

(19) Ethiopia

(20) Poly Styrene (Marianne Joan Elliott-Said)

SOUTH AFRICA QUESTIONS

(1) South Africa has an executive, a judicial and a legislative capital. Name two of the cities.

(2) What is the largest city?

(3) What is the unit of currency?

(4) With which sport do you associate Gary Player and Ernie Els?

(5) True or false: The Cape of Good Hope is the southernmost point of the African continent.

(6) What is the name of the famous black township outside of Johannesburg?

(7) What overall name is given to the wars which took place in South Africa in the late 19th and early 20th centuries and which included the famous Siege of Ladysmith?

(8) What alcoholic drink is associated with the names Constantia, Stellenbosch and Paarl?

(9) Name two of the four most spoken first languages in South Africa.

(10) Which South African singer and civil rights activist, famous for The Click Song and Pata Pata, was briefly married to the well-known trumpeter, Hugh Masekele of Grazin' In The Grass fame?

(11) What is the name of the island in Table Bay where Nelson Mandela was imprisoned for 18 of the 27 years he served behind bars?

(12) Which famous Indian activist spent 21 years in South Africa from 1893 to 1914?

(13) In which three major sports has South Africa been the host of the World Cup competition: one in 1995, one in 2003 and one in 2010?

(14) What name is given to the eastern portion of the Great Escarpment, the highest point of which in South Africa is Mafadi at 3,450m?

(15) Name one of the two South African writers who have been awarded the Nobel Prize for Literature.

(16) Together with which South African President was Mandela awarded the Nobel Peace Prize in 1993?

(17) Why do people remember the name Louis Washkansky?

(18) Which archbishop first used the term Rainbow Nation to describe post-apartheid South Africa?

(19) Which 2009 science fiction action film set in Johannesburg starring Sharlto Copley became an unexpected cult hit?

(20) What is the name of the national park in north-eastern South Africa, named after the third President of the South African Republic?

SOUTH AFRICA ANSWERS

(1) Pretoria (executive), Bloemfontein (judicial) and Cape Town (legislative)

(2) Johannesburg

(3) The rand

(4) Golf

(5) False; Cape Agulhas about 150 km. to the east-southeast is the southernmost point.

(6) Soweto

(7) The Boer Wars

(8) Wine

(9) Two from Zulu (22.7%), Xhosa (16.0%), Afrikaans (13.5%) and English (9.6%)

(10) Miriam Makeba

(11) Robben Island

(12) Mahatma Gandhi

(13) Rugby (1995), Cricket (2003) and Football (2010)

(14) The Drakensberg

(15) Nadine Gordimer (1991) or JM Coetzee (2003)

(16) F.W. de Klerk

(17) He was the first heart-transplant patient in 1967 of Dr. Christian Barnard at the Groote Schur Hospital in Cape Town.

(18) Desmond Tutu

(19) District 9

(20) The Kruger National Park (named after Paul Kruger)

SOUTH KOREA QUESTIONS

(1) What important sporting event was held in the capital Seoul in 1988?

(2) Which country is bigger in area, North Korea or South Korea?

(3) In what year was the armistice which ended fighting in the Korean War?

(4) The abbreviation ROK is sometimes used to denote South Korea. What does it mean?

(5) Which South Korean company with its headquarters in Suwon is one of the world's largest manufacturers of consumer electronics?

(6) What is the name of South Korea's second-largest city and most important port situated in the south-east of the country?

(7) What is the name of the South Korean film which won the 2020 Best Film Oscar?

(8) What is the most popular Korean surname?

(9) Which South Korean motor group produces the Elantra and the Ioniq?

(10) What is the name of the Korean who was Secretary-General of the United Nations from 2007 to 2016?

(11) Which South Korean singer had an international hit with Gangnam Style?

(12) Which martial art involving kicking techniques was developed in Korea in the 1940s and 1950s?

(13) What is Jeju?

(14) Is the flag of Korea known as the Hanbok or the Taegukgi?

(15) What name is given to the famous traditional side dish of salted and fermented vegetables?

(16) Born in Seoul, but now a citizen of New Zealand, with what sport do you associate Lydia Ko?

(17) Where were the Winter Olympics held in 2018?

(18) By what name are the Bangtan Boys normally known in Europe and America?

(19) Which Korean was the founder of the Unification Church of the United States, noted for its mass wedding ceremonies?

(20) Which Japanese island is closest to South Korea: Honshu, Okinawa or Tsushima?

SOUTH KOREA ANSWERS

(1)   The Summer Olympic Games

(2)   North Korea (120,540 sq. km.) South Korea is 100,363 sq. km.

(3)   1953

(4)   The Republic of Korea (ROK is used as the international vehicle registration code for South Korea).

(5)   Samsung

(6)   Busan

(7)   Parasite

(8)   Kim

(9)   Hyundai

(10)   Ban Ki-Moon

(11)   Psy

(12)   Taekwondo

(13)   South Korea's biggest island

(14)   The Taegukgi (The hanbok is the traditional Korean dress.)

(15)   Kimchi

(16)   Golf

(17)   Pyeongchang

(18)   BTS (one of the most successful K-pop groups)

(19)   Sun Myung Moon

(20)   Tsushima (about 50 km. from Busan)

SOUTH SUDAN QUESTIONS

(1)   From which country did South Sudan gain independence in July 2011?

(2)   Is the capital of South Sudan Juba or Khartoum?

(3)   True or false: The majority of the population are Arabs.

(4)   True or false: English is the official language of South Sudan.

(5)   In the independence referendum, what percentage voted for independence: (a) over 85% (b) over 90% or (c) over 95%?

(6)   In which direction do you have to travel to get from South Sudan to Ethiopia?

(7)   True or false: Oil is important for the economy.

(8)   Does the White Nile or the Blue Nile flow through South Sudan?

(9)   Six colours feature on the flag of South Sudan. Name three of them.

(10)   In what field has Wau-born Alek Wek made a name for herself?

(11)   True or false: South Sudan and the rest of Sudan co-existed fairly peacefully until South Sudan gained independence.

(12)   What event between 2013 and 2020 killed thousands of people in South Sudan?

(13)   Do more Christians or more Muslims live in South Sudan?

(14)   What sport does Juba-born Deng Adel play in the USA: baseball, basketball or volleyball?

(15)   SSP is the abbreviation for the currency. What is it?

(16)   What would a South Sudanese do with Kisra: (a) eat it (b) drink it (c) wear it?

(17)   What is the Sudd, formed by the White Nile's Bahr al-Jabal section?

(18)   With which of its neighbours, capital Nairobi, is South Sudan involved in an ongoing dispute over the Ilemi Triangle, an area of land in East Africa?

(19)   With which neighbouring country did South Sudan clash over oil-rich regions in the Heglig Crisis of 2012?

(20)   How did John Garang de Mabior, who led the SPLA, a guerrilla movement which fought against the government of Sudan and after independence became the South Sudanese Army, die in 2005: (a) assassinated (b) died in a helicopter crash (c) natural causes?

SOUTH SUDAN ANSWERS

(1) The Republic of Sudan

(2) Juba

(3) False; the majority are Nilotic e.g. Dinka, Nuer, Shilluk and Bari.

(4) True

(5) (c) Over 95% (98.83%)

(6) East

(7) True

(8) The White Nile

(9) Three from black, white, red, green, blue and yellow

(10) Modelling and designing

(11) False; Sudan was involved in two long civil wars between 1955 – 1972 and 1983 and 2005.

(12) The South Sudanese Civil War

(13) More Christians (c 61%) (Muslims c 6%)

(14) Basketball

(15) The South Sudanese Pound

(16) (a) Eat it; it's a thin fermented bread, the national dish of South Sudan.

(17) A vast swamp

(18) Kenya

(19) Sudan

(20) (b) He died in a helicopter crash.

SPAIN QUESTIONS

(1) Which is officially correct: the Kingdom of Spain or the Republic of Spain?

(2) Who is the King of Spain?

(3) What is the name of the peninsula on which Spain is situated?

(4) True or false: Spain is the only European country to have a physical border with an African country.

(5) Put the three biggest Balearic Islands in order of size.

(6) True or false: Madrid lies on the River Ebro.

(7) Is the city of Granada in the region of Andalusia, Aragon or Asturias?

(8) What position does Spanish hold in the list of most-spoken native languages?

(9) Name three of the eight main islands of the Canary Islands.

(10) What lies on the other side of the border to the town of La Linea de la Concepción?

(11) In which century did the Spanish Empire reach its maximum extension?

(12) What famous work was first published in Spain in two parts between 1605 and 1615?

(13) Which two artists recorded the song Barcelona in 1988?

(14) What is the Sagrada Família?

(15) The marriage of Queen Isabella and King Ferdinand in 1469 is often seen as the beginning of the unification of Spain. From which two Spanish kingdoms did the pair come?

(16) Name the husband and wife who won Best Supporting Acting Oscars for No Country for Old Men and Vicky Cristina Barcelona.

(17) Which Spanish painter, born in 1746 who painted The Nude Maja and The Clothed Maja among many other famous paintings, has the most works on display in the Prado, the national art museum of Spain in Madrid?

(18) Which football club won the UEFA Champions League three times in a row from 2016 to 2018?

(19) Between what years did the Spanish Civil War take place?

(20) With what two typical Spanish traditional activities do you associate the words corrida and palo?

SPAIN ANSWERS

(1) The Kingdom of Spain

(2) Felipe VI

(3) The Iberian Peninsula

(4) True; with Morocco through the enclaves Ceuta, Melilla and Penón de Vélez de la Gomera.

(5) Mallorca (3,640 sq. km.), Menorca (695 sq. km.) and Ibiza (571 sq. km.)

(6) False; it's on the River Manzanares.

(7) In Andalusia

(8) Second, after Mandarin Chinese

(9) Three from Tenerife, Fuerteventura, Gran Canaria, Lanzarote, La Palma, La Gomera, El Hierro and La Gracioso

(10) Gibraltar

(11) The 18th century

(12) Don Quixote by Cervantes

(13) Freddie Mercury and Montserrat Caballé

(14) The large unfinished Roman Catholic basilica in Barcelona designed by Antoni Gaudi.

(15) Isabella from Castile and Ferdinand from Aragon

(16) Javier Bardem and Penelope Cruz

(17) Francisco Goya

(18) Real Madrid

(19) 1936 – 1939

(20) Bullfighting (corrida de toros) and flamenco (palos are flamenco styles)

SRI LANKA QUESTIONS

(1) By what name was Sri Lanka known until 1972?

(2) True or false: The legislative capital Sri Jayawardenepura Kotte is located within the urban area of Sri Lanka's biggest city and executive and judicial capital Colombo.

(3) Sinhala or Sinhalese is one of the official languages. What is the other?

(4) In which ocean is Sri Lanka situated?

(5) What is the main religion, Buddhism or Hinduism?

(6) What animal appears on the flag of Sri Lanka, the elephant or the lion?

(7) The name Ceylon comes from Ceilao, a name given to the country by settlers from which European country?

(8) Sri Lanka is the world's fourth largest producer of which aromatic beverage?

(9) Which city in central Sri Lanka is the home of the Temple of the Tooth Relic, one of the most sacred places of worship in the Buddhist world?

(10) Sri Lanka-born Duncan White was the first athlete from the country to win an Olympic medal at the 1948 Olympics. In which city did the games take place?

(11) Roughly how long did the Sri Lankan Civil war, which began in 1983, last: 5 years, 15 years or 25 years?

(12) What did the Tamil Tigers hope to achieve in the civil war?

(13) In which sport did Sri Lanka win the World Cup in 1996?

(14) Which British singer who was born in Colombo in 1963 had a number three hit in the UK in 1991 with Promise Me?

(15) Which Sri Lankan became the world's first elected female prime minister in 1960?

(16) What is the name of the chain of limestone shoals between southern India and north-western Sri Lanka which could have been a former land connection between the two countries?

(17) What is located near the summit of Adam's Peak and is revered as a holy site by Buddhists, Hindus, some Muslims and Christians?

(18) Which Booker-Prizewinning novel by Colombo-born writer Michael Ondaatje was made into a 1996 film starring Ralph Fiennes, Juliette Binoche and Kristin Scott-Thomas?

(19) What is the name of the strait which separates Sri Lanka from India: (a) the Bass Strait (b) the Palk Strait or (c) the Torres Strait?

(20) Which presenter of BBC News was born in Colombo in 1955?

SRI LANKA ANSWERS

(1)   Ceylon

(2)   True

(3)   Tamil

(4)   The Indian Ocean

(5)   Buddhism (70%), Hinduism (13%)

(6)   The lion

(7)   Portugal

(8)   Tea

(9)   Kandy

(10) London; White won the silver medal in the 400-metre hurdles.

(11) 25 years, until 2009

(12) An independent Tamil state in the north-east of Sri Lanka

(13) Cricket

(14) Beverley Craven

(15) (Mrs) Sirimavo Bandaranaike

(16) Adam's Bridge

(17) A footprint, said to be the footprint of Buddha or Shiva or Adam etc.

(18) The English Patient

(19) (b) The Palk Strait; the Bass Strait is between Australia and Tasmania and the Torres Strait between New Guinea and Australia.

(20) George Alagiah

ST KITTS & NEVIS QUESTIONS

(1)   Is St Kitts & Nevis in the East Indies or the West Indies?

(2)   Is it in the Leeward Islands or the Windward Islands?

(3)   The capital has a French name which means low ground. What is it?

(4)   Is Basseterre on St Kitts or on Nevis?

(5)   Which Italian explorer was the first European to see the islands in 1493?

(6)   Of which English first name is Kit(t) a diminutive?

(7)   The Narrows Strait separates the two islands. How wide is it at its narrowest point: 2km, 3km or 4km?

(8)   True or false: St Kitts & Nevis is the smallest country in the Caribbean.

(9)   Which of the two islands is roughly oval in shape?

(10) Is the capital of Nevis (a) Andrewtown (b) Charlestown or (c) Edwardtown?

(11) In which sprinting discipline did Kim Collins become World Champion in 2003?

(12) Is St Kitts & Nevis one of the Lesser Antilles or the Greater Antilles?

(13) The fortress on the hill on St Kitts is a UNESCO World Heritage Site and its name includes an alternative name for sulphur. What is its name?

(14) Is the country's national cricket or football team known as the Sugar Boyz?

(15) What was traditionally the islands' main agricultural export until the early 2000s?

(16) Which Nevis-born statesman and founding father of the USA was the subject of a 2015 Broadway musical written by Lin-Manuel Miranda which won 11 Tonys?

(17) What cute animal which was introduced to the islands in the 17th century has become something of a pest, particularly for local farmers?

(18) Which British singer-songwriter who recorded the top ten albums Me Myself I and Walk Under Ladders was born in Basseterre in 1950?

(19) Which British maritime hero married his Nevis-born wife Fanny on the island of Nevis in 1787?

(20) Although 62% voted for independence from St Kitts in Nevis in 1998, why did the referendum fail?

ST KITTS & NEVIS ANSWERS

(1)   In the West Indies

(2)   In the Leeward Islands

(3)   Basseterre

(4)   On St Kitts

(5)   Christopher Columbus

(6)   Christopher

(7)   3 km

(8)   True

(9)   Nevis

(10) (b) Charlestown

(11) 100 metres

(12) The Lesser Antilles

(13) The Brimstone Hill Fortress

(14) The national football team

(15) Sugar

(16) Alexander Hamilton

(17) The (vervet) monkey

(18) Joan Armatrading

(19) Horatio Nelson

(20) A higher percentage (two thirds) was necessary for the referendum to succeed.

ST LUCIA QUESTIONS

(1) Which two European nations vied with each other in the 17th and 18th centuries for control of St Lucia?

(2) Which nation took definitive control of the island in 1814?

(3) Is St Lucia located in the eastern or the western Caribbean?

(4) True or false: The island was named after one of Columbus's ships.

(5) What is the capital?

(6) Which yellow fruit is now the principal crop of the island?

(7) Which group of islands lies to the south-west of St Lucia?

(8) True or false: The flag of St Lucia includes the British Union Jack.

(9) For what sort of alcoholic beverage is Roseau Valley famous?

(10) What sort of bird is the Saint Lucia amazon, sometimes known as Jacquot?

(11) What is most important for St Lucia's economy: (a) the service sector (b) industry or (c) agriculture?

(12) With which sport do you associate Darren Sammy?

(13) True or false: St Lucia is a member of the Commonwealth of Nations and the Organisation internationale de la Francophonie.

(14) What is the name of the Castries-born poet and playwright who won the Nobel Prize for Literature in 1992?

(15) Which singer who had a number one hit in the UK in 1959 with What Do You Want to Make Those Eyes at Me For? was born in Castries in 1937?

(16) Which British actor, real name Maurice Joseph Micklewhite, starred in the 1985 comedy film Water which was largely shot on St Lucia?

(17) As the French name suggests, what sort of springs can be found near the town of Soufrière on the island?

(18) What are the Gros Piton and the Petit Piton?

(19) Which of the Nobel prizes was Castries-born Sir Arthur Lewis awarded in 1979?

(20) Diana Ross, Rihanna, John Legend, Luther Vandross and Amy Winehouse have all performed at which annual event in St Lucia?

ST LUCIA ANSWERS

(1) Britain and France

(2) Britain

(3) The eastern Caribbean

(4) False; it was named after the third century Catholic Saint Lucy of Syracuse.

(5) Castries

(6) The banana

(7) St Vincent and the Grenadines

(8) False; the flag consists of a light blue field with a yellow triangle in front of a white-edged black isosceles triangle.

(9) Rum

(10) A parrot; it is endemic to St Lucia.

(11) (a) The service sector (82.8%) (Industry 14.2% and Agriculture 2.9%)

(12) Cricket; he was Captain of the West Indies team between 2010 and 2014.

(13) True

(14) Derek Walcott

(15) Emile Ford

(16) Michael Caine

(17) Sulphur

(18) Two mountainous volcanic peaks, a famous landmark of the island and a World Heritage Site

(19) The Nobel Memorial Prize in Economic Sciences

(20) The St Lucia Jazz Festival

ST VINCENT AND THE GRENADINES QUESTIONS

(1) In which part of the world are the islands situated?

(2) Two of the following apply to St Vincent and the Grenadines. Which two? Greater Antilles, Lesser Antilles, Leeward Islands, Windward Islands

(3) True or false: All of the Grenadines are inhabited.

(4) Is the capital Kingston or Kingstown?

(5) Are the Grenadines located north or south of St Vincent?

(6) To which other island nation does the southern end of the Grenadines belong?

(7) From which fruit is the syrup grenadine made?

(8) Do pomegranates grow on the islands?

(9) What is La Soufrière?

(10) Which of the Grenadines was often visited by Princess Margaret who owned a house there?

(11) Which fruit is most important to the economy: banana, kiwi or pineapple?

(12) The first three films of which series starring Johnny Depp had many scenes which were filmed in St Vincent and the Grenadines?

(13) The capital of the Grenadine island of Bequia has the same name as a port in the Eastern cape province of South Africa. What is its name?

(14) Who is the head of state?

(15) What was the title of the song with which Kingstown-born Kevin Lyttle had a worldwide hit in 2003?

(16) Which captain of the ship HMS Bounty brought the breadfruit plant to the islands in 1793?

(17) The motto of the country is Pax et Justitia. What does this mean?

(18) Vincentian foot baller Wesley Charles who often played in Canada and Ireland in his career was born in a village with the same name as a large resort in East Sussex on the south coast of England. What is its name?

(19) Which of the Grenadine islands is closest to St Vincent: Bequia, Mustique, Canouan or Tobago Cays?

(20) Which position which represents the British monarch have Sir David Jack, Sir Frederick Ballantyne and Susan Dougan held in St Vincent and the Grenadines?

ST VINCENT AND THE GRENADINES ANSWERS

(1)   In the West Indies (Caribbean)

(2)   Lesser Antilles and Windward Islands

(3)   False; there are 32 Grenadines, some inhabited, some not.

(4)   Kingstown

(5)   South

(6)   Grenada

(7)   Pomegranate

(8)   No

(9)   A volcano on St Vincent and the island's highest peak (1,234m)

(10) Mustique

(11) The banana

(12) Pirates of the Caribbean

(13) Port Elizabeth

(14) The British monarch

(15) Turn Me On

(16) Captain Bligh

(17) Peace and Justice

(18) Brighton

(19) Bequia

(20) Governor-general

SUDAN QUESTIONS

(1) What is the capital?

(2) At the confluence of which two rivers is Khartoum situated?

(3) The city of Port Sudan is the country's main port on which sea?

(4) Sudan used to be the biggest country in area in Africa before the independence of South Sudan. Name one of the two countries which is now bigger in area.

(5) The Nubian Desert in the north-east of Sudan is part of which much larger desert?

(6) With which country does Sudan share Lake Nasser?

(7) The flag of Sudan consists of the four Pan-Arab colours, also used in the flags of Iraq, Syria and Yemen, among others. Name two of the colours.

(8) What happened to Sudan's territory in 2011?

(9) Which famous army officer and administrator was killed at the Siege of Khartoum in 1885?

(10) What title did Gordon's opponent in the siege Muslim religious leader Muhammad Ahmad give himself?

(11) Which famous British actor of stage and screen played the Mahdi in the 1966 film Khartoum?

(12) Sudan has more of these constructions than Egypt. What are they?

(13) Which famous Riyadh-born terrorist leader spent the first half of the 1990s in Sudan?

(14) Who was in charge of the British forces at the Battle of Omdurman in 1898 which ensured British control over Sudan?

(15) What is the name of the gum of which Sudan produces about 80% of the world's supply?

(16) What is the name of the region in western Sudan where two rebel groups started to fight the Sudanese government in 2003 with devastating consequences for the population?

(17) Which present-day African country used to be known as French Sudan?

(18) What is the name of the dictatorial President of Sudan who was in power from 1989 until he was deposed in 2019?

(19) In what field has Khartoum-born Zeinab Badawi made a name for herself?

(20) Sudan-born actor Alexander Siddig appeared in the film Syriana alongside which actor who won Best Supporting Oscar for his role in the film and who has also campaigned for a resolution of the Darfur conflict?

SUDAN ANSWERS

(1) Khartoum

(2) The Blue and the White Nile

(3) On the Red Sea

(4) Either Algeria or Democratic Republic of the Congo

(5) The Sahara Desert

(6) Egypt

(7) Two from black, red, white or green

(8) It was reduced by 619,745 sq. km. (about 25%) due to the independence of South Sudan.

(9) General Gordon

(10) The Mahdi

(11) Laurence Olivier

(12) Pyramids

(13) Osama bin Laden

(14) Lord Kitchener

(15) Gum arabic

(16) Darfur

(17) Mali

(18) Omar al-Bashir

(19) TV and radio journalism in the UK

(20) George Clooney

SURINAME QUESTIONS

(1) In which continent is Suriname situated?

(2) Is it on the north-east or the north-west coast?

(3) Which country in South America is smaller in area than Suriname?

(4) What is the capital?

(5) Under which country's rule did Suriname come in the late 17th century until independence in 1975?

(6) True or false: Suriname has a border with France.

(7) By what name was Suriname previously known?

(8) What is the official language?

(9) There are many famous sportsmen with Surinamese descent. With which sport are the following associated: Ruud Gullit, Frank Rijkaard, Edgar Davids and Patrick Kluivert?

(10) Is Paramaribo located on the Paramaribo River or the Suriname River?

(11) Put the religions in order of popularity: Christianity, Hinduism, Islam.

(12) What sedimentary rock with a relatively high aluminium content is important for Suriname's economy?

(13) Suriname has territorial disputes with its two small neighbouring countries. One is the French overseas department of French Guiana. What is the other one?

(14) For which British football team based in North Yorkshire did Suriname-born Jimmy Floyd Hasselbaink play between 2004 and 2006?

(15) Is the currency the euro, the gulden or the Surinamese dollar?

(16) The highest mountain in Suriname is named after a Dutch Queen. Is it called Beatrixtop, Julianatop or Wilhelminatop?

(17) What colour is the poison dart frog, Dendrobates tinctorius azureus, which is endemic to Suriname?

(18) Created between 1961 and 1964, what is the Brokopondostuwmeer?

(19) With which swimming style did Anthony Nesty win the gold medal for Suriname at the 1988 Olympics?

(20) What is the name of the controversial president who was elected in 2010 who is believed to have been involved in murders and drug trafficking?

SURINAME ANSWERS

(1) In South America

(2) On the north-east coast

(3) None; it is the smallest (163,820 sq. km.)

(4) Paramaribo

(5) Under the Netherlands' rule

(6) True; it has a border with French Guiana, an overseas department and region of France.

(7) Dutch Guiana

(8) Dutch

(9) Football

(10) On the Suriname River

(11) Christianity (48.4%), Hinduism (22.3%) and Islam (13.9%)

(12) Bauxite

(13) Guyana

(14) Middlesbrough

(15) The Surinamese dollar

(16) Julianatop (1,280 metres)

(17) Blue

(18) A large reservoir near the town of Brokopondo, one of the largest in the world.

(19) Butterfly; he won the 100 metres.

(20) Dési Bouterse

SWEDEN QUESTIONS

(1) What colour is the cross on the Swedish flag?

(2) Which city in Sweden hosts the annual Nobel Prize ceremonies and is home to the ABBA Museum and the Karolinska Institute?

(3) What is the Swedish name for Sweden?

(4) Name the second-largest and third-largest city in Sweden.

(5) How many times did Björn Borg win the Wimbledon tennis championship?

(6) Roughly what percentage of Sweden lies north of the Arctic Circle: 5%, 10% or 15%?

(7) Which Swedish company with its headquarters in Gothenburg is particularly famous for manufacturing cars?

(8) The 1956 Summer Olympics were held in Melbourne, but which of the events were actually held in Stockholm?

(9) What is the name of the Stockholm-born actress who retired at the age of 35 in 1941 after making the film The Two-Faced Woman?

(10) Which company was founded in Sweden in 1943 by Ingvar Kamprad?

(11) What is the name of the red-haired, freckled, unpredictable girl created by author Astrid Lindgren?

(12) What is the name of the royal house of Sweden, rulers of the country since 1818?

(13) What are Vänern and Vättern?

(14) What relation was Swedish actress Ingrid Bergman to Swedish director Ingmar Bergman?

(15) What name is given to the type of meal, originating in Sweden, where a selection of hot and cold dishes are served buffet-style?

(16) In what field has Stockholm-born Max Martin been particularly successful?

(17) What is the name of the 18th century botanist and zoologist whose binomial classification enable plants and animals to be consistently named and classified into families?

(18) What animal is traditionally carved out of wood and usually painted bright red in the Swedish province of Dalarna?

(19) Which Swedish economist and diplomat, the second Secretary-General of the United Nations, was killed in a plane crash in Northern Rhodesia in 1961?

(20) Which novelist is best known for writing the Millennium trilogy?

SWEDEN ANSWERS

(1)   Yellow

(2)   Stockholm, the capital

(3)   Sverige

(4)   Gothenburg and Malmö

(5)   Five times (1976 – 1980)

(6)   About 15%

(7)   Volvo

(8)   The equestrian events (due to the Australian quarantine regulations)

(9)   Greta Garbo

(10) IKEA

(11) Pippi Longstocking

(12) The House of Bernadotte

(13) The two largest lakes in Sweden

(14) No relation

(15) Smorgasbord

(16) Songwriting; he has written many number 1 hits including Baby One More Time for Britney Spears

(17) Carl von Linné (Carl Linnaeus)

(18) A horse

(19) Dag Hammarskjöld

(20) Stieg Larsson

SWITZERLAND QUESTIONS

(1) What colour is the cross on the Swiss flag?

(2) Which large lake does Switzerland share with Germany and Austria?

(3) Which famous mountain is known as Mont Cervin in French?

(4) The capital city of Bern is the fifth-biggest city in Switzerland. Can you name three of the four biggest cities?

(5) Name three of the four official languages.

(6) Which language is spoken most as a first language?

(7) Which multinational food and drink company was founded in Switzerland in 1866?

(8) Which famous person has the Swiss Guards as his bodyguards?

(9) Which of the Grand Slam tournaments has Swiss tennis legend Roger Federer only won once?

(10) What is the name of the railway tunnel which connects Brig in Switzerland with Domodossola in Italy?

(11) Which Swiss town hosted the Winter Olympics in 1928 and in 1948?

(12) Which Geneva-born humanitarian and businessman's experience of the Battle of Solferino in 1859 led to the founding of the Red Cross?

(13) What character did Swiss-born actress Ursula Andress play in the James Bond film Dr. No?

(14) Which legendary Swiss marksman was the subject of a play by the German playwright Friedrich Schiller?

(15) What is the name of the young girl living in the Swiss Alps created by the children's author Johanna Spyri?

(16) With what product do you associate the names Appenzeller, Gruyère, and Sbrinz?

(17) Which two towns does the famous Glacier Express train link?

(18) What is the usual abbreviation for the European Organization for Nuclear Research based in Geneva?

(19) On which lakes are the towns of Locarno and Lucerne and Lugano situated?

(20) What is the name of the largest glacier in the Alps which is located in Switzerland?

(1)   White

(2)   Lake Constance (Bodensee)

(3)   The Matterhorn

(4)   Three from Zürich, Geneva, Basel and Lausanne

(5)   German, French, Italian and Romansh

(6)   German (62.8%), then French (22.9%), then Italian (8.2%) and Romansh (0.5%)

(7)   Nestlé

(8)   The Pope

(9)   The French Open

(10) The Simplon Tunnel

(11) St. Moritz

(12) Henri Dunant

(13) Honey Ryder

(14) William Tell

(15) Heidi

(16) Cheese

(17) Zermatt and St. Moritz

(18) CERN (Conseil européen pour la recherche nucléaire)

(19) Locarno: Maggiore, Lucerne: Lucerne and Lugano: Lugano

(20) The Aletsch Glacier

SYRIA QUESTIONS

(1) What is the capital, the oldest continuously inhabited city in the world?

(2) On which sea does Syria have a coast?

(3) Which country borders Syria to the north?

(4) Are there two blue stars or two green stars on the flag?

(5) What is the name of the late co-founder and CEO of Apple Inc. whose father was born in Homs, Syria?

(6) What type of cloth derives its name from the city of Damascus?

(7) The abbreviation for the currency is SYP. What does it stand for?

(8) What did Syria form with Egypt from 1958 to 1961?

(9) Which family have held the presidency since 1971?

(10) In which year did the current civil war in Syria start: 2009, 2010 or 2011?

(11) Which major historic city in the north of Syria has suffered badly as a result of the war?

(12) Which river, one of the two defining rivers of Mesopotamia, flows from Turkey through Syria for 710 kilometres and then into Iraq?

(13) True or false: The River Tigris also flows through Syria.

(14) Which pope visited the Umayyad Mosque in Damascus in 2001, the first pope to visit a mosque?

(15) What is the name of the heights which were captured from Syria by Israel in the Six Day War?

(16) From which European nation did Syria become independent in 1946?

(17) Which ancient city in the Homs Governorate was badly damaged by ISIL terrorists in 2015?

(18) Which European country accepted hundreds of thousands of Syrian refugees in the period from 2015 to 2016?

(19) The father of Oscar-winning actor F. Murray Abraham was born in Syria. For which film did the actor win his Oscar?

(20) What sort of building is the Krak des Chevaliers?

SYRIA ANSWERS

(1)   Damascus

(2)   On the Mediterranean Sea

(3)   Turkey

(4)   Two green stars

(5)   Steve Jobs

(6)   Damask

(7)   The Syrian pound

(8)   The United Arab Republic

(9)   The al-Assad family (Hafez al-Assad 1971 – 2000 and then his son Bashar)

(10) 2011

(11) Aleppo

(12) The Euphrates

(13) True, but only for 44 kilometres on the border with Turkey.

(14) Pope John Paul II

(15) The Golan Heights

(16) France (Syria became independent from the French Mandate of Syria and Lebanon.)

(17) Palmyra

(18) Germany

(19) Amadeus

(20) It's a Crusader castle, one of the most important preserved medieval castles in the world.

TAIWAN QUESTIONS

(1) Is the capital Kaohsiung, Taichung or Taipei?

(2) True or false: Taiwan is not a member of the United Nations.

(3) With which countries does Taiwan have a land border?

(4) Which country lays claim to the island of Taiwan?

(5) By what name was Taiwan often known previously in the English-speaking world?

(6) Are the colours of the flag the same as the British flag or the German flag?

(7) What is Taiwan's national sport: baseball, basketball or volleyball?

(8) With what sort of product is the Taiwanese company Acer associated?

(9) What nationality were the discoverers of Taiwan who named it Ilha Formosa or Beautiful Island in 1590?

(10) What was the name of the Chinese nationalist politician, revolutionary and military leader who retreated to Taiwan in 1949 when defeated by Mao Zedong's communist forces?

(11) By what name is Taiwan known to the People's Republic of China, a name which Taiwan uses, for example, when participating in the Olympics?

(12) What trendy type of tea was invented in Taiwan in the 1980s?

(13) What is the name of the Taiwanese director who won Best Director Oscars for Brokeback Mountain and Life of Pi?

(14) What is one of the main attractions of Taroko National Park which has been carved out by the Liwu River?

(15) What superlative record did the Taipei 101 hold between 2004 and 2010?

(16) Apart from Taiwan, name two of the other four countries which lay claim to the Spratly Islands and have military installations there.

(17) Taiwan is one of the Four Asian Tigers, economies which underwent rapid industrialisation and experienced high growth rates between the 1960s and 1990s. Can you name one of the other tigers?

(18) Which country invaded Taiwan in 1895 and remained there until 1945?

(19) Yani Tseng won five major championships and was number one in the rankings for 109 consecutive weeks. In which sport?

(20) Which Chinese nationalist political party co-founded by Sun Yat-sen was for many years Taiwan's sole ruling party?

TAIWAN ANSWERS

(1) Taipei

(2) True; it was replaced by the People's Republic of China in 1971.

(3) None, it's an island.

(4) The People's Republic of China

(5) Formosa

(6) The same as the British flag, red, white and blue.

(7) Baseball

(8) Computers and electronics

(9) Portuguese

(10) Chiang Kai-shek

(11) Chinese Taipei

(12) Bubble tea

(13) Ang Lee

(14) A gorge

(15) It was the tallest building in the world. It was superseded by the Burj Khalifa in Dubai, United Arab Emirates.

(16) Two from China, Malaysia, the Philippines and Vietnam.

(17) One from Hong Kong, Singapore or South Korea

(18) Japan

(19) Golf

(20) Kuomintang

TAJIKISTAN QUESTIONS

(1) Where is Tajikistan: in Central Africa, Central America or Central Asia?

(2) From which country did Tajikistan gain independence in 1991?

(3) To which language is the language Tajik closely related: Arabic, Persian or Chinese?

(4) Does Tajikistan have a border with Iran?

(5) Is the capital Ashgabat, Bishkek, Dushanbe, Nur-Sultan or Tashkent?

(6) What does the Persian suffix -stan mean?

(7) What devastating event lasted in the country from 1992 to 1997?

(8) After which 4th century BC King of Macedonia, famous for his military campaigns and empire, is the lake Iskanderkul named?

(9) The Wakhan Corridor is a narrow strip of territory which separates Tajikistan from Pakistan. To which country does the corridor belong?

(10) What is the somoni?

(11) True or false: The present flag of Tajikistan is the same flag that was used under Soviet rule.

(12) Under Soviet rule, Dushanbe was named after an infamous dictator who died in 1953. Which dictator?

(13) Fedchenko is the longest what in the world outside of the polar regions?

(14) Tajikistan has a remittance-dependent economy. What does that mean?

(15) What is the Pamir?

(16) Which silvery-white, soft metal is particularly important to the Tajikistan economy?

(17) What post has Emomali Rahmon held since 1994?

(18) The word Dushanbe means a day of the week in Persian. Which one?

(19) With which sport do you associate the Tajik athlete Nellie Kim?

(20) In which neighbouring country is about 27% of the population from the Tajik ethnic group?

TAJIKISTAN ANSWERS

(1)   In Central Asia

(2)   The Soviet Union

(3)   Persian

(4)   No; it has borders with Afghanistan, China, Kyrgyzstan and Uzbekistan.

(5)   Dushanbe

(6)   Place of or country/land

(7)   Civil war

(8)   Alexander the Great (Iskander is the Persian pronunciation of Alexander; kul means lake.)

(9)   Afghanistan

(10) The unit of currency

(11) False; the new flag was adopted on 24 November 1992.

(12) Stalin; it was called Stalinabad.

(13) Glacier

(14) A large part of GDP comes from money sent by Tajik workers abroad, especially in the Russian Federation.

(15) The mountain range which covers a large part of the country.

(16) Aluminium

(17) President of Tajikistan

(18) Monday

(19) Gymnastics

(20) Afghanistan

TANZANIA QUESTIONS

(1) Is the capital Dar es Salaam or Dodoma?

(2) On which coast is Dar es Salaam situated?

(3) True or false: Dodoma is also situated on the Indian Ocean.

(4) Africa's largest lake is situated in the north-west of Tanzania on the border with Kenya and Uganda. What is its name?

(5) Does Dar es Salaam mean Place of Peace or Place of Welcome?

(6) What is the name of the archipelago off the coast of Tanzania which includes the Islands of Unguja and Pemba?

(7) Africa's highest mountain is located in Tanzania. What is its same?

(8) Which famous rock star was born in Zanzibar in 1946 as Farrokh Bulsara?

(9) True or false: Dala-dala is made from lentils and is the national dish of Tanzania.

(10) Which national park, famous for its mammal migration covers parts of northern Tanzania and joins with the Masai Mara Game Reserve in southern Kenya?

(11) Who was President of Tanzania from 1964 to 1985?

(12) Lake Nyasa in the south-west of Tanzania is also known as Lake what?

(13) Apart from English, which other Bantu language is widely spoken in Tanzania?

(14) What is the name of the lake in the west of Tanzania, the world's second-deepest after Lake Baikal and one of the world's largest, which shares its name with the previous name of Tanzania?

(15) With which country did Zanzibar go to war in 1896, the war lasting about 45 minutes?

(16) People go to Ngorongoro to visit the caldera. What is a caldera?

(17) Which island in the North Sea did Germany gain control over in 1890 in return for recognizing British authority in Zanzibar?

(18) Which island off the coast of Tanzania has the same name as an Italian crime syndicate?

(19) Which expert on chimpanzees started her research at the Gombe Stream National Park in Tanzania in 1960?

(20) Do you associate the name Filbert Bayi with athletics or football?

(1)   Dodoma

(2)   On the Indian Ocean

(3)   False; it's in the centre of the country.

(4)   Lake Victoria

(5)   Place of Peace

(6)   Zanzibar

(7)   Mount Kilimanjaro

(8)   Freddie Mercury

(9)   False; they are minibuses used for passenger travel.

(10) Serengeti

(11) Julius Nyerere

(12) Malawi

(13) Swahili

(14) Lake Tanganyika

(15) The United Kingdom

(16) A large crater which has become a conservation area.

(17) Heligoland

(18) Mafia Island

(19) Jane Goodall

(20) Athletics; he was a middle-distance runner.

THAILAND QUESTIONS

(1)   What is the capital of Thailand?

(2)   What is the former name of Thailand?

(3)   What is the country's main religion?

(4)   True or false: One baht is 100 satang.

(5)   What is the official language?

(6)   What is the name of the gulf which is surrounded on the north, west and southwest by Thailand?

(7)   What is the name of Thailand's largest island which has become a tourist hotspot?

(8)   Which famous river forms quite a lot of the border between Thailand and Laos?

(9)   Who is Maha Vajiralongkorn?

(10) What was the name of the previous king who ruled for over 70 years?

(11) One of Thailand's favourite sports is Muay Thai. By what name do we know it in the English-speaking world?

(12) In which 1955 Walt Disney cartoon does The Siamese Cat song feature?

(13) With which of the Indochina countries does Thailand not have a border?

(14) Which American golfer who has won numerous major championships has a Thai mother?

(15) What is a khlong?

(16) Who were Chang and Eng Bunker?

(17) Which James Bond film starring Roger Moore and Christopher Lee had many scenes shot in Thailand?

(18) Which sport is played on elephants in Thailand?

(19) Who or what is Tom Yum: (a) a Thai TV star (b) a type of hot and sour Thai soup (c) the Thai for Tom Thumb?

(20) Who was the star of the 1999 film The Beach which was filmed on the Thai island Ko Phi Phi Leh?

THAILAND ANSWERS

(1) Bangkok

(2) Siam

(3) Buddhism

(4) True; it's the currency.

(5) Thai

(6) The Gulf of Thailand

(7) Phuket

(8) The Mekong

(9) The current King of Thailand, also known as Rama X.

(10) King Bhumibol

(11) Thai boxing or kickboxing

(12) Lady and the Tramp

(13) Vietnam

(14) Tiger Woods

(15) A canal; Bangkok has a number of them.

(16) 19th century conjoined twins from Thailand whose fame popularised the expression Siamese twins

(17) The Man with the Golden Gun

(18) Elephant polo

(19) (b) A type of hot and sour Thai soup

(20) Leonardo DiCaprio

TIMOR-LESTE QUESTIONS

(1) In which continent is Timor-Leste situated?

(2) What is the alternative name of Timor-Leste?

(3) Which large country is separated from Timor-Leste by the Timor Sea?

(4) Which European country colonized Timor-Leste from the 16th century until 1975?

(5) Which country invaded Timor-Leste in 1975 and declared it as its 27th province in 1976?

(6) Did Timor-Leste finally become an independent state in the 20th century or the 21st century?

(7) True or false: Timor-Leste is the only Asian country to be located completely in the Southern Hemisphere.

(8) Is the capital of Timor-Leste Dili, Parsli or Sagi?

(9) The word Timor means east in Indonesian. Does the word Leste mean north, south, east or west in Portuguese?

(10) True or false: The majority of the inhabitants are Muslim.

(11) What important award did politician José Ramos-Horta and Bishop Carlos Belo receive in 1996?

(12) Timor-Leste is a member of the organisation sometimes known as the Lusophone Commonwealth. What does the word Lusophone mean?

(13) Does the island of Timor belong to the Greater or Lesser Sunda Islands?

(14) Timor-Leste made its official debut at the Summer Olympics in 2004. In which country?

(15) Which crop is of importance to Timor-Leste's economy, tea or coffee?

(16) What is Tetum?

(17) To which country does West Timor belong?

(18) True or false: Timor-Leste's Special Administrative Region of Oecusse is totally surrounded by Indonesia.

(19) What major world currency is also the currency of Timor-Leste?

(20) True or false: The population of Timor-Leste is less than one million.

TIMOR-LESTE ANSWERS

(1)   In Asia

(2)   East Timor

(3)   Australia

(4)   Portugal

(5)   Indonesia

(6)   In the 21st century (2002)

(7)   True

(8)   Dili

(9)   East

(10) False: They are Christian (97% Roman Catholic)

(11) The Nobel Peace Prize (for working "towards a just and peaceful solution to the conflict in East Timor").

(12) Portuguese-speaking

(13) The Lesser Sunda Islands

(14) In Greece

(15) Coffee

(16) One of the official languages of Timor-Leste (along with Portuguese)

(17) Indonesia

(18) False; it has a sea coast (The Savu Sea)

(19) The US dollar

(20) False; it's about 1.3 million.

TOGO QUESTIONS

(1) Is Togo in Central Africa?

(2) Is the capital Abuja, Accra, Lomé or Porto-Novo?

(3) From which country did Togo gain its independence in 1960?

(4) Name one of the countries beginning with the letter B which has a border with Togo.

(5) What adjective can be formed from the word Togo?

(6) Which one of these colours does not feature on the Togolese flag: white, red, black, green and yellow?

(7) Name one of the three Cs which generate 20% of Togo's exports.

(8) True or false: The official language is English.

(9) Is the major river of Togo called the Mono River or the Stereo River?

(10) Togo has the second largest population of Ewe people in Africa. Which neighbouring country, with the capital Accra, has the largest population?

(11) Between 1884 and 1914 Togoland was a protectorate of which European country?

(12) True or false: The capital city Lomé is situated inland.

(13) What is more important for Togo's economy, oil or phosphates?

(14) The Togo national football team has only taken part in one FIFA World Cup Finals competition in 2006. In which country did the finals take place?

(15) True or false: Togo is one of the ten smallest countries in area in Africa.

(16) Historically was Togo part of the Barbary Coast, the Gold Coast or the Slave Coast?

(17) Gnassingbé Eyadéma was President of Togo for 38 years until his death in 2005. What relation to him is the new president, Faure Gnassingbé?

(18) The footballer Emmanuel Adebayor played for three teams in England, Manchester City, Crystal Palace and for which team did he earn his spurs between 2012 and 2015?

(19) Alexandre Grimaldi-Coste, the son of Togo-born Nicole Coste, is the illegitimate son of whom?

(20) In the 2008 Olympic Games in Beijing Benjamin Boukpeti won the bronze medal in which palindromic boating event?

TOGO ANSWERS

(1) No, it's in West Africa.

(2) Lomé

(3) France

(4) Benin or Burkina Faso

(5) Togolese

(6) Black doesn't feature on the flag.

(7) One from cocoa, coffee or cotton.

(8) False; it's French.

(9) The Mono River

(10) Ghana

(11) Germany

(12) False; it's situated on the Gulf of Guinea.

(13) Phosphates

(14) Germany

(15) False; 13 countries are smaller.

(16) The Slave Coast

(17) Son

(18) Tottenham Hotspur

(19) Prince Albert of Monaco

(20) Kayak

TONGA QUESTIONS

(1) Is Tonga a kingdom or a republic?

(2) What relation is the present king, Tupou VI to the previous king Tupou V?

(3) What is the capital?

(4) With which seaside port on the east coast of Yorkshire, near Scarborough, is Nuku'alofa twinned?

(5) What is the dominant colour of the flag of Tonga, red or white?

(6) How many islands make up Tonga: (a) 69 (b) 169 (c) 269?

(7) True or false: Tonga has never been colonized.

(8) Brought by a ship from New Zealand, what killed 1,800 Tongans in 1918?

(9) Which famous British explorer and navigator landed in Tonga in the 1770s?

(10) What sport do the national team the Sea Eagles play?

(11) What name did Captain Cook give to Tonga because of the warm welcome that he received on his second visit there in 1774?

(12) How many groups of islands make up Tonga: one, two or three?

(13) The mutiny on which famous ship took place in Tongan waters in 1789?

(14) Which Queen of Tonga attended the 1953 coronation of Queen Elizabeth II?

(15) Is the unit of currency (a) the pa'anga (b) the tonga or (c) the New Zealand dollar?

(16) Does Tonga lie east or west of the International Date Line?

(17) What name is given to the major area in the Pacific where many earthquakes and volcanic eruptions occur and which includes Tonga?

(18) The island of Niue is the nearest foreign territory to Tonga. It is a self-governing state in free association with which much bigger island country?

(19) Some Tongans consume quite a lot of kava. What is it?

(20) Which famous All-Black rugby player who died unexpectedly in 2015 spent some of his early childhood in Tonga with his aunt and uncle and had parents who originally came from the islands?

TONGA ANSWERS

(1)   A kingdom

(2)   They are brothers.

(3)   Nuku'alofa

(4)   Whitby

(5)   Red

(6)   (b) 169

(7)   True; from 1900 to 1970 it had British protected state status, but it never lost its sovereignty.

(8)   The 1918 flu pandemic

(9)   James Cook

(10) Rugby Union

(11) The Friendly Islands

(12) Three: from north to south - Vava'u, Ha'apai and Tongatapu.

(13) The Bounty

(14) Queen Salote

(15) (a) The pa'anga

(16) West, and so it is one of the first nations to celebrate the New Year.

(17) The Ring of Fire

(18) New Zealand

(19) A drink made from the root of the kava plant which has sedative and intoxicating properties.

(20) Jonah Lomu

TRINIDAD AND TOBAGO QUESTIONS

(1) Off the coast of which South American country is Trinidad and Tobago situated?

(2) Have the islands always been a single unit?

(3) What is the capital?

(4) Which island is further south, Trinidad or Tobago?

(5) Is the head of state the president or the British monarch?

(6) In which film did Trinidad-born Billy Ocean's song When the Going Gets Tough, the Tough Get Going feature?

(7) True or false: Trinidad and Tobago has large reserves of gas and oil.

(8) What is the name of the dance contest where the aim is to pass under a low bar without dislodging it, which originated on the island of Trinidad?

(9) With what musical instrument do you associate Trinidad-born Winifred Atwell?

(10) Was Trinidad-born cricketer Brian Lara a great batsman or a great bowler?

(11) What shade of red is the ibis which is the national bird of the country?

(12) What style of music, originally from Trinidad, was popularised in the 1950s by Harry Belafonte with his Banana Boat Song?

(13) The capital and largest town on Tobago is named after a famous seaside resort in North Yorkshire. What is its name?

(14) Which rapper, whose albums include Pink Friday, The Pinkprint and Queen was born in Port of Spain in 1982?

(15) With which television station do you associate Trinidad-born Trevor McDonald?

(16) Which running event did Trinidad-born Hasely Crawford win at the 1976 Summer Olympics, the first Caribbean athlete to do so?

(17) Which 1960 Walt Disney film from a novel by Johann Wyss starring John Mills and James MacArthur was filmed almost entirely on Tobago?

(18) Which Tobago-born football player, who played for Aston Villa, Manchester United and Blackburn Rovers amongst others, also captained the Trinidad and Tobago national team at the 2006 FIFA World Cup?

(19) Which Trinidad-born writer, famous for the novels A House for Mr. Biswas and In a Free State, was awarded the Nobel Prize for Literature in 2001?

(20) What name is given to the lake which contains the largest natural deposit of asphalt in the world?

TRINIDAD AND TOBAGO ANSWERS

(1) Off the coast of Venezuela

(2) No; they were united in 1889.

(3) Port of Spain

(4) Trinidad

(5) The president

(6) The Jewel of the Nile starring Michael Douglas, Kathleen Turner and Danny DeVito

(7) True; that's why it is one of the wealthiest countries in the Caribbean.

(8) Limbo

(9) The piano

(10) A great batsman

(11) Scarlet

(12) Calypso

(13) Scarborough

(14) Nicki Minaj

(15) ITV (News presenter with ITN)

(16) 100 metres

(17) Swiss Family Robinson

(18) Dwight Yorke

(19) V.S. Naipaul

(20) Pitch Lake

TUNISIA QUESTIONS

(1)　What is the capital city?

(2)　Which two of these four countries have a border with Tunisia: Algeria, Egypt, Libya, Morocco?

(3)　Which sea borders Tunisia?

(4)　True or false: Arabic and French are the official languages.

(5)　What is the closest European country in distance to Tunisia?

(6)　Which of these two is a city in Tunisia, Tataouine or Tatooine?

(7)　What famous ancient city, supposedly founded by Dido, was situated on the coast in the north of Tunisia?

(8)　What is significant about Cape Angela in Tunisia?

(9)　Did Tunisian-born Alain Boublil co-write the music or the lyrics for the musical Les Misérables?

(10)　To what ethnic group do the indigenous population of Tunisia belong?

(11)　What name is given to the series of anti-government protests, uprisings and armed rebellions which started in Tunisia in 2011 and then spread to other Arab countries?

(12)　What name is given to the wars fought between Rome and Carthage between 264 BC and 146 BC?

(13)　Which Italian-Tunisian actress, star of Once Upon a Time in the West and Fitzcarraldo, was born in Tunis in 1938?

(14)　The second-biggest and third-biggest cities in Tunisia both begin with S. Can you name one of them?

(15)　What name is given to the crushed durum wheat semolina which is an important part of Tunisian cuisine?

(16)　What is the name of the holiday island situated in the Gulf of Gabès used as a location for the Star Wars film?

(17)　Who served as Tunisia's leader from independence in 1956 until 1987?

(18)　What is the name of the Carthaginian general who commanded Carthage's main army against Rome during the Second Punic War (218 – 201 BC)?

(19)　What is the title of the song with which Tunisia-born F.R. David had a worldwide hit in 1982?

(20)　What international prize was the Tunisian National Dialogue Quartet awarded in 2015?

TUNISIA ANSWERS

(1) Tunis

(2) Algeria and Libya

(3) The Mediterranean Sea

(4) False; only Arabic

(5) Italy (Sicily)

(6) Tataouine; Tataooine is Luke Skywalker's home planet in Star Wars named after the Tunisian city.

(7) Carthage

(8) It's the northernmost point on the African continent.

(9) The original French lyrics with Jean-Marc Natel. Claude-Michel Schönberg wrote the music.

(10) Berber

(11) The Arab Spring

(12) The Punic Wars

(13) Claudia Cardinale

(14) Sfax and Sousse

(15) Couscous

(16) Djerba

(17) Habib Bourguiba

(18) Hannibal

(19) Words

(20) The Nobel Peace Prize, for their attempts to form a lasting constitutional settlement in Tunisia following the 2011 Jasmine Revolution.

TURKEY QUESTIONS

(1) True or false: Istanbul is the capital of Turkey.

(2) The flag of Turkey is red with what two features on it?

(3) In which continent is Turkey?

(4) Is the currency (a) the Turkish dollar (b) the Turkish pound or (c) the Turkish lira?

(5) What is the largest minority ethnic group living in Turkey?

(6) What is the name of the Turkish sea which connects the Black Sea to the Aegean Sea?

(7) What two straits connect the Sea of Marmara to the Black Sea and the Aegean Sea?

(8) Which empire controlled Turkey and much of South-eastern Europe and North Africa between the 14th and early 20th centuries?

(9) Apart from Asia Minor, what other name is often given to most of Asian Turkey?

(10) What is Turkey's highest mountain on which Noah's Ark is said to have landed?

(11) Which Turkish field marshal and statesman was founder of the Republic of Turkey and served as the first president from 1923 until his death in 1938?

(12) What is the Turkish national football team's best position in the finals of the FIFA World Cup: first, second, third, fourth or fifth?

(13) Which province in south-western Turkey is the centre of the country's tourist industry?

(14) Who became the 12th President of Turkey in August 2014?

(15) Name one of the two Seven Wonders of the Ancient World which was located in Turkey.

(16) What did Istanbul-born Sertab Erener win in 2003?

(17) What is the Golden Horn?

(18) Which historical city from Homer's Iliad did the German Heinrich Schliemann help to discover in the 19th century?

(19) Which Greek-American director of films such as A Streetcar Named Desire and On the Waterfront was born in Istanbul in 1909?

(20) For what is the Turk Mehmet Ali Agca remembered?

TURKEY ANSWERS

(1)   False; the capital is Ankara.

(2)   A white crescent and a white star

(3)   Largely in Asia, with a small part in South-eastern Europe.

(4)   (c) The Turkish lira

(5)   The Kurds (c. 15% to 20%)

(6)   The Sea of Marmara

(7)   The Bosporus Strait connects it to the Black Sea and the Dardanelles Strait to the Aegean Sea.

(8)   The Ottoman Empire

(9)   Anatolia or the Anatolian peninsula

(10) Mount Ararat

(11) Kemal Atatürk

(12) Third in 2002

(13) Antalya

(14) Recep Tayyip Erdogan

(15) Either the Temple of Artemis at Ephesus or the Mausoleum at Halicarnassus

(16) The Eurovision Song Contest with the song Every Way that I Can.

(17) It is an important waterway into the Bosporus, the estuary of two rivers.

(18) Troy

(19) Elia Kazan

(20) For shooting and wounding Pope John Paul II

TURKMENISTAN QUESTIONS

(1) Which sea does Turkmenistan border to the west?

(2) Name one of the -stan countries with which Turkmenistan does not have a border.

(3) The capital city begins with the letter A. Is it Almaty, Ashgabat or Astana?

(4) True or false: The Silk Road passed through Turkmenistan.

(5) Ashgabat is situated very close to the border with which major Middle Eastern country?

(6) True or false: Turkmenistan was not part of the Soviet Union.

(7) Is the official language Turkish, Turkic or Turkmen?

(8) What position did Saparmurat Niyazov hold in Turkmenistan from 1990 until his death in 2006?

(9) Which desert covers much of Turkmenistan: the Gobi, the Karakum or the Thar?

(10) In the Turkmen language, does Karakum mean (a) black sand (b) gold sand or (c) brown sand?

(11) True or false: Turkmenistan has large reserves of oil and natural gas.

(12) What devastating event happened in Ashgabat on 6 October 1948?

(13) What is the biggest ethnic minority living in Turkmenistan, Uzbeks or Russians?

(14) For what traditional craft is Turkmenistan particularly noted: (a) basket weaving (b) carpet weaving (c) wine making?

(15) What is Kopet Dag: (a) a mountain range in southern Turkmenistan (b) the national drink of Turkmenistan or (c) a port on the Caspian Sea?

(16) The Akhal-Teke, the national animal of Turkmenistan noted for its shiny coat and speed and intelligence, is a breed of which mammal?

(17) Is the currency the dinar, the rial or the manat?

(18) What classical material has been used to construct many buildings in Ashgabat?

(19) To prevent the spread of which gas did experts set fire to the Darvaza gas crater in the Karakum Desert?

(20) The ancient town of Merv was an important oasis on the Silk Road. Nowadays the town that has replaced it has an English girl's name beginning with the letter M. What is its name?

TURKMENISTAN ANSWERS

(1) The Caspian Sea

(2) One from Kyrgyzstan, Pakistan or Tajikistan

(3) Ashgabat

(4) True

(5) Iran

(6) False; it became independent from the Soviet Union in 1991.

(7) Turkmen

(8) President of Turkmenistan; he was declared President for Life in 1999!

(9) The Karakum; the Gobi is in China and Mongolia and the Thar in India and Pakistan.

(10) (a) Black sand

(11) True

(12) An earthquake of the magnitude 7.3 which killed thousands of people.

(13) Uzbeks (c. 5%), Russians (c. 4%)

(14) (b) Carpet weaving

(15) (a) A mountain range in southern Turkmenistan

(16) Horse

(17) The manat

(18) Marble

(19) Methane; the crater has been burning for many years and has become a tourist attraction.

(20) Mary

TUVALU QUESTIONS

(1) In which ocean is Tuvalu situated?

(2) To which continent does Tuvalu belong?

(3) Is Tuvalu north or south of Fiji?

(4) Is Tuvalu in Melanesia, Micronesia or Polynesia?

(5) What was the former name of Tuvalu?

(6) The Ellice Islands were part of a colony with which other islands?

(7) Of which European country were the Gilbert and Ellice Islands a colony until 1976?

(8) What is the capital of Tuvalu?

(9) True or false: Funafuti is the capital, but it is an atoll rather than a town.

(10) True or false: the British Union Jack features on the flag of the country.

(11) Why is Tuvalu's Internet country code top level domain a valuable one?

(12) How high is the highest point on Tuvalu: 3.5metres, 4.5 metres or 5.5 metres?

(13) What do the nine stars on the flag represent?

(14) What nationality was the first European to see the islands?

(15) Name one of the three countries in the world that is smaller in area than Tuvalu.

(16) True or false: Funafuti is the only one of the nine islands that does not begin with the letter N.

(17) What are the two official languages?

(18) True or false: Tuvalu has the smallest population (c. 10,200) of any sovereign state in the world.

(19) Who is the current heir to the throne of Tuvalu?

(20) Is Te Ano (a) the national drink of Tuvalu (b) a welcome greeting in Tuvaluan or (c) the national sport of Tuvalu?

TUVALU ANSWERS

(1) The Pacific Ocean

(2) Oceania

(3) North

(4) In Polynesia

(5) The Ellice Islands

(6) The Gilbert Islands

(7) The United Kingdom

(8) Funafuti

(9) True

(10) True

(11) It is .tv and income is created for the country by leasing it out.

(12) 4.5 metres

(13) The nine islands of Tuvalu

(14) Spanish (Álvaro de Mendana)

(15) One from Vatican City, Nauru or Monaco

(16) False; 7 of the islands begin with N: Nanumea, Nui, Nukufetau, Nukulaelae, Nanumanga, Niulakita and Niutao. Vaitupu, the biggest atoll, begins with the letter V!

(17) English and Tuvaluan

(18) False; the Vatican City has a smaller population (c. 800)

(19) Prince Charles

(20) (c) The national sport of Tuvalu, with similarities to volleyball, but with two balls used at the same time..

UGANDA QUESTIONS

(1) Is the capital Entebbe, Kampala or Nansana?

(2) True or false: Both Entebbe and Kampala are located on the shores of Lake Victoria.

(3) With which new nation does Uganda have a border in the north?

(4) In which British sitcom did Kampala-born Richard Gibson play the part of Herr Flick?

(5) In the basin of which great river does Uganda lie?

(6) Which great lake in Uganda is named after Queen Victoria's consort?

(7) What is the name of the infamous military officer who served as President of Uganda from 1971 to 1979?

(8) Which actor won an Oscar for portraying Idi Amin in the film The Last King of Scotland?

(9) From which airport did Israeli soldiers free over 100 hostages following a hijacking by a group of Palestinian and German militia?

(10) The currency has the same name as an old English coin. What is it?

(11) Which endangered mountain animal can be found in Uganda's Bwindi Impenetrable National Park?

(12) Which long-distance athletics event did Stephen Kiprotich win at the 2012 London Olympics?

(13) What is Buganda, a separate nation or a kingdom within Uganda?

(14) Name one of the two British kings after whom a lake in Uganda has been named.

(15) Which Milton served as President of Uganda from 1966 to 1971, was then overthrown by Idi Amin, but regained power from 1980 to 1985?

(16) Which British archbishop was born in Kampala in 1949?

(17) Which British statesman is said to have described Uganda as the Pearl of Africa because of its flora and fauna?

(18) Which British singer-songwriter who has released the successful albums Home Again and Love & Hate is the son of Ugandan parents who escaped the Amin regime?

(19) Who or what is the Kabaka of Buganda?

(20) Which mountain on the border with the DRC, named after the explorer famous for his search for David Livingstone, is the third highest in Africa?

UGANDA ANSWERS

(1) Kampala

(2) True

(3) South Sudan

(4) 'Allo 'Allo

(5) The Nile

(6) Lake Albert

(7) Idi Amin

(8) Forest Whitaker

(9) Entebbe airport

(10) The (Ugandan) shilling

(11) The mountain gorilla

(12) The marathon

(13) A kingdom within Uganda including the capital Kampala

(14) George V and Edward VII (Both lakes were named before they became king.)

(15) Milton Obote

(16) John Sentamu, Archbishop of York

(17) Winston Churchill

(18) Michael Kiwanuka

(19) The King of Buganda

(20) Mount Stanley (also known as Mount Ngaliema), 5,109m

UKRAINE QUESTIONS

(1) The two colours of the Ukrainian flag represent the sky and the wheat. What are the colours?

(2) What is the capital?

(3) Which peninsula in Ukraine did Russia annex in 2014?

(4) True or false: The language Ukrainian is not written in Cyrillic script.

(5) What was the occupation of Volodymyr Zelenskyy before he became president?

(6) With the same name as a colour and a fruit, what name was given to the series of protests that took place in Ukraine from November 2004 to January 2005?

(7) The delta of which major river forms the border between Ukraine and Romania?

(8) The first and only woman to hold the office of prime minister in Israel was born in Kiev in 1898. Who is she?

(9) Which body of water borders Ukraine in the south?

(10) In which Ukrainian city would you find the Potemkin Steps featured in Sergei Eisenstein's 1925 silent film Battleship Potemkin?

(11) In which year did the nuclear accident at Chernobyl take place?

(12) Which river, the fourth-longest in Europe, flows through the centre of Kiev?

(13) Which three statesmen met at the Yalta conference in 1945?

(14) Which city, the unofficial capital of the Donbass region, has been one of the major sites of fighting in the ongoing Donbass War?

(15) Which Kiev football team won the UEFA Cup Winners' Cup twice?

(16) Which actress, who starred in the films The Fifth Element and Resident Evil, was born in Kiev in 1975?

(17) Under what name is Independence Square in Kiev often known?

(18) Called Lemberg by the Germans, this city is one of the main cultural centres of Ukraine, famous for its many cafés. What name do we know it by?

(19) Which famous classical pianist and composer, who lived most of his life in the USA, was born in Kiev in 1903?

(20) Name one of the two winning Ukrainian songs in the Eurovision Song Contest.

UKRAINE ANSWERS

(1) Blue and yellow (two equally sized horizontal bands)

(2) Kiev

(3) The Crimean Peninsula

(4) False; Cyrillic script is used.

(5) Comedian, actor

(6) The Orange Revolution

(7) The Danube

(8) Golda Meir

(9) The Black Sea

(10) Odessa

(11) 1986

(12) The Dnieper

(13) Churchill, Roosevelt and Stalin

(14) Donetsk

(15) Dynamo Kiev

(16) Milla Jovovich

(17) Maidan (the word means square)

(18) Lviv

(19) Vladimir Horowitz

(20) Wild Horses (2004 by Ruslana) and 1944 (2016 by Jamala)

UNITED ARAB EMIRATES QUESTIONS

(1) On which large peninsula is the UAE situated?

(2) How many emirates are there: three, five or seven?

(3) On which gulf does the UAE have most of its coastline?

(4) Ajman, Fujairah, Ras Al Khaimah, Sharjah and Umm Al Quwain are five of the emirates. Can you name the other two?

(5) With which two countries does the UAE share a border?

(6) What is the capital of the UAE?

(7) Known as the Trucial States until 1971, of which European country were the states a protectorate?

(8) What are the official language and the official religion of the UAE?

(9) What is the name of the world's tallest building situated in Dubai which was used in the filming of Mission: Impossible – Ghost Protocol?

(10) The emir of which of the emirates is usually the President of the UAE?

(11) What is the national bird of the UAE?

(12) The currency of the UAE is the dirham. Which country in North Africa with the capital Rabat also has the dirham as its currency?

(13) Which is the largest of the emirates in area?

(14) About 38% of the population come from which South Asian country?

(15) The Burj al-Arab is another tall building in Dubai. What is it used as?

(16) Which German driver won the inaugural race of the 2009 Abu Dhabi Grand Prix?

(17) Does the Emirate of Fujairah have a coastline on the Gulf of Oman or on the Persian Gulf?

(18) Which northern English football club was bought by the Abu Dhabi United Group in 2008?

(19) What is the name of the airline based in Dubai which is the largest airline in the Middle East?

(20) What sort of race is run in the Dubai World Cup?

UNITED ARAB EMIRATES ANSWERS

(1)   The Arabian Peninsula

(2)   Seven

(3)   The Persian Gulf

(4)   Abu Dhabi and Dubai

(5)   Oman and Saudi Arabia

(6)   Abu Dhabi

(7)   The United Kingdom

(8)   Arabic and Islam

(9)   Burj Khalifa

(10) The Emir of Abu Dhabi

(11) The (peregrine) falcon

(12) Morocco

(13) Abu Dhabi

(14) India

(15) As a hotel

(16) Sebastian Vettel

(17) On the Gulf of Oman

(18) Manchester City

(19) Emirates

(20) A thoroughbred horse race

(1) What is the full name of the United Kingdom?

(2) Which of the capitals of Northern Ireland, Scotland and Wales has the biggest population?

(3) Which university is older, Oxford or Cambridge?

(4) Who was Queen when the Acts of Union were passed in 1707?

(5) Which three crosses make up the Union Flag?

(6) What is the tallest building in the UK?

(7) At which ancestral home was Winston Churchill born in 1874?

(8) What is the longest river in Scotland?

(9) Who was the first Labour Prime Minister of the UK?

(10) Of the three popular soaps Coronation Street, Emmerdale and EastEnders which one is the youngest?

(11) What is the highest mountain in England?

(12) Which English football club has won the most Premier League titles?

(13) Not including the islands of Great Britain and Ireland, what is the biggest island in the UK?

(14) Which play by Shakespeare with the characters Valentine and Proteus is believed by many to be his first play?

(15) What are the largest lakes in the four home countries, natural or man-made?

(16) Name one of three Brits who has won an EGOT – an emmy, grammy, Oscar and tony.

(17) Which British city on the River Lagan is famous for shipbuilding?

(18) Chris Hoy and Jason Kenny have won the most Olympic gold medals of any British sportsmen or women. With which sport are they associated?

(19) What is the largest mammal that can be found in the UK?

(20) Which theoretical physicist did Eddie Redmayne portray in the film The Theory of Everything?

UNITED KINGDOM ANSWERS

(1) The United Kingdom of Great Britain and Northern Ireland

(2) Edinburgh

(3) Oxford (c. 1167) Cambridge (c. 1209)

(4) Queen Anne

(5) The Cross of St. George (England), the Cross of St. Patrick (Ireland) and the Cross or Saltire of St. Andrew (Scotland)

(6) The Shard

(7) Blenheim Palace

(8) The River Tay (188 km.)

(9) Ramsay MacDonald

(10) EastEnders (1985) (Coronation Street 1960, Emmerdale 1972)

(11) Scafell Pike (978m)

(12) Manchester United (13 titles)

(13) Lewis and Harris

(14) The Two Gentlemen of Verona

(15) Northern Ireland: Lough Neagh (383 sq. km.) Scotland: Loch Lomond (71 sq. km.) England: Windermere (14.73 sq. km.) and Wales: Lake Vyrnwy (4.54 sq. km.)

(16) One from John Gielgud, Andrew Lloyd Webber or Tim Rice

(17) Belfast

(18) Cycling

(19) The Red Deer

(20) Stephen Hawking

UNITED STATES OF AMERICA QUESTIONS

(1)   What does the D.C. stand for in Washington D.C.?

(2)   What was the exact date of the Declaration of Independence?

(3)   What are the two assemblies which make up Congress?

(4)   What is Old Glory?

(5)   What is the oldest and largest national park in the USA?

(6)   How many cents make up a nickel?

(7)   How many states have the word New in their name?

(8)   From which Italian explorer does America take its name?

(9)   What is the USA's biggest lake?

(10)   Between which years did the American Civil War take place?

(11)   Who wrote the plays A Streetcar Named Desire and The Glass Menagerie?

(12)   The previous name of the highest mountain in the USA was Mount McKinley. By what name is it now known?

(13)   Which American swimmer is the most decorated Olympian of all time, having won a total of 28 medals?

(14)   Which amendment to the constitution abolished slavery?

(15)   The heads of which four former presidents can be seen at Mount Rushmore?

(16)   Which individual has won the most Oscars?

(17)   Who was the first American in space?

(18)   In which Mississippi city was Elvis Presley born?

(19)   What is the name of the stock market index which measures the stock performance of 30 large companies listed on stock exchanges in the USA?

(20)   In which decade was the Golden Gate Bridge built in San Francisco?

(1)   District of Columbia

(2)   4th July 1776

(3)   The Senate and the House of Representatives

(4)   A nickname for the flag of the USA.

(5)   Yellowstone National Park

(6)   Five cents

(7)   Four: New Hampshire, New Jersey, New Mexico and New York

(8)   Amerigo Vespucci

(9)   Lake Superior

(10) 1861 - 65

(11) Tennessee Williams

(12) Denali

(13) Michael Phelps

(14) The 13th Amendment

(15) George Washington, Thomas Jefferson, Theodore Roosevelt and Abraham Lincoln

(16) Walt Disney (22)

(17) Alan Shepard in 1961 (His craft entered space, but he was not able to achieve orbit. This was achieved by John Glenn in 1962.)

(18) Tupelo

(19) The Dow Jones Industrial Average

(20) The 1930s

(1) What is the capital city?

(2) With which two large South American countries does Uruguay have a border?

(3) Which capital city is further south, Buenos Aires or Montevideo?

(4) What is the currency: the peso, the real or the sol?

(5) The motto of Uruguay is Libertad o Muerte. What does it mean?

(6) By what name is the Río de la Plata sometimes known in English?

(7) Which European country established the town of Colonia del Sacramento, now a UNESCO World Heritage Site, in 1680?

(8) How many times has Uruguay won the FIFA World Cup Football Championship?

(9) Which company associated with tinned processed meat products has the same name as a port on the Uruguay River?

(10) In which category did Montevideo-born Jorge Drexler win an Oscar in 2004: Best Actor, Best Song or Best Cinematography?

(11) True or false: Footballer Diego Forlán never played for an English football club.

(12) Only one country in South America is smaller in area than Uruguay. Which one?

(13) What is the international vehicle registration code for Uruguay?

(14) Is the town of Artigas in the north of Uruguay named after a national hero of Uruguay or a huge gas field located near the town?

(15) What was the name of the left-wing urban guerrilla group active in Uruguay in the 1960s and 1970s?

(16) What is pictured on the Uruguayan flag with a face: the sun, the moon or a star?

(17) Which famous Uruguayan footballer who has played for Liverpool is famous for biting his opponents?

(18) In which two months of the year does Uruguayan Carnival usually take place?

(19) What took place on 27 June 1973, the outcome lasting until 1985, the official reason for it being to crush the Tupamaros?

(20) Which resort on the Atlantic coast in south-eastern Uruguay is famous for the La Mano sculpture and the Casapueblo complex and is sometimes called "the Monaco of the South"?

URUGUAY ANSWERS

(1) Montevideo

(2) Argentina and Brazil

(3) Montevideo

(4) The Uruguayan peso

(5) Freedom or Death

(6) The River Plate

(7) Portugal

(8) Twice, in 1930 and 1950.

(9) Fray Bentos

(10) Best Song, Al Otro Lado del Rio from the 2004 film The Motorcycle Diaries. He was the first Uruguayan to win an Oscar.

(11) False; he played for Manchester United between 2002 and 2004.

(12) Suriname

(13) ROU (República Oriental del Uruguay)

(14) It is named after José Artigas (1764 – 1850), sometimes called "the father of Uruguayan nationhood".

(15) The Tupamaros

(16) The sun

(17) Luis Suárez

(18) (Mid) January to (late) February

(19) A military coup

(20) Punta del Este

UZBEKISTAN QUESTIONS

(1) What is the capital city?

(2) True or false: the official language is Uzbek.

(3) What is the predominant religion in the country?

(4) The currency could be said to be the addition of a sequence of any kind of numbers. What is its name?

(5) What is the second biggest ethnic group in the country: Kazakhs, Russians or Tajiks?

(6) Which is the only other country in the world which is doubly landlocked, i.e. it is surrounded by landlocked countries?

(7) True or false: Uzbekistan borders all the other four Central Asian states, Kazakhstan, Kyrgyzstan, Tajikistan and Turkmenistan.

(8) What is the name of the shrinking lake which lies on the border between Uzbekistan and Kazakhstan?

(9) What is the name of one of the oldest inhabited cities on the Silk Road beginning with the letter S?

(10) Which soft fluffy staple fibre is one of the most important crops in Uzbekistan?

(11) What natural disaster took place in Tashkent in 1966?

(12) Which Macedonian emperor conquered parts of Uzbekistan in the 4th century BC?

(13) What precious metal is mined in Muruntau in the Navoiy Region of Uzbekistan?

(14) Which Serbian tennis player did Tashkent-born Denis Istomin defeat in the second round of the Australian Open in 2017?

(15) Which is the only -stan country with which Uzbekistan does not have a border?

(16) What is the population of Uzbekistan: between (a) 10 and 20 million (b) 20 and 30 million or (c) 30 and 40 million?

(17) The first name of the president who ruled Uzbekistan for 25 years until his death in 2016 is the same as a world religion. What is it?

(18) What is the name of the city rich in historical sites, located on the Silk Road and the birthplace of Imam Bukhari?

(19) Ruslan Chagaev held a WBA title twice from 2007 to 2009 and from 2014 to 2016. In which sport?

(20) With which of the -stan countries does Uzbekistan have its shortest border?

UZBEKISTAN ANSWERS

(1)   Tashkent

(2)   True

(3)   Islam

(4)   The sum

(5)   Tajiks (4.8%) Kazakhs (2.5%) and Russians (2.3%)

(6)   Liechtenstein

(7)   True; it's the only one of the five states to do so.

(8)   The Aral Sea

(9)   Samarkand

(10) Cotton

(11) An earthquake

(12) Alexander the Great

(13) Gold

(14) Novak Djokovic

(15) Pakistan

(16) (c) 30 and 40 million (c. 34m)

(17) Islam (Karimov)

(18) Bukhara

(19) Boxing (heavyweight)

(20) Afghanistan (144 km.)

VANUATU QUESTIONS

(1) Sounding like some new Scottish islands, what name was given to Vanuatu during the colonial period?

(2) Two European powers shared sovereignty over New Hebrides until independence in 1980. Which two powers?

(3) Is Bislama an official language of Vanuatu or the official currency?

(4) The first explorer to visit the islands in 1606 was the Portuguese Pedro Fernandes de Queirós, but for which country was he sailing?

(5) Which letter of the alphabet best describes the shape of Vanuatu, X, Y or Z?

(6) The largest island of Vanuatu is Espiritu Santo. What do the Spanish words mean?

(7) The two largest towns are Luganville on Espritu Santo and Port Vila on Efate. Which is the capital?

(8) What sort of natural disaster destroyed a lot of Vanuatu in March 2015?

(9) Is the currency the Vanuatu vanu or the Vanuatu vatu?

(10) Which famous 18th century explorer coined the name New Hebrides for the islands?

(11) Which musical was created from James Michener's stories collected while stationed on the island of Espiritu Santo?

(12) Vanuatu first competed in the Summer Olympic Games in 1988. In which country?

(13) Which male member of the British royal family do the Kastom people on the island of Tanna believe to be a divine being?

(14) Which popular jumping activity was influenced by the Vanuatu ritual of Nanggol, performed by men of the southern part of Pentecost Island?

(15) Is laplap (a) the national dish of Vanuatu (b) the national dance or (c) the national drink?

(16) Which sea does Vanuatu border to the east?

(17) Which American reality show was filmed in Vanuatu in 2004?

(18) True or false: The national anthem of Vanuatu is called Yumi, Yumi, Yumi.

(19) Which is the closest capital to Port Vila: Honiara, Nuku'alofa or Suva?

(20) What domestic animal is considered to be a symbol of wealth in Vanuatu?

VANUATU ANSWERS

(1)   New Hebrides

(2)   France and the United Kingdom

(3)   An official language, along with English and French

(4)   Spain

(5)   The archipelago is best described as Y-shaped.

(6)   Holy Spirit

(7)   Port Vila

(8)   A cyclone (Cyclone Pam)

(9)   The Vanuatu vatu

(10) Captain James Cook

(11) South Pacific (Michener's book was Tales of the South Pacific).

(12) In South Korea (Seoul)

(13) Prince Philip

(14) Bungee jumping; Nanggol is a form of land diving and involves men jumping off wooden towers with two tree vines wrapped around their ankles.

(15) (a) The national dish

(16) The Coral Sea

(17) Survivor

(18) True (In English We, We, We)

(19) Suva (c. 1,067 kms.)

(20) The pig

VATICAN CITY QUESTIONS

(1)   Of which city is the Vatican City an enclave?

(2)   True or false: The Vatican City is the smallest sovereign state in the world by both area and population.

(3)   What is the name of the famous Renaissance-style basilica, held to be the burial site of the saint after which it is named?

(4)   From whom does the Sistine Chapel get its name?

(5)   Who is famous for having painted the ceiling of the Sistine Chapel?

(6)   Who is the Bishop of Rome?

(7)   Name the last three popes.

(8)   After what is the Vatican City named?

(9)   What is the name of the treaty of 1929 which recognized the Vatican City as an independent state under the sovereignty of the Holy See?

(10) Who was Prime Minister of Italy at the time of the Lateran Treaty?

(11) In which country was Pope Benedict XVI born?

(12) Name three of the five requirements needed to be a member of the Papal Guard.

(13) What is Peter's Pence?

(14) What body elects the Pope?

(15) The flag consists of two vertical bands with the crossed keys of St. Peter and the Papal Tiara. What colour are the two vertical bands?

(16) What is the official language of the Vatican City?

(17) In which French city did several popes reside in the 14th century rather than in Rome?

(18) What blessing does the Pope usually give at Easter and Christmas from the loggia balcony of St. Peter's Basilica?

(19) Which ancient construction is located in the centre of St. Peter's Square?

(20) What name is given to the central governing body of the entire Roman Catholic Church which is located within the Vatican City?

(1) Rome

(2) True; Area: 0.44 sq. km. Population: 825

(3) St. Peter's Basilica

(4) From Pope Sixtus (IV)

(5) Michelangelo

(6) The Pope

(7) John Paul II (1978 – 2005), Benedict XVI (2005 – 2013) and Francis (2013 -)

(8) After the Vatican Hill

(9) The Lateran Treaty

(10) Benito Mussolini

(11) Germany

(12) You have to be (1) Swiss (2) male (3) Catholic (4) Between 19 and 30 (5) unmarried.

(13) Donations or payments made directly to the Holy See of the Catholic Church.

(14) The College of Cardinals

(15) Yellow and white

(16) It doesn't have one, although Italian and Latin are often used.

(17) In Avignon

(18) Urbi et orbi

(19) An Egyptian obelisk

(20) The Holy See

VENEZUELA QUESTIONS

(1)   What is the capital city?

(2)   On which sea does Venezuela have a coastline?

(3)   Name two of the three countries with which Venezuela has a border.

(4)   Which great river flows through Colombia and Venezuela and empties into the Atlantic Ocean near the island of Trinidad?

(5)   Of which commodity has Venezuela the largest reserves in the world?

(6)   Of which European city was Amerigo Vespucci allegedly reminded when he saw some stilt villages in Venezuela in 1499, naming the region Veneziola?

(7)   Is Joropo Venezuela's national dance, dish or drink?

(8)   Who was President of Venezuela from 1999 until his death in 2013?

(9)   Name one of the two politicians in dispute over the presidency of the country.

(10) What is the name of the vast tropical grassland plain shared with Colombia, the main river of which is the Orinoco?

(11) Which famous liberator and military and political leader was born in Caracas in 1783?

(12) What is the nickname of the Venezuelan-born terrorist, one of the most notorious political terrorists of the 1970s and 1980s, who is now serving life sentences for murder in France?

(13) What is the name of the large tidal bay connected to the Gulf of Venezuela by the Tablazo Strait and often regarded as the largest lake in South America?

(14) What is the name of the world's highest uninterrupted waterfall situated in the Canaima National Park?

(15) What nationality was Jimmie Angel after whom the falls are named?

(16) Who recorded the international hit song Orinoco Flow?

(17) The third-largest city in Venezuela has the same name as the third-largest city in Spain. What is it?

(18) What title have the Venezuelans Susana Duijm, Pilín León, Astrid Carolina Herrera, Ninibeth Leal, Jacqueline Aguilera and Ivian Sarcos all won?

(19) What is the name of the holiday island off the coast of Venezuela which has recently been affected by organised crime and the illegal drug trade?

(20) Which French award did Venezuelan actor Edgar Ramirez win for his performance as Carlos the Jackal in the 2010 film Carlos?

(1) Caracas

(2) The Caribbean Sea

(3) Two from Brazil, Colombia and Guyana

(4) The Orinoco

(5) Oil

(6) Venice (Veneziola means Little Venice.)

(7) National dance

(8) Hugo Chavez

(9) Nicolás Maduro or Juan Guaidó

(10) Los Llanos

(11) Simon Bolivar

(12) Carlos the Jackal (Ilich Ramirez Sánchez)

(13) Lake Maracaibo

(14) The Angel Falls

(15) American; the falls were not known to the outside world until Jimmie Angel flew over them in 1933.

(16) Enya

(17) Valencia

(18) Miss World

(19) Isla Margarita

(20) César Award (for Most Promising Actor)

VIETNAM QUESTIONS

(1)   Is the capital Hanoi or Ho Chi Minh City?

(2)   What is the former name of Ho Chi Minh City?

(3)   Is the unit of currency the Dang, Deng, Ding, Dong or Dung?

(4)   What colour is the background of the flag which also features a yellow star?

(5)   True or false: The delta of the Mekong River is situated in Vietnam.

(6)   What is the official language of Vietnam?

(7)   In which decade did people first become aware of the Vietnamese boat people?

(8)   Does Tet, the Vietnamese New Year, usually take place in (a) January or February or (b) November or December?

(9)   Who was the Vietnamese general, diplomat and politician who was awarded the Nobel Peace Prize jointly with Henry Kissinger, but refused it?

(10) By what name was the National Liberation Front that fought against the USA and the South Vietnamese government in the Vietnam War often known?

(11) What sort of dish is the popular street food Pho?

(12) What is the name of the sea off the east coast of Vietnam?

(13) What is the most widespread surname in Vietnam?

(14) What is the name of the city in Central Vietnam, a former capital, famous for its Imperial City?

(15) Of which type of nut, commonly used in Indian cooking, is Vietnam the world's leading producer?

(16) What type of puppet theatre in Vietnam is a tradition that dates back to the 11th century?

(17) What is the name of the bay in Northern Vietnam which contains thousands of isles in various shapes and sizes?

(18) The airport of which important port in Central Vietnam was used extensively by the South Vietnamese and American forces during the Vietnam War?

(19) What is the name of the American filmmaker who directed three films about the Vietnam War including Platoon and Born on the Fourth of July?

(20) With what sport do you associate Vietnam-born Yvon Petra?

VIETNAM ANSWERS

(1)   Hanoi

(2)   Saigon

(3)   The Dong

(4)   Red

(5)   True

(6)   Vietnamese

(7)   In the (late) 1970s, following the end of the Vietnam War in 1975.

(8)   (a) In January or February

(9)   Le Duc Tho

(10) The Viet Cong

(11) A soup consisting of broth, rice noodles, herbs and meat.

(12) The South China Sea

(13) Nguyen

(14) Hué

(15) The cashew nut

(16) Water puppet theatre

(17) Ha Long Bay

(18) Da Nang

(19) Oliver Stone

(20) Tennis

YEMEN QUESTIONS

(1)   On which peninsula is Yemen situated?

(2)   With which two countries does Yemen share a border?

(3)   What is the capital?

(4)   True or false: Yemen has a coastline on the Gulf of Aden and the Red Sea.

(5)   The flag of Yemen is basically the Arab Liberation Flag of 1952. What are the three colours of it?

(6)   Is the capital Sana'a situated on the coast or inland?

(7)   What is the official language?

(8)   What was the name of the British Protectorate where a state of emergency was declared in the 1960s due to fighting between the British and Arab nationalist guerrilla forces?

(9)   In what year did the two Yemeni states unite to form the Republic of Yemen: 1980, 1990 or 2000?

(10) Is the currency the dinar, the dirham or the rial?

(11) What does a Yemeni do with Khat or qat: (a) chew it (b) eat it or (c) drink it?

(12) What archipelago between the Arabian Sea and the Gulf of Aden is politically part of Yemen which is in Asia, but geographically part of Africa?

(13) What sort of beverage is associated with the Red Sea port of Mocha?

(14) Sana'a is situated at 2,250 metres. Name one of the seven capital cities in the world which is situated at a higher elevation.

(15) Name one of the two African countries on the other side of the Bab-el-Mandeb, the strait at the end of the Red Sea separating the Arabian peninsula from the Horn of Africa.

(16) Which golden bird is featured on the emblem of Yemen?

(17) Which controversial British Labour Party politician who served as Minister for Europe between 1999 and 2001 was born in Aden in 1956?

(18) Which disease, an infection of the small intestine, has been particularly prevalent in Yemen since it began in October 2016?

(19) Which stand-up comedian and actor who appeared as Bertie, Prince of Wales, in the 2017 film Victoria and Abdul, was born in Aden in 1962?

(20) What was the name of the president whose resignation was demanded in the Yemeni Revolution, part of the Arab Spring protests, and who was assassinated in 2017?

(1)   The Arabian Peninsula

(2)   Oman and Saudi Arabia

(3)   Sana'a

(4)   True

(5)   Red, white and black

(6)   Inland

(7)   Arabic

(8)   Aden Protectorate

(9)   1990

(10) The (Yemeni) rial

(11) (a) Chew it (It's a plant which acts as a stimulant when chewed.)

(12) Socotra

(13) Coffee (Mocha used to be an important marketplace for coffee.)

(14) One from La Paz (3,640m), Quito (2,850m), Sucre (2,750m), Bogota 2,625m), Addis Ababa (2,355m), Thimphu (2,334m) or Asmara (2,325m)

(15) Djibouti or Eritrea

(16) The golden eagle

(17) Keith Vaz

(18) Cholera

(19) Eddie Izzard

(20) Ali Abdullah Saleh

ZAMBIA QUESTIONS

(1)   What is the capital?

(2)   What was the name of Zambia before it became independent in 1964?

(3)   With which geographical feature does the word Zambia have a connection?

(4)   Which KK became first President of the independent Zambia?

(5)   Into which ocean does the Zambezi River flow?

(6)   What animal appears on the Zambian flag: an eagle, a hippo or a lion?

(7)   Is singer Emeli Sandé's mother or father originally from Zambia?

(8)   What city in the south of Zambia to the north of the Zambezi River is named after a Scottish explorer?

(9)   With the mining of what element is Zambia particularly associated?

(10) After whom was Rhodesia named in 1895?

(11) In what field is Northern Rhodesia-born Wilbur Smith famous?

(12) What is the name of the dam constructed on the Zambezi between Zambia and Zimbabwe, finally completed in 1977?

(13) Zambia won the 2012 Africa Cup of Nations Final, beating the country with the capital Yamoussoukro on penalties. Which country?

(14) In 1953 Southern Rhodesia was grouped into a federation with Northern Rhodesia and one other country. Which country?

(15) What is referred to by Zambians as Mosi-oa-Tunya, "The smoke that thunders"?

(16) With what sport do you associate Lusaka-born Phil Edmonds?

(17) What is Zamrock?

(18) Of which of the African Great Lakes does Zambia have a small share in the north?

(19) Born in Northern Rhodesia in 1948, Mutt Lange produced the 1997 album Come On Over with his then-wife, a famous Canadian singer and songwriter. Who is she?

(20) Although sometimes contested, Zambia seems to be part of a quadripoint along with Namibia, Botswana and Zimbabwe. What is a quadripoint?

ZAMBIA ANSWERS

(1)   Lusaka

(2)   Northern Rhodesia

(3)   The Zambezi River

(4)   Kenneth Kaunda

(5)   The Indian Ocean

(6)   A (fish) eagle

(7)   Her father

(8)   Livingstone

(9)   Copper

(10)   Cecil Rhodes

(11)   Novel writing

(12)   The Kariba Dam

(13)   Cote d'Ivoire (Ivory Coast)

(14)   Nyasaland (nowadays Malawi)

(15)   The Victoria Falls

(16)   Cricket

(17)   A style of music from Zambia, a combination of traditional African music with psychedelic rock and funk.

(18)   Lake Tanganyika

(19)   Shania Twain

(20)   A quadripoint is a point that touches the borders of four distinct countries or territories.

ZIMBABWE QUESTIONS

(1) What is the capital city?

(2) By what name was Harare known until 1982?

(3) Who became President of Zimbabwe in 1980?

(4) By what name was Zimbabwe known before 1980?

(5) In 1965 the conservative white minority government declared UDI. What does the abbreviation mean?

(6) Who was prime minister during this period?

(7) What is the name of the bishop who was briefly Prime Minister from June 1979 to April 1980?

(8) After which British monarch were the famous falls between Zambia and Zimbabwe named?

(9) Apart from Zambia, name one other country with which Zimbabwe has a border.

(10) What is the name of the man-made lake, the largest in the world, formed on the border with Zambia by the construction of the Kariba Dam?

(11) Is Shona (a) a TV star in Zimbabwe (b) the currency or (c) a language?

(12) Who was Prime Minister of the UK when Southern Rhodesia declared UDI?

(13) Having been suspended in 2002, from which international institution did Zimbabwe withdraw in 2003?

(14) What is the name of Zimbabwe's second-biggest city?

(15) With what sport do you associate the Black family, Byron, Cara and Wayne?

(16) Born in Bulawayo, what is the name of the creator of the series of novels The No.1?

(17) What is the connection between the first President of Zimbabwe and an elongated, edible, yellow fruit?

(18) Which famous river does the Beitbridge cross on the southern border with South Africa?

(19) Is the mbira a musical instrument or a village chieftain?

(20) In which Far Eastern island country did Robert Mugabe die in September 2019?

ZIMBABWE ANSWERS

(1) Harare

(2) Salisbury

(3) Robert Mugabe

(4) Southern Rhodesia

(5) The Unilateral Declaration of Independence

(6) Ian Smith

(7) Bishop Abel Muzorewa

(8) Victoria

(9) One from Botswana, Mozambique, Namibia or South Africa

(10) Lake Kariba

(11) A language, spoken by about 70% of the population. English is also widely spoken.

(12) Harold Wilson

(13) The Commonwealth of Nations

(14) Bulawayo

(15) Tennis

(16) Alexander McCall Smith

(17) Banana (The first president was Canaan Banana.)

(18) The Limpopo

(19) It's a musical instrument traditional to the Shona people of Zimbabwe.

(20) Singapore